Start of 2004
Tour de France

Stage 1
Stage 3
Stage 4
Stage 5
Stage 2
Stage 20
Paris
Stage 6

FRANCE

Stage 9
Stage 19
Stage 18
Stage 10
Stage 17
Stage 11
Stage 15
Stage 16
Stage 14
13
Stage 1

July 3–9 Stages 1–6

Hell Week: The Tour de France's first seven days bring 99 crashes, three broken collarbones, two fractured vertebrae, and 12 rider withdrawals. Armstrong crashes on stage 6, but is unhurt.

June 20 Lugano, Switzerland

Germany's Jan Ullrich, Armstrong's most feared—and erratic—rival, proves he's reaching good form by scoring a dramatic, one-second comeback to win the Tour of Switzerland.

July 21 Stage 16, Alpe d'Huez

Half a million screaming people, ten legendary miles of switchback road, one anonymous death threat – and, for Armstrong, the chance to clinch an historic sixth Tour victory.

June 10 Mount Ventoux

In the key stage of the biggest Tour-preparation race, Armstrong is humiliated by American Tyler Hamilton and Spain's Iban Mayo. "If they keep improving, we're in trouble," says Armstrong's team director, Johan Bruyneel.

Early February Girona, Spain

Five weeks after his $15 million divorce is finalized in Texas, Lance Armstrong lands at his European training base accompanied by new girlfriend, Sheryl Crow, two bikes, and four of her guitars.

Illustration: Matthew Pollock

LANCE ARMSTRONG'S WAR

LANCE ARMSTRONG'S WAR

One Man's Battle Against Fate,
Fame, Love, Death, Scandal,
and a Few Other Rivals on the
Road to the Tour de France

Daniel Coyle

HarperCollins*Publishers*

HarperCollins books may be purchased for educational, business, or sales promotional use. For information, please write: Special Markets Department, HarperCollins Publishers, 10 East 53rd Street, New York, NY 10022.

FIRST EDITION

Portions of Chapters 4 and 10 first appeared in slightly different form in the July 2004 issue of *Outside* magazine. Copyright © 2004 by Daniel Coyle.

Designed by Nancy Singer Olaguera

Printed on acid-free paper

Library of Congress Cataloging-in-Publication Data is available upon request.

ISBN 0–06–073497–3

05 06 07 08 09   ❖/RRD   10 9 8 7 6

To Aidan, Katie, Lia, and Zoe,
the best adventurers I know

CONTENTS

LANCE ARMSTRONG'S WAR

Will and intellect are one and the same thing.

—*Benedict Spinoza*

In early February 2004, my wife Jen, our four kids, and I buttoned up our house in Alaska and traveled to the city of Girona, Spain. The night we arrived we drove its medieval maze of cobbled streets for three hours before finding our hotel, which was next to the cathedral. For the first few nights, we bolted upright in our beds each time the church bell boomed out the hour.

We'd come here to follow a cycling season, as Lance Armstrong attempted to win his historic sixth Tour de France. Like most people, I knew something about Armstrong, and what I knew I liked. I had read his autobiography *It's Not About the Bike,* and watched him win the Tour each year. I admired his commitment to fighting cancer, his charismatic presence, and his ability to inspire. Here was an amazing human being by any measure, trying to do what nobody had ever done, in the planet's hardest race.

At the same time, I was curious. Like most Americans, I didn't know much about the inner workings of professional bike racing. Most of what I'd read and watched about Armstrong amounted to retellings of the same powerful, mythic story—a story that, while undeniably moving, still left me wanting to know more. I felt like a new baseball fan watching Babe Ruth blast titanic home runs. I admired the spectacle, but found myself wanting to move down from the grandstand into the box seats, to step out onto the infield grass. I wanted to get closer, to find the answers to basic questions. What, exactly, gave Armstrong his edge over his rivals? What sacrifices did he make to keep that edge? What was his greatness made of, and what happened when that greatness was pushed to its limits?

A month earlier, I'd attended U.S. Postal's team training camp in Solvang, California, and received my first up-close view of the man. Or, rather, nonview. Armstrong was hard to see, appearing and disappearing, usually surrounded by a whirling group of people. Sebastian Moll, a veteran German journalist, pulled me aside. "You see, it's Planet Lance," he said, pointing. "He is in the middle, and here you have the satellites."

The satellites seemed like an intriguing bunch. There was his team director, a dark-eyed, watchful Belgian named Johan Bruyneel. There were more Belgians on the team staff, tough-talking, pompadoured types who reminded me of Chicago tough guys, some of whom worked as *soigneurs* ("healers" in French), performing massage and other team-support tasks. Farther afield, there were The Kid, aka Chris Carmichael, Armstrong's longtime coach, and Mr. Magic, aka Jeff Spencer, the team's Tour de France chiropractor. There was also Dr. Evil, aka Dr. Michele Ferrari, Armstrong's trainer, who was on trial in Italy for allegedly administering performance-enhancing drugs, a case that did not involve Armstrong. By moving to Girona, a city of 50,000 that served as Armstrong's European home, I hoped to find a way into their orbits—and into his.

That first sunny morning in Girona, I walked out of the hotel and bumped into Dr. Evil himself, who, it turned out, was staying in the room directly above ours. Ferrari, an ebullient, dark-haired man who vaguely resembled Snidely Whiplash without the mustache, referred to Armstrong as "The King." His cell phone rang, playing Scott Joplin's "Entertainer." We made plans to meet for dinner.

The next afternoon, I rounded a corner to hear a voice call my name. I saw three slender, slow-walking young men I recognized from Postal's training camp—Floyd Landis, Michael Barry, and George Hincapie, Armstrong's support riders, or *domestiques*. We had a coffee.

A day or so later, my eight-year-old son was standing on a

bridge, lobbing bits of his sandwich to the fish below. A cyclist in blue rolled past.

"Don't jump," Armstrong said with a smile.

So began our journey to Planet Lance. Over the course of fifteen months in Europe, I followed Armstrong and his top rivals, a trio that included American rider Tyler Hamilton, Armstrong's upstairs neighbor. I attended training sessions, fitness tests, and six-hour training rides. I visited human-testing labs, team buses, the smoky backrooms of Belgian bars, and far too many Girona coffee shops, which serve as gathering places for the twenty or so American cyclists who make their homes here. In our dusty blue Peugeot minivan, I drove to races across the continent, a job made convenient, if not comfortable, by the sleeping bag and foam mattress stowed in the back.*

Along the way, I kept in contact with Armstrong's director, coach, trainer, technical advisors, *soigneurs,* and close friends. All were generous about sharing their knowledge and offering their insights, which frequently circled back to a common theme: Armstrong's complexity. "He seems so simple from a distance," was how Landis put it. "But the closer you get, the more you realize—this is one very, very complicated guy."

I soon came to find out that reporting on Armstrong meant that he was also reporting on you. Throughout the season, Armstrong kept track of me, always letting me know he knew who I was talking with. Sometimes he let me into his inner circle; other times he chose not to. It evolved into a kind of game, and, under the circumstances, probably a fair one.

After the season ended, Armstrong and I sat down in his Austin, Texas, living room. It was a faultless fall afternoon, clear and cold. We had a lot to catch up on: races, his Tour performance, his new Discovery Channel team. Some battles were drawing to a close, others beginning.

---

*For a brief explanation of how bike racing works, please turn to "Notes on the Sport" on page 315.

He wore an orange T-shirt, baggy brown shorts, and leather slippers. His ankles were marked with small red hieroglyphs of cuts and scrapes. He leaned back in an armchair, his face half in light, half in shadow. Before I could start my questions, he spoke.

"Well," he said, "how do you like me now?"

CHAPTER 1

HE OF THE DOUBLE DOOR

Each morning, even in winter, the European continent looks as if it is simmering over a cookfire. Not one big fire, but a thousand tiny blazes exhaling threads of smoke and steam until everything is bathed in a white-gray haze. The haze rolls over the countryside, concealing borders, filling hollows, flowing over the steeples of the thousand sleepy villages that float in and out of view like so many ghost towns, half-dissolved in the heat of the modern world.

Over the simmering haze, screaming eastward at five hundred miles an hour, came a silvery white Gulfstream aircraft, with its wings turned up at their tips like a fighter jet. Inside its sleek cocoon, Lance Armstrong was peering down into the mist, trying to spot the trolls.

That's what Armstrong called them, the sneaky lowlifes who tried to snare him, to pull him down into the muck. The landscape was crawling with them. A month ago, a troll had swiped his Visa card and gone on a spree at JC Penney's ("They must not have known which Armstrong they had," he said). Then, a couple days later, some troll had jimmied his way into a cabin on one of his properties outside Austin, and had set up camp there. Dozens of media trolls were whispering that Armstrong was too old, too distracted, washed up. An Italian troll named Filippo Simeoni—a cyclist, no less—was suing him for libel. The biggest trolls were David

Walsh and Pierre Ballester, journalists who were writing a book claiming that Armstrong may have used performance-enhancing drugs. Trolls were down there in the mist, creeping around, grasping at him with hairy fingers, daring him to fight. All of which made Armstrong happy.

"Fucking trolls!" he said when he watched Walsh, Simeoni, or any of the others on the liquid-crystal display of his handheld personal organizer, which sent him constant updates on their activities. "Little fucking goddamn trolls!"

Well, perhaps "happy" is the wrong word. "Enlivened" is more like it. Others might have been tempted to ignore the trolls, or at least pretend to ignore them, but not Armstrong. He watched them obsessively, getting ready to fight, to go to battle, to *take the bastards on*. Armstrong is fascinating for many reasons, but mostly because he's our purest embodiment of the fundamental human act—to impose the will on the uncaring world—an act that compels our attention because it seems so simple and yet is secretly magical. Because at its core, will is about belief, and with Armstrong we can see the belief happening.

It's etched on his face, in that narrow-eyed expression Armstrong's friends warily refer to as The Look. His is the latest rendition of the gunfighter's squint, a look made more powerful because the weapon Armstrong brandishes is no more or less than himself. He is a living fable, the man who had cancer and who came back to win the hardest athletic event on the planet five times. He's been fighting from the start, starting out as Lance Edward Gunderson, the willful son of a seventeen-year-old mother in Plano, Texas. He fights to survive, to win, and also to show us his force, and he has been successful enough that his face, like that of Joe DiMaggio in the forties or the Mercury astronauts in the sixties, has become America's face, a hero who embodies many people's best idea of what they want to be.

What Armstrong wants to be? That's a tougher question.

You can attempt to find out by asking him, to which he'll respond that he wants to (1) be a good dad, (2) fight cancer, and

(3) ride his bike. Or you can examine the causes into which he channels his energy: the tens of millions of dollars raised by the Lance Armstrong Foundation. Or you can add up his business interests: the $19 million in annual endorsements and his part-ownership of his cycling team. Or you can peruse the family drama: his fatherless childhood, his intense bond with his mother, his refusal to meet his birth father. Or you can look at the topography of his relationships; the walled kingdom of close friends and business associates; the warm, endless expanse of acquaintances; the icy archipelagoes filled with former friends who have been, as one puts it, excommunicated. Or you can look at the range of emotion he inspires. There are not many people whose mailbox regularly receives both death threats and calls for his beatification.

"People find this hard to believe, but he's not a happy-go-lucky, Mr. Smiley, save-the-world-from-cancer type of person," said John Korioth, nicknamed College, who is one of Armstrong's closest friends. "I look on it as almost an animalistic thing. In sports or business or anywhere there's always the question of who's the alpha, who's the meanest, who's the toughest? And it's Lance. Always Lance."

"It is simple, no?" said Armstrong's longtime trainer, Dr. Ferrari, smiling. "Lance wishes to swallow the world."

Two thousand years ago, Greek storytellers told of young commoners who ventured alive into the kingdom of the dead. They survived with the aid of magical helpers, then returned in a kind of second birth to perform a triumphant act, bringing their teaching to the rest of humanity. One was called Dithyrambos, or "He of the Double Door."

Funny thing is, the Greeks were a little fuzzier about endings. Without the escape hatch of "happily ever after," their death-venturing heroes tended to fade into obscurity, or sulk as the world refused to hear their teachings. Now, flying to Spain, Armstrong was embarking on his attempt to break one of the more legendary marks in sport. His first step, as it happened, was also one of the trickiest. He had to be calm.

The difficulty of this lay in the fact that Armstrong's life was usually anything but calm, particularly at the moment. The trolls were the least of it: a few weeks before, he had finalized a painful, expensive divorce from Kristin, his wife of five years and mother to their three young children. He was coming off his worst season in half a decade, an injury- and accident-riddled tour he'd politely termed a near-disaster. To top it off, he'd just lost his best teammate, Roberto Heras, who'd unexpectedly defected to the powerful Liberty Seguros team.

But even in the face of such facts—especially in the face of such facts—Armstrong's instinct had called for a response; in this case, a show of off-season contentedness that was also a show of control. He'd smiled. He'd spoken cheerily about his new role as a single divorced father ("Kristin and I are better friends than ever," he said). He attended movie premieres, NBA games, and award ceremonies with his new girlfriend, rock singer Sheryl Crow. He proclaimed to *USA Today* that he'd "never been happier."

Less debatable was the fact that he was older: thirty-two, to be exact. Looking at side-by-side photos from his first Tour win in 1999 was like examining before-and-after photos of a one-term U.S. president. The rosy boyishness had been replaced by a drier, hard-cut look, along with a salting of gray hairs which were duly noted, if not actually counted, by cycling cognoscenti all too aware of the pertinent statistic: none of the four previous five-time winners had won after the age of thirty-one. (Indeed, only four men older than thirty-one had won the Tour in the previous seventy-three years.) Five wins, thirty-one years; the numbers hardened into a wall. Perhaps, the thinking went, there was some physiological odometer, some secret number of pedal strokes or heartbeats, beyond which the human body simply collapsed.

Examining attempts for number six was akin to examining early attempts to climb Mount Everest: long, steady progress to a certain height, ending in dazzlingly swift demise in the Death Zone. You could look it up: Miguel Induráin at Les Arcs in 1996; Bernard Hinault on Superbagneres in 1986; Eddy Merckx at Pra Loup in 1975; Jacques Anquetil on the road from Chamonix to St. Etienne in 1966—boom, boom, boom, boom. More mysteriously, few had seen it coming. The crack, as the event is aptly called, opened with the hungry suddenness of a crevasse. One moment, the five-time champions rode supreme, sailing toward the holy shores of number six. The next they were simply gone, swept down as if by the hand of God. The 2004 season existed as nothing so much as a question: Would Armstrong crack or not? Behind the question stood perhaps a more interesting possibility: when Armstrong's time arrived, nobody would know, perhaps not even he.

"Lance does not admit weakness," said his trainer Ferrari. "It is not a possibility. Even last year, when he was weak, he would not show it."

"I think he's often a lot closer to the edge than he lets on," Carmichael said. "The ability to hide weakness at all costs is his great strength, and like any strength it can sometimes be a handicap."

"The mental edge is important this year," Bruyneel said. "He must show them how strong he is. And show himself, too."

Or, put another way, "The game is to show them nothing," said teammate Landis. "If they get a whiff, they'll be on him."

The game had already started, the preseason intelligence-gathering that Armstrong loved, where he peered through the mist to check on his rivals. He knew, for instance, that Jan Ullrich had suffered a cold and had skipped the first days of team training. He knew that Tyler Hamilton was angling to sign another top Spanish climber to strengthen his Phonak team. Armstrong also knew they were all watching him, and he did his best to make sure they couldn't see much (in fact, Armstrong had a cold at his training camp and quit his first ride early, too, though it wasn't reported). What they could see—well, Armstrong did what he could to influence their vision.

A good example of this involved Armstrong's newly departed teammate. Before Heras left, he was a hero. Heras had twice won the Vuelta a España, a three-week tour; he was the second-highest-paid member of the team, the key lieutenant, the one whom Armstrong called "a really special talent," and the keystone of his 2002 win ("It was Roberto who made the difference. He made the pace and all I had to do was follow," Armstrong said after the decisive mountain stage). A few days after he left, Heras was rechristened Roberto Who?

"If you add up all his good days, his really good days, at the

Tour, there were what, three? Four?" Armstrong said at training camp. "I think that can be replaced. You watch."

Armstrong beamed them The Look, which morphed into a smile of contentment, the mug of a guy who's got the world on a string. Everything was in place. He was in good shape, his tech team was cooking up a top-secret new bike, last year's troubles were gone, banished.

The white jet zoomed over the mist, and when it landed the usual things would happen. Mike Anderson, Armstrong's trusty mechanic and assistant, would be waiting. The golf cart would whisper out to the plane and take its passengers and their luggage to the BMW 540i. They would drive into the ancient walled city of Girona, bumping along the narrow cobbled streets of its medieval core. They would walk through the inner gate of the rebuilt palace that now held his apartment. And tomorrow Armstrong would climb on his bike, and his cycling season in Europe would officially begin.

A couple of days later, after he awoke to the sound of somebody pounding at the door, Armstrong would tell the story of the latest invasion. A random troll—an autograph hunter, it turned out—finding his way past the twenty-foot-tall front door, through the inner iron bars, then up the stone stairs to his very door, bellowing Armstrong's name and banging with relentless fist—*boom, boom, boom*—like some avenging angel or bill collector looking for his due.

"Pretty funny, huh?" Armstrong said, though he wasn't smiling when he said it.

As Armstrong prepared for his first ride in Spain, his rivals were posted around him like so many Shakespearean sentries. The three rode for different teams, each choosing his own path of attack.

In Mallorca, off the coast of Spain, Jan Ullrich chose power. The T-Mobile rider, already regarded as the sport's greatest talent, had embarked on a weight-training program. His goal was to strengthen his right leg, which had been weakened by surgery two years earlier.

"He raced last year with a muscle imbalance," said his physiotherapist, Birgit Krohme. "Now we must balance him out, add power, and then lose the weight."

Ullrich was a child of power, a thirty-year-old East German who had used cycling to escape his family's poor roots, rising through Berlin's Soviet-model sports schools. Since his unexpected Tour win in 1997, Ullrich struggled with injuries and what the German press referred to as "the appetite issue." Each year, however, he snapped into form in time for the Tour. In six tours, Ullrich had never finished lower than second.

"Jan waits until the water is up to his nose. Then he starts swimming," is how T-Mobile's team manager Walter Godefroot put it.

As fate and race organizers would have it, the 2004 Tour would suit such an approach. The race could well be decided on the next-to-last stage, a long, hilly time trial in Besançon that closely mirrored the 2003 time trial in which Ullrich had beaten Armstrong by 1:36, the cycling equivalent of two touchdowns. Indeed, the time trial potentially looked to be Armstrong's Achilles' heel: he'd won only one long Tour time trial since 2001. By adding power, Ullrich was playing to his natural strengths, pushing all his chips on that day.

"I do not race by numbers," Ullrich said cryptically. "When my power comes, it will come, and we will see who is the strongest."

In Girona, ahead of Armstrong, awaited his former teammate Tyler Hamilton, a thirty-three-year-old from Marblehead, Massachusetts. Hamilton was known as the nicest and toughest man in the sport, a reputation he'd earned by demonstrating an ungodly tolerance for pain. Hamilton smiled as he rode with broken bones; smiled as he ground his teeth to their nerves. Smiling was part of the bargain he'd made, a bargain built on the old Protestant belief that modesty and perseverance would be rewarded.

For Hamilton, the key to beating Armstrong lay in his team. Hamilton, who had served Armstrong in three tours, was attempting to build his new Phonak team into one worthy of taking on Armstrong's vaunted U.S. Postal squad. For the first time in his long career, Hamilton would be in charge. He would be the unquestioned leader; he would call the shots, pick his riders, control their efforts, build a team in his modest, gritty image.

"This is what it takes to win the Tour," he said in March. "A team with full commitment, one goal. And a bit of luck."

The luck Hamilton needed most was to ride through a Tour without crashing. He'd finished second in the 2002 Tour of Italy with a broken shoulder; fourth in the 2003 Tour de France with a broken collarbone. His perseverance had brought him a measure of fame, but it was a skill that he was weary of displaying.

"I don't mind doing those things, but I don't want to have to do them. Because I always wonder what might have happened if I was at full strength. And this year I hope to find out the answer to that question."

In the hills of northern Spain, Iban Mayo was preparing in the best Basque style, which is to say by instinct. Mayo, a twenty-six-year-old welder's son, was considered the best pure climber in the world, with a swashbuckling personality and a knack for defeating Armstrong. He'd beaten the champion several times head to head, most famously last Tour on Alpe d'Huez, a mountain that happened to be the site of a time trial that would serve as the centerpiece of this year's Tour. For the Basques, a rebellious, cycling-mad people who'd lived under the boot of occupying governments for two thousand years, most recently Spain, Mayo wasn't just a rider. He was a conquering knight, the pride of a lost nation.

To prepare, Mayo rode the climbs of his youth, near the village of Igurre. He rode without sophisticated powermeters, without a detailed training program. He raced the same way. He'd attacked Armstrong last year at a pre-Tour race called the Dauphiné Libéré. He'd attacked by intuition, varying the tempo, pushing Armstrong to his limit and past it. It had worked.

"The time Mayo tried to kill me," was the way Armstrong referred to the race.

"Mayo, he is the one we don't understand," Postal director Bruyneel said. "I don't think he is close to anybody."

Nobody, perhaps, but the Basques, whom Mayo passed on the roads as he trained. Old men and children who needed a hero. Kids from poor villages who raised their fists and shouted the words from their nation's anthem: *Gora, gora, gora*—up, up, up.

CHAPTER 2

HARD BOYS

> In case of fatal accident, I beg of the spectators not to feel
> sorry for me. I am a poor man, an orphan since the age of
> eleven, and I have suffered much. Death holds no terror for
> me. The record attempt is my way of expressing myself. If
> the doctors can do no more for me, please bury me by the
> side of the road where I have fallen.
>
> —Cyclist Jose Meiffret, in a note carried in his
> pocket as he attempted to set a world speed
> record in 1962

Bike racers are good at hoping. You can see it in their eyes at the start of a race, that glimmering look of "maybe today." You can also see it in the casual, aristocratic way they escort their bikes to the start, as if they were guiding horses—which might be the most hopeful part, because, as a rule, none of them comes from a background that's remotely aristocratic.

As boxing once was to the American underclass, so cycling has long been to poor European kids, a magnet for foundlings and farm kids, the hard-eyed lads with the least to lose and the most to prove. Small-town boys who worked like stevedores during the week and spent each Sunday on wooden kneelers, surrounded by images of bodily sacrifice. The roster of Tour de France champions is a chronicle of successful escapes: Charly Gaul, butcher; Frederico Bahamontes, vegetable-stand boy; Lucien Aimar, carpenter; Roger Pingeon, plumber; Bernard Hinault, farmboy; Miguel Induráin the same. Both Armstrong and Ullrich were abandoned by their fathers at a young age, a biographical detail that strikes some veteran observers as so predictable as to be unworthy of mention. *Of course* they are fatherless; *of course* they are ghosted. How else could they possibly have what it takes? Jacques Anquetil's father was rumored to beat him. Maurice Garin, who won the first Tour de France in 1903, was a chimney sweep whose parents, legend has it, gave him away in exchange for a wheel of cheese.

Just as with boxing, hope is not merely helpful; it is indispensable. Boxers can at least fool themselves into thinking they have a fifty-fifty shot of winning each match; pro cyclists routinely go winless for seasons, even careers. The money is small compared to other professional sports (minimum salary of $30,000; most in the $50,000—$80,000 range, a handful cross the million-dollar mark), the season is long, careers are cup-of-coffee short, and the injury rates are high enough that Lloyd's of London is one of the few firms willing to provide health insurance for professional cyclists—and even they are picky about it. For example, Lloyd's insures Tyler Hamilton's body with the exception of his left shoulder, which they deemed too likely to be rebroken in a crash.

That is the great open secret of bike racing—how often and how terribly they crash. They crash in sprints and on downhills, on greasy roundabouts and on sun-melted tar. They lose eyes. They go into comas. They break their backs with such regularity that they have a nifty-sounding term for it: "percussion fracture."

Here's the report for two weeks in March 2004: On Tuesday, March 16, Gaizka Lejarreta crashed and went into a coma. That Saturday, Carlos Da Cruz broke his back and wrist, and Rik Reinerink fractured his shoulder blade. The following Wednesday, Pietro Caucchioli broke his collarbone. On Thursday, Armstrong's teammate Dave Zabriskie suffered a severe concussion and tore off the flesh over his eye, cheek, and ear. In the same race, but a different crash, Ted Huang broke his cheekbone and also received a concussion, and Mariano Friedick broke his collarbone. Also on Thursday, but in a different race, Michael Rasmussen broke his collarbone and Rafael Casero broke three ribs. The following Monday, Paul Van Hyfte broke his elbow, and Stuart O'Grady broke a rib. On Wednesday, March 31, Michael Skelde broke two vertebrae (percussion fracture) and received a concussion.

On average, it works out to about five serious injuries a week shared among the four hundred or so professional cyclists. Over the course of a six-month season, that amounts to a one-in-four chance that they'll log hospital time. In the 2002 NASCAR season, by comparison, there were five serious injuries all year.

Luck, therefore, is regarded as a skill, and is maximized through a complex grid of superstition that is equal parts Catholicism and old-time cyclist voodoo. Dutch rider Michael Boogerd carried a medallion crammed with his first tooth, his girlfriend's first tooth, and a four-leaf clover. The wife of Bernard Thévenet, the French Tour winner who cracked Eddy Merckx in the 1975 Tour, used tarot cards. The U.S. Postal support staff is aware that Viatcheslav Ekimov cannot abide a race jersey or hotel room number containing the number 13; his teammate Chechu Rubiera rides with a tiny Virgin of Asturias dangling from his brake cable.

Not everyone is a believer, of course. During the 2002 Tour de France, Michael Sandstod of Team CSC decided to perform a demonstration at the team dinner. First, Sandstod knocked over the salt shaker. Everyone waited for him to perform the usual ritual passing of the shaker, the pitching of salt over the left shoulder. But to his teammates' horror and disbelief, Sandstod didn't pick up the salt—no, he spilled it again on purpose, letting the grains sprinkle on the tablecloth, on the carpet. He poured out the salt in his hand and threw it around in the smiling, imperturbable manner of a missionary priest in a pagan temple.

"Don't you see?" Sandstod said. "It's just *salt!*"

The following afternoon brought the second half of Sandstod's demonstration, as he crashed on a steep downhill section, breaking his shoulder, fracturing eight ribs, and puncturing a lung. He nearly died, and spent that evening attached to a respirator in the intensive care unit while the story of his apostasy was repeated in hushed tones around team dinner tables.

So they do not talk about it. They chat endlessly about indigestion or a poor night's sleep, but crashes? "I will not speak of that," says Ekimov. Better to talk of overcooking turns, of touching the floor, of losing bark, of leaving meat on the road. Everyone else, the obedient media, the teams, the families, plays along, so that crashes seem like afterthoughts, such as in the 2003 Milan–San Remo race, when Martin Derganc fell, suffered a severe head injury, and was choking to death on his tongue until a mechanic, realizing what was happening, jammed in a screwdriver and opened his airway. It's good fun, no big deal! Never mind that nearly naked bodies are routinely flung into masses of sharp metal. Never mind that crashes carry an acrid smell that veterans recognize as the smell of burning flesh—it's fine, somebody just overcooked! Someone touched the floor!

But there is something far worse than crashing: being left behind. Not wanting to be left behind is the main cause of a primal scene that is enacted every few days during the cycling season. A rider crashes and is badly injured—like U.S. Postal rider Michael Barry was in the 2002 Tour of Spain. He touched the floor hard on a downhill and got tagged by a motorcycle and dragged seventy feet. He had road rash on every part of his body but the soles of his feet. He was bleeding—not the dull surface stuff, but bright, arterial blood. And Barry got back on his bike and rode for two hours to the finish. He had to quit the next day, but he had done the important thing: he had proved he would not be left behind.

Mothers, of course, have an instinctive grasp of these facts, and so racers' early years brim with illicit tales of bicycles stashed behind barns, scabs clumsily explained away, shiny jerseys hidden beneath mattresses. Long after they make good, the figure of the disapproving mother looms: Rubiera might have ridden on three Tour de France—winning teams, but his mother still lights a candle at the beginning of each season, praying that he'll come to his senses and quit.

But they can't resist. Bike racing contains everything a boy could love: speed, danger, heroism, and, most of all, the promise of change.

Because cycling is nonimpact—which is to say, gentle on bones and joints—it opens the door to the deepest of impacts, the pushing of the human body to its limits. This property, when mixed with the human will, creates some impressive numbers. The average pro cyclist will pedal far enough in training each year to encircle the globe; the daily metabolic rate of a Tour de France cyclist exceeds that of Everest climbers and comes close to matching the highest rates found in any other animal species. But for these hard-eyed boys, as they work themselves into men worthy of winning the Tour de France, the hope lies in the idea that pouring all your energy into a bicycle can raise you up, make you different than you are.

In the winter of 2004, hope was swirling mightily in the misty air. Armstrong's rivals might have been different nationalities, riding for different teams, but the hope moving inside them was identical, a kind of quickening that could be summed up by a single image that glowed in each of their minds: the Dead Elvis Grin.

The Dead Elvis Grin is a term coined by a German journalist, which refers to Armstrong's facial expression when he's pushed to the edge, when he can go no harder. In bike racing, as in poker, looking cool and impervious is the same as being cool and impervious. Racers thus spend a lot of time studying one another for what card players refer to as tells: the imminent signs of cracking, the moments of supreme vulnerability, when one good push can decide a race. Some tells are so obvious as to be regarded as amateurish: the pleading downward glance at the legs, the death-grip on the handlebars. But since champions don't exceed their limits as much or as often, their tells tend to be more subtle, and gaining knowledge of them is akin to cracking the entry code to a bank door: it doesn't get you the cash, but it gets you inside the building.

For Fausto Coppi, the two-time Tour champion, it was a vein behind his right knee, which bulged prominently (his rivals would assign teammates to shadow Coppi, shouting a predetermined code word when the vein appeared). For three-time Tour winner Greg LeMond, it was a pattern of sitting and standing, combined with the distinctive way he rocked his shoulders. Eyes tend to be a giveaway, the soft tissue reddening and puffing. Cyclists were among the first sportsmen to take to wearing sunglasses during competition—not to help them see out, but to prevent others from seeing in.

When it came to concealing his tell, Miguel Induráin was the modern era's king, so much so that when he cracked on Les Arcs in 1996 while trying for his sixth Tour victory, none of his rivals could comprehend what had happened. They looked around, half panicked—where's Mig? Had he fallen? The knowledge gradually dawned: Induráin had indeed fallen, in the largest sense. Later, explanations abounded: he was too heavy, he'd overtrained, he had forgotten to eat, but the bottom line was that he'd cracked right next to them, and he'd done it so beautifully that nobody had noticed. It was the perfect cyclist's demise: five and a half years of impermeable stoicism followed by a few seconds of collapse, the sphinx crumbling into dust.

Armstrong had been Induráin's worthy successor, often ascending the steepest climbs with such seeming ease as to make the mere opening of his mouth worthy of note. His full-blown crack had not been sighted in years, not since a day on the Col de Joux-Plane in the 2000 Tour when the mercurial Italian, 1998 Tour de France champion Marco Pantani, famously put him over the edge by charging off 130 kilometers from the finish of a particularly hard six-climb day, forcing Armstrong to chase, and ultimately to suffer what he'd called "my hardest day on a bike."

All that changed at the 2003 Tour, as the peloton had a front-row seat for a new show: Armstrong's almost-crack. It was unveiled on stage 8 to Alpe d'Huez, exhibited vividly during the stage 12 time trial in Gaillac, and continued on the following stage to Plateau de Bonascre. It was a little different every time, but it usually began with Armstrong changing positions on his bike—standing, sitting, standing again, rooting around for more power. Then he would lean forward on the handlebars, throwing his body weight into the pedals, his head tipping forward and his eyes peering out of the tops of their sockets, as if he were resisting an invisible hand pushing his head down. His face would turn red, then ashen. The furrows in his forehead would deepen, and his eyes fix, and as they did, his upper lip would slowly rise up over his front teeth, a half-snarl, half-smile that resembled a . . . Dead Elvis Grin! Bingo!

But through the winter, few spoke openly of Armstrong's vulnerability, not Ullrich, not Mayo, and certainly not the ever-polite Hamilton. Why should they? Everybody knew that Armstrong used detraction as fuel, reading every article, remembering every quote. Why not just let the forces in play—fate, fame, age, scandal—do their silent work?

Exhibit A was the divorce. When Lance and Kristin Armstrong had separated in January of 2003, it was seen as an abrupt fracture in what had been a storybook marriage. Both Armstrongs attributed their split to the stress the past five years had brought. When they'd married, Armstrong was a recovering cancer patient with a questionable future. When they divorced, he was one of the planet's best-known, best-paid athletes.

"[The split] was brought on gradually by a number of pressures, rather than one big blow-up," Kristin said in 2003. "We've been together four and a half years, and we've had six homes, three languages, three countries, one cancer comeback, three children, four Tour de France wins, and one rise to celebrity. You're not supposed to cram such a huge amount of events into such a small period of time."

For Kristin Armstrong, post-divorce life moved slowly. After the final separation in September 2003, she withdrew, grew melancholy, lost weight. That fall, at the encouragement of concerned friends, she started distance running. In December, a few days after the divorce papers were finalized, she entered the White Rock Marathon in Dallas.

"In my first marathon, I tried to be like Lance, who, as long as he's pushing himself as an athlete and going fast, doesn't have to deal with his emotions," she said. "But I realized that I didn't need to run away from my despair or misery, that I could handle things. I realized that we were not alike in that way."

"Divorce has been harder than dealing with cancer," Lance said in the fall of 2004. "It's not just the breakup of an unhappy marriage. There are three other people to consider. But I think she's a good mom, and I know I'm a good dad, and that's what counts."

On the surface at least, Armstrong seemed to adjust quickly to single life, which the tabloids recounted in detail. There he was in October, canoodling with actress Sandra Bullock, reportedly giving her a golden necklace inscribed "You Keep My Heart Racing." Two weeks later, reports had him dating forty-two-year-old singer Crow. Within a month, Crow was a constant public presence, as the couple snuggled at the Country Music Awards, took newlywed-style quizzes on AM radio, and strode red carpets alongside Jennifer Aniston and Brad Pitt.

"His life is huge, and it keeps getting bigger and crazier," said Bob Roll, the cyclist-turned-television-commentator. "I don't know how he keeps it all together."

It was in this atmosphere of wonder that the shrimp-surfing story began to circulate. According to it, Armstrong and some of his friends were on the jet on their way back from a Washington, D.C., function, and they were having fun, you know, popping a beer or two, enjoying that we're-in-a-private-jet buzz. When the jet revved, seatbelts clicked. Then Armstrong stood up in the aisle and assumed the classic surfer's stance. Others joined him. The jet accelerated, hurtling down the runway, hitting 100, 150 miles an hour, and Armstrong was there—look ma! No hands!—hanging ten, riding that sucker into the air, and as the jet tilted skyward, a large, round crystal bowl of shrimp tumbled off the front table and rolled down the aisle, accelerating like some boulder out of an *Indiana Jones* movie, scattering shrimp like pink confetti, and Armstrong was dodging the boulder and now he was surfing the blue sky and everybody on board was howling with delight, and the bowl crashed into the back of the plane as it zoomed into the stratosphere.

"He will be tired after touring with Sheryl Crow," Spanish rider Francisco Mancebo blurted out during an interview in training camp. Then, realizing with horror what he had done, and who would soon be reading his words, quickly corrected himself: "No no, I am only joking!"

CHAPTER 3

INSIDE THE VAULT

"The king! Where is the king?"

Dr. Michele Ferrari, Armstrong's fifty-year-old trainer, stood on the cobbled street with his long arms outstretched in the golden Spanish sunlight. He was dark-haired and darty-eyed. He wore a shiny, robin's-egg blue sweatsuit, a red nylon backpack, and a broad, teasing smile.

"The king, he is late," Ferrari announced in the manner of the town crier, gesturing theatrically toward the tall wooden doors. "But that is why he is the king, no? A king should not have to hurry."

Ferrari was here because he had what was widely acknowledged as one of the two most brilliant minds in cycling. The other belonged to fellow Italian Dr. Luigi Cecchini, who trains several of Armstrong's top rivals. Ferrari and Cecchini, former colleagues, were usually described in the media as "notorious." Exactly what notorious meant was difficult to say, but it seemed based on three qualificiations: (1) Ferrari and Cecchini, who each worked as independent contractors, had trained many extremely successful cyclists; (2) Italian authorities and the European cycling media had raised questions over whether they had used entirely legal means to do so; and (3) it was a compelling notion. Can any reader remain uninterested in a story that mentions one of the planet's best athletes being advised by "the notorious Doctor Ferrari"?

By any measure, Michele (pronounced mi-KEL-ay) Ferrari had

been a key part of Armstrong's Tour preparation since 1999, and part of his life since they had met in 1995. The Italian was the lesser known of Armstrong's duo of key advisors, the other being Armstrong's longtime personal coach, Chris Carmichael. Carmichael, who lived in Colorado Springs, gathered and analyzed Armstrong's training data via e-mail. Ferrari, who lived in northern Italy, spent a good portion of the season with Armstrong, including five to six weeks immediately prior to the Tour, an event Ferrari was famous for not attending.

"Eh, the Tour, it is a big show," Ferrari said, frowning. "I do not wish to go to a big show."

Due to his regular presence, Ferrari had been granted the honor of a nickname: Dr. Evil. It was a good nickname, partly because of Ferrari's dark features and partly because it poked fun at the pesky cloud of questions that followed him, questions that Armstrong had always dismissed with the affirmation that Ferrari was a smart, honest trainer who provided Armstrong with training programs and advice, period. As it happened, Ferrari was currently on trial on three counts of doping-related offenses in Italian court (charges against Cecchini had been dropped in 2001 due to lack of evidence). Ferrari's trial did not involve Armstrong, who has always tested clean, and who expressed confidence that his trainer would be acquitted. But it was a concern. My conversations with Ferrari took place, in part, because I agreed not to ask questions about doping.

"I believe all these charges are groundless," Armstrong told the newspapers. "Michele is telling the truth. I will back him until I see evidence otherwise. The man is extremely talented; he's more than a coach, he's like a mathematician or a physicist."

As mathematics went, this qualified as an important day. Dr. Evil had flown to Girona from his home in northern Italy to administer Armstrong's first conditioning test of the season—to listen to the engine, as Ferrari put it.

But as the clock ticked and His Majesty did not show, Ferrari's smile grew broader and a touch strained. Ferrari had the same concerns as everyone else about the challenges of the coming year, plus a few that were his alone. Originally, the plan had been to train and test Armstrong a week ago at the remote island of Tenerife, off the coast of Africa, which was one of their favorite training haunts. But Armstrong had canceled at the last minute and had told Ferrari to come to Girona instead.

"I think I know why," Ferrari had said, looking distressed at dinner the previous night. "It was Sheryl Crow's birthday. He wanted to be with her, to show her this place." He grimaced and took a sip of his wine.

When he talked about Armstrong, Ferrari's face functioned as a kind of Geiger counter, twitching and flexing in response to the level of risk. It was easy to pick out the risk factors, because Ferrari stretched out the word in his rich Italian accent. Muscles became *maaaaahhhssscles*. Stress became *streeeeehhhsss*. Blood became *blaaaaahhhd*. And the latest factor—a mathematically significant factor, in Ferrari's view—was that his newly divorced client appeared to be in *laaaaahhhve*.

"Marriage, divorce, these things happen," Ferrari said, fiddling with his wineglass. "With Lance, they perhaps happen more quickly."

The effects of the Sheryl factor were already being felt. For instance, as Ferrari outlined the coming season's schedule with Armstrong, I inquired where their next training session would take place. Ferrari's lips pursed; his forehead suddenly resembled an accordion.

"Lance is talking about going to Nice," Ferrari said, extending the word. "But this makes no sense to go there in March, it is not time to do those tests." Then he raised his finger in the *a-ha* gesture. "But I think that perhaps he wishes to show Sheryl the Cote d'Azur."

I responded by telling Ferrari about a recent *New York Post* gossip column that said Crow wanted to have Armstrong's baby.

At the word "baby," the Geiger counter began to spark and smoke: Ferrari's eyes bugged out, his head tipped sideways until his cheek was almost touching his Serrano ham.

"Sheryl is *preeehhhgnant*? *Now*?" he asked incredulously. He regained his composure only when I reassured him several times that the article had said no such thing, that it was merely gossip. It didn't seem to relax him much.

"Ahhh," he said, mopping sweat from his brow. "Ahhh, well."

Ferrari's attentiveness was shared by many in Armstrong's circle. Cyclists' superstitions about crashing were exceeded only by their superstitions about their bodies in general, especially food and sex. Routine prohibitions included:

- No ice cream (causes indigestion)
- No air conditioners (cause illness due to bacteria growing on the filter)
- No hot sauce (indigestion)
- No carbonated water (diarrhea)
- No soft center of bread (same)
- No tomato sauce (acidity)
- No chocolate mousse (excessive sweating)
- No shaving of legs the night before a race (energy lost in regrowing hair)
- Minimal contact between skin and water (softens the muscles). A few riders take this so far so as to shower with uniforms on; another rider, Isidro Nozal of Liberty Seguros, is believed (with pungent evidence) to forego showers during a stage race.

Few of these prohibitions make scientific sense, of course, but that is not the point. They are ancient laws, handed down by elders and violated at a racer's imminent peril. And none is more ancient or perilous than the presence of a woman, except perhaps a woman who wishes to become pregnant. Celibacy before races is routine— two weeks before a one-day race, six weeks before a grand tour, advised Irish great Sean Kelly. To prevent temptation, wives and girlfriends are not permitted in team hotels or at team dinners, and certainly never during races—a Spanish rider was booted from his team last year for that offense. When Stephen Roche's chain fell off in the 1981 Tour, his director remarked, "This is the kind of thing that happens when women are brought to races." But word was already out: not only had Sheryl Crow stayed in Armstrong's room during training camp, she was eating meals with the team.

"She's *what*?" said president of USA Cycling and Armstrong's friend Jim Ochowicz, when he was informed of the arrangement. "She's *where*?"

"This is not completely usual," Ferrari had said tactfully last night. "But what is usual for Lance is not usual for everyone. If it makes him happy, then it is good. Happiness, that is a good factor."

Back on the street in Girona, Ferrari found his own measure of happiness in the arrival of Floyd Landis and George Hincapie, Armstrong's teammates and two of the twenty or so American cyclists who make their homes in Girona. Hincapie was a dark-haired and languid New Yorker; Landis a red-haired and springy Pennsylvanian. Hincapie and Landis, veteran Tour riders, knew Ferrari well, having been tested by him many times previous.

Hincapie waved his hello, leaned his bike against a tree, and quickly slipped into a wicker chair in obedience to bike racing's first rule of energy conservation: *Never stand when you can sit; never sit when you can lie down.* Never walk, that goes without saying. Walking, particularly upstairs, makes their legs ache. Cyclists congregate in Girona for several reasons—it's near the Pyrenees, the cost of living is lower than in France, but also because its tight medieval layout keeps perambulation to a happy minimum. Armstrong, who lives on the second floor, frequently uses the elevator.

Landis, though, did not sit down. Neither did Ferrari, who shifted his weight from leg to leg.

"We must search for the king," Ferrari said. "We should perhaps have a look inside, no?"

"He's been late the last couple days," Landis said in a joking tone.

"Really?" Ferrari leaned in, interested. This was not a joke to him. "How late? Half an hour?"

"Don't sweat it, Michele," Landis said, trying to placate the doctor. "Ten, fifteen minutes, tops."

"Hmmm," Ferrari said. "So we go in now, yes?"

With the lanky Ferrari in the lead, we ventured through the tall wooden doors, through the iron-bar gate, and into the shared inner courtyard of the renovated palace that holds nine apartments, including Armstrong's. Light filtered down, showing smooth stone walls and balconies on three sides, an abrupt change from the rougher textures outside. The impression was of entering a bank vault, and it wasn't lessened by the bluish glint in the security camera lens aimed at a pair of massive steel doors at the courtyard's far end.

Ferrari strode across the stone floor and poked his head through a crack in the doors, finding not the hoped-for Armstrong but rather the tall, amiable figure of Mike Anderson, Armstrong's mechanic and assistant, who was prepping a bike for today's ride.

Anderson pushed the steel doors further open, revealing, with a B-movie creak, the sanctum sanctorum, a dark, narrow, stone-walled room about the size of a studio apartment. A dozen or so bikes dangled from ceiling hooks, wheels and tires were stacked like cordwood along the walls, the wooden workbench held a neat assortment of shoes, helmets, and shark-toothed cogsets.

One way to look at this room was to imagine all the stuff that was *not* here—the millions of dollars in bike frames, wheels, helmets, and shoes that had failed to pass through the needle's eye of Armstrong's standards. Everything in here had been sorted, tested, and designated by its curator as The Shit. That's what Armstrong called something he liked, and when he really liked something, which happened perhaps three times a year, he granted that item his ultimate accolade: he said it would kill them.

Here then, outlined in white halogen light, lay the Museum of Shit That Will Kill Them. There, glistening silver on the workbench, were the new Nike shoes with the Texas flag on one buckle and the world-champion rainbow insignia on the other. There, in the drawer below, were the twenty identical Selle San Marco brand saddles, the ones Armstrong had just sorted through as if he were selecting a cantaloupe, squeezing each until he found one or two keepers. There, above a bright plastic kiddie car and lawn mower, hung Crow's birthday present, the buffed-out silver team-edition Trek, along with a helmet inscribed with her equally new nickname, Juanita Cuervo ("cuervo" is Spanish for "crow"). And there, swoopy and black in its stand, stood the piece de resistance, the new top-secret time-trial bike, the one that Trek had been building since the summit meeting in Austin last August, the one whose features Armstrong had cryptically referred to in the press, about whose details the mechanics had been sworn to secrecy.

Standing just outside the room, Landis and Hincapie couldn't help but sneak an admiring look around. Ferrari glanced impatiently, unimpressed. He was a cyclist himself, but these were not the machines in which he was interested.

The courtyard echoed with the promising tap-dancer click of bike cleats, and Ferrari's eyes flashed hopefully to see . . . not Armstrong but Juanita Cuervo herself, looking decidedly unpregnant in lavender top, black tights, and cycling shoes that, while fine for a bike, produced rather less elegance on a stone floor.

"Hello hello hello," she called.

Crow click-clacked gamely toward us, a fluoro-pink piece of gum being worked over by what a British music reviewer famously deemed "the sexiest mouth in rock." She smiled and did her nice-to-meet-yous. With her new friend Odessa Gunn, the wife of American cyclist Levi Leipheimer, she seized her bike from Anderson and wheeled it into the courtyard.

"You ready, girlfriend?" Gunn asked.

"Ready as I'm gonna be, babe," Juanita replied, grasping the saddle and handlebars in the classic cyclist's pose. She leaned it casually against her thigh as she cinched her helmet.

Hincapie and Landis watched with anesthetized expressions. They'd met her before, but it was still a lot to absorb: Sheryl Crow, a bona fide rock star—Eric Clapton's old squeeze, for God's sake, a Grammy winner—kitting up for a morning spin.

"You look ready, George," Crow said.

"Nuh-uh." Hincapie managed a shy smile. "I don't feel ready."

"Now now," Crow warned. "Don't try to fool me."

Crow made microadjustments to the sleeves of her lavender top. She checked her shoes. She lifted her bike and thudded it testingly against the ground.

Landis and Hincapie stared with respectful detachment, like amateur chemists who had accidentally created a powerful explosive. It didn't make sense—Sheryl Crow, here, with them. Cyclists were dorks, weren't they? That was the term they had used in high school, still used, "cycle dorks." As in, skinny, equipment-obsessed Euro-dweebs. Like most American cyclists, they'd always identified themselves as uncool—in fact, that was the cool thing about it, the spectacular private uncoolness of it, so much that their sport became their secret. And here was this MTV star, with her juicy pink gum and her tawny hair who not only wanted to be with them, she wanted to be *like* them, with the tights and the duckfoot shoes. They stood transfixed, memorizing her outline in case she should evaporate.

To their left, out of Crow's line of sight, Ferrari's face started twitching and clicking. He had heard that she would be around . . . but riding a bike? Riding *with* Lance? His eyebrows began to jump seismically.

Behind Ferrari and Crow, a large yellow duffel bag on his shoulder, the king walked into the courtyard. This was the way he entered most rooms, checking things out from the jump with clear, assessing glances—or, preferably, even before he came into the room, doing the various background checks that he called his homework. He was forever surprising people with how much he already knew about them—a flattering, slightly disconcerting moment for the visitor, but one that Armstrong handled with marked casualness. Because it was not his knowing that concerned him. It was yours.

We shook hands, his grip cool and light. We chatted for a while. He knew my family had moved to Girona. I asked about schools.

"My wife looked at sending our oldest—" he came up short. "My *ex-wife*, I mean," he said, enunciating the words as if practicing the phrase.

He stared at the ground, kept going.

"But the Spanish school day is really long, and when the kids are young, you want to be with them. So that wasn't going to work for her—for us, I mean."

He blinked. For a half-second, it was officially awkward: his rock-star girlfriend a few steps away, his kids' toys gathering dust in the bike room, his pronouns getting tangled up. He had an air of surprise.

Then he blinked and looked around intently, and the moment was gone—not dissipated, but actively pressed away. He started over, bending and rooting through his yellow duffel. He pulled out a map.

"You guys ready?" he called to Gunn.

"Almost," she said.

"I'm a map *freak*," he said, shaking the map open. "There are some roads out here you guys wouldn't believe."

"I believe," Crow piped in, "after what I saw the other day."

"There's better," Armstrong said to her, tipping his head, letting us mark his meaning. "There are some spots that are crazy cool, way wilder than that, like the backside of Hell's Angels."

"The backside of Hell's Angels," Anderson echoed appreciatively.

"We'll get you up there," Armstrong said to Crow. "You'll love it."

"I know you will," she said, and the sexiest mouth smiled, and everybody else couldn't help but smile too, even Dr. Evil. All that ex-wife awkwardness of a moment ago was a million miles away—or, rather, it was still there, buried but somehow fueling the quickness and the energy of the new thing, this moment, *now*.

"Here, and here, and here," Armstrong said, pointing to the map, where only he could see. "Oh, and over here too. This, *this* is a great spot."

Armstrong is a map guy, in the largest sense of the word. No matter how marvelous some place is, there's always some place higher and more beautiful, and he knows exactly where it is and he wants to show you. To be with him is to receive doses of certitude and mystery, together. After he won his first few Tours, Armstrong's friends would occasionally get calls at odd hours, and pick up to hear Armstrong's voice asking, "Guess where I am right now?" Those calls tailed off for a while, but this winter he started making them again.

Now Armstrong walked toward Anderson. "Ready?" Meaning, was the bike ready?

"Ready," Anderson replied in the practiced, easy rhythm of an air-traffic controller, and just then Armstrong's cell phone rang.

"Yeah, what's going on?" Armstrong answered. "Yeah, yeah. How come?" He listened, staring intently at the floor drain. "No, I'll take care of it. Right."

This conversation was repeated in various forms, dozens of times a day. Sometimes it was about Tailwind Sports, the management company that ran the U.S. Postal team (and which Armstrong partly owned), or his new top-secret bike (which he was in the process of finding brakes for), or about his race schedule, or about the pending endorsement renewal with Coca-Cola, or about any of a zillion projects for his cancer foundation, or about how they were going to sue the everloving shit out of the *Weekly World News* if they published that photo of Lance with a pregnant woman and claimed falsely it was his love child (the woman was Allison Anderson, his mechanic's wife), or how the president of Spain was asking President Bush to ask Lance to ride the Tour of Spain, or how his buddy Korioth might come out in March, or how Bruyneel had just seen a photo of Ullrich (he looked fat!), or how his agent had heard that Matt Damon might be interested in playing Armstrong in the movie they were putting together on Armstrong's life, or how there was a cyclist in California who had just been killed by a mountain lion and could Armstrong write a quick letter to be read at the funeral, nothing big, just a few words, please.

"It seems like he has about five lives, living them all at once," says Haven Hamilton, the wife of cyclist Tyler Hamilton, and a neighbor. "When you're with him, it's all so casual, and then later when you think about everything that's going on, you realize that his life is . . ." she struggles for the word, "humongous."

Well-meaning friends over the years have tried to persuade Armstrong to hire an assistant. But he won't. And why should he? He has a system. He has his BlackBerry—or CrackBerry, as he calls it, giving a nod to its addictive hold. He has a few trusted guys, his satellites, each assigned to a specific orbit. There are Ferrari and Carmichael for training, Bill Stapleton and Bart Knaggs at Capital Sports & Entertainment (CS&E) for sponsorship and legal stuff, Mark Higgins and Jogi Muller for media, Bruyneel for team and tactics and equipment and everything else, Scott Daubert for Trek bike stuff. The satellites know the rules—four or five lines per e-mail, max. Quick updates and questions—nothing squishy, everything wound nice and tight, like a Super Ball. All these projectiles come whizzing in, and he fires them back with spin, challenging, provoking, pushing, all of it adding up to a hot infochemical flow that tracks his rivals and his many projects. Hire an assistant? This is the interaction he lives for, to answer and then to ask a question, which is itself another answer. *Guess where I am right now?*

"We have three rules," says Stapleton, his agent. "Keep. Lance. Informed. Nothing bothers him more than not knowing something."

"Lance has a very well-defined decision-making mechanism within him," says Knaggs, a former riding buddy who works as CS&E's marketing director. Prior to his present job, Knaggs designed artificial-intelligence software.

"He got confidence that he was smart through cancer," Knaggs continues. "Before, he'd say he was just a dumb bike racer. But after, he realized there wasn't anything magic to oncology, to anything, and he started getting involved in everything. And by everything, I do mean everything."

Like all effective software, Armstrong's mind functions along a handful of basic principles:

1. Everything is evaluated on a binary scale. On or off, good or bad. "Lance hates gray areas; he doesn't have time for them," Knaggs says. "He sets out to determine very quickly if something or someone is useful to him. If you're not useful, you won't be around long."
2. Attacking is better than defending. In situations of conflict, Armstrong provokes, asks questions, inflicts himself. "He's only

comfortable when he's pushing people to the next level, upping the ante, daring you to match him," Carmichael says. "Whatever the game, whatever the contest, Lance's message is, 'You're a pussy if you don't match me.' And he's tough to match."

3. He is able to block out the negative. "You could give him the most horrible piece of news," his chiropractor Jeff Spencer says. "And he would be able to absorb it, deal with it, and move past it very quickly and never, ever, ever go back to it. He has no fear paralysis, and it frees him up to be optimistic about everything, even when it makes no rational sense to be."

This third quality is perhaps the most interesting, because it is selective. Armstrong is skilled at remembering his detractors, to the point of repeating their names to himself during training rides. His ability to block out—to effectively forget—is applied mostly to his own vulnerabilities, as the following story attests.

At seven p.m. the night before the 2003 tour, Armstrong found himself unable to walk. His hip, which he'd injured in a crash three weeks earlier, had become jammed in its socket. He was due on stage in half an hour for the team-introduction ceremony, but he was unable to climb a single stair. He hobbled to the bus and beckoned for Spencer.

There was no time for X-rays or a full workup. With the music and crowd noise rising, Armstrong lay on his back on the gray leather seat. Spencer leaned and pulled sharply. The air resounded with a concussive pop.

"It was horrifying," Spencer said later. "I was positive I'd broken or torn something. It wasn't the kind of sound that comes from a body, more like something you hear in the forest. Like a ten-inch-thick dry tree snapping across a hollow log."

For a moment, the two men stared at each other. Then Armstrong stood up. Flexed the hip. Tested it on some stairs. Then thanked Spencer and walked off the bus and onto the stage. Armstrong never spoke to Spencer about it again.

"For you or me or almost anyone else on the planet, that's an unbelievably traumatic, scary moment," Spencer said. "He clicks past it, and gets on with the next question."

Put together, the three qualities form a potent combination, a system of ascertaining, attacking, and blocking out that requires vast quantities of fresh stimulus, new contests to engage in. The process is applied with equal vigor to each question, be they small or large. Whom do we pick for the Tour team? What are tech stocks going to do? What's Ullrich doing right now? And one that seemed to be on his mind at the moment—what the hell was this book all about?

I'd done the customary journalistic groundwork, written letters describing the book I planned to write, explained my project to Stapleton and others. But Armstrong wasn't about to fling open his door on my say-so (and, frankly, I would have been surprised if he had). No, this book was a question to be analyzed, another game to be played. I recalled speaking with the journalist Eric Hagerman, who had worked six months on a perceptive profile of Armstrong for *Outside* magazine.

"His people were doing background checks, interviewing people after I spoke with them, watching my every step," Hagerman had told me. "I felt like I was reporting on Watergate."

Due to the obscurity of cycling in America, Armstrong had enjoyed an unprecedented degree of control over the telling of his story, a telling that had occurred largely through his two bestselling memoirs, and the enthusiastic, if not adoring, coverage provided by the Outdoor Life Network (which had just made the marriage official, coming onboard as a formal team sponsor). On the other hand, there was no questioning the fact that there were some journalists and cycling authorities who strongly believed Armstrong had used performance-enhancing drugs, and who would like nothing better than to bring the American down. The result of those two factors was that Armstrong and his people had become skilled at dividing journalists into friends and enemies, and at letting potential enemies know what lay in store for them.

When I first visited CS&E's casual-cool offices in Austin, Texas,

Knaggs started things off with an office tour, lingering in front of a large aquarium filled with a dozen or so dull-looking brown fish. After ten seconds in front of the aquarium, I was ready to move on. But Knaggs wasn't. He knelt in front of the glass, gazing in. I got the distinct impression that I was meant to notice something.

"Are those piranhas?" I finally asked.

Knaggs nodded, pleased. "Look at those teeth," he murmured. "Like razors."*

But for now, here in the courtyard, life was good. Armstrong tip-tapped away on his BlackBerry, then tucked it in his pocket. He turned to Sheryl and Odessa. His eyes roved, checking that they were equipped with water bottles, sunglasses, jackets. Satisfied, he took his bike and wheeled it toward the door, pausing on the threshold. He smiled into the sunshine.

It might have been the first test-day of the year, but it was also a day—a damn fine day, and now he was noticing that, too, breathing it in, letting everyone mark it together. A *kick-ass* day, as a matter of fact, here in Girona's maze of medieval streets, with cool facts clicking all around—the sun bouncing off the cobbles, guitar music trickling from an unseen window, the leathery old ladies scouring their porches with those bristly witches' brooms, the bell of the cathedral exploding *bong bong bong* and scattering the sparrows out into the blue—and he was going to chase that day, track it down, taste it. With Armstrong, there was the feeling of heading out on a big weekend. Bags, bikes, maps, cars, rock stars—we could end up anywhere.

---

*To help ensure openness, I showed Armstrong and his people drafts of what I wrote, in order that they might respond and offer corrections.

The development that helped most, however, occurred early on, when Johan Bruyneel asked if I had any inside information on the condition of Jan Ullrich's oft-injured knee. I passed on a few tidbits (nothing earth-shattering—in fact, I'd seen some of the same material on cycling Web sites). But from that moment on, Bruyneel became a model of helpfulness. As with so many things related to Armstrong and his team, it wasn't about the information; it was about demonstrating loyalty.

"Ladies," he said, ushering Sheryl and Odessa chivalrously out the door.

He walked quickly; Ferrari rushed to fall in step with him, hobbling a bit on the uneven stones.

"This new bike is fast, Michele," Armstrong said, flashing the big-weekend grin. "You're going to love it."

"And you are comfortable with your position? The feelings, they are good?"

"They're good," he said, turning to give Ferrari the high-beams. "Very good."

"We shall see, then." Ferrari was circumspect. He knew from experience that Armstrong could occasionally be romanced by the idea of something new. The conversation flagged, but only for a half-second.

"So they're working on this new jersey for Alpe d'Huez," Armstrong said. "It's made of a kind of new mesh—you know?"

"Eh?" Ferrari said, uncomprehending.

"Mesh, you know?" Armstrong rubbed his thumb and index finger together. "Like a woman's stocking."

"Ahhh." Ferrari smiled lasciviously. "A woman's stocking. That is good. You will ride fast."

"Italians!" Armstrong hooted to no one in particular. "Only thinking of one thing."

"We think of other things," Ferrari said. "Sometimes."

CHAPTER 4

THE NICEST GUY

The multiple difficulties of defeating Lance Armstrong in the Tour de France have been distilled into a theorem by Bob Roll, the former professional cyclist and OLN commentator. Roll's Law consists of two axioms set against each other like a riddle:

1. The way to beat Armstrong is not to make him mad.
2. Beating Armstrong makes him mad.

However, Roll's Law does contain a small opening of logic, and it is this: The way to beat Armstrong is to do it so that he doesn't know you are beating him. To catch him by surprise.

Tyler Hamilton resided in this opening. He also resided, along with his wife Haven, and his golden retriever, Tugboat, in a spacious apartment one floor upstairs from Armstrong in Girona. Armstrong and Hamilton, who were former teammates, shared the same entrance, the same elevator, and the same goal to which they'd devoted their lives. Surprising Armstrong may have been a tall order, but it was one that Hamilton was uniquely well suited for, having built his life around the act of surprising people.

It began with his appearance. Hamilton stood 5' 8", and weighed around 130 pounds. His shoulders were narrow; his hair prep-school short, his ears prominent, his eyes green and alert. He favored checked button-down Oxford shirts, white crewneck undershirts, and well-pressed khakis. He was extraordinarily polite. He had an awareness of small needs, his hands reaching out to open doors, tickle babies, pay for coffees, scratch exactly the right spot behind a dog's ears. He was, in short, the living image of the nicest boy you've ever met. He was also, as he had proven on several well-documented occasions, secretly insane.

This was, after all, the same Tyler Hamilton who slowly ground a dozen teeth down to the nerves after breaking his shoulder early in the 2002 Giro d'Italia, and finished second. Who fractured his collarbone in the first stage of the 2003 Tour and went on to finish such a strong fourth that everyone—Armstrong included—couldn't help but wonder where Hamilton might have finished if only he hadn't crashed.

"It's like there are two people in one body," was how his wife, Haven, explained it. "There's this nice guy you see most of the time, and inside, there's this warrior that comes out on the bike."

Hamilton and Armstrong were profoundly different people on nearly every measurable level. Armstrong was Texan, and had been a dominating force from the moment he stepped onto the bike as a teenager. Hamilton was from Massachusetts, and had spent most of his career in obscurity. Armstrong admitted to few, if any, vulnerabilities. Hamilton was a walking amalgam of vulnerability, a teller of self-deprecating stories. Reporters joked that it would be simpler to interview Tugboat, since his master's repertoire of peerlessly bland quotes had appeared in print a thousand times before: "I was just doing my job." "It hurt a lot, but I kept going." "I'm grateful to my team."

Of course, the rest of his body was not exactly uncommunicative. There was the ugly white scar along the index finger of his left hand, the result of a bloody crash in last year's Tour of Holland, in which he also cracked his femur. There was the tentacle of a scar above his eyebrow, courtesy of a car door he encountered while warming up for a 2002 race in Brussels. And the fine spray of lines at the corners of his eyes, those eyes which, on closer examination, weren't nearly so boyish as they first appeared.

"He's extremely nice and he's extremely tough," said former Postal teammate Jonathan Vaughters. "Somewhere deep inside he's got that edge, that urge to kill—the sport's too hard not to have it. But he buries it very well. I'm not saying he does it intentionally as a tactic. But as a tactic, it works well."

"Tyler doesn't get angry, he gets even in his own way," said Peter Kaiter, a former East German cyclist who helped introduce Hamilton to the sport. "He's very smart, he thinks everything through. Then when it's time to let it all out, he lets it all out."

Exactly what Hamilton was reserving was the more interesting question. It would have been easy to mistake all this for mere niceness and to miss what dwelled quietly beneath, namely a massive deposit of granitic reserve, a quality invented by English Protestants and exported in pure form to Hamilton's hometown of Marblehead, Massachusetts. It was a quality built on one simple rule: the bolder you were, the more deferential you must be. The higher your reach, the more you must, as much as possible, disappear. In time past, the idea was to avoid offending God. In Hamilton's world, the power in question was not quite so distant.

Richard Fries, a longtime friend of Hamilton's and editor of *The Ride* magazine, was visiting with Hamilton recently in his Girona home and made the obvious joke.

"So you think it might get a little chilly around here if you win the tour?" Fries asked, gesturing downstairs, toward Armstrong's apartment.

He waited for the inevitable smile, the Hamiltonian burst of niceness. But Hamilton did not respond. "He stared straight ahead—he gave me nothing. It was like he didn't hear me. He is not going there, not at all."

When Hamilton was thirteen, he helped found a group called Crazykids. At least the kids at the ski school called it that; the parents didn't know about it—or, if they found out, quickly wished they hadn't. The group's purpose was simple: to go out in the woods every day and do something big. Climb a mountain. Cross a frozen river—or, better yet, a partially frozen one. The group included Mark Synnott, who would grow up to be a famed rock-climber, and Robert Frost, now a noted adventure filmmaker. But for now they were just a bunch of restless pups enthralled by the idea of seeing how close they could sneak toward the edge and not get hurt.

If they did get hurt, they were usually too numb from cold to notice. Wildcat Mountain—in New Hampshire, near Mount Washington—was a squat, north-facing slab of ice to which the term "resort" was usually applied ironically. Godawful weather was the norm, and from a tender age Hamilton was faithfully submitted to its charms, his family making the three-hour trip from their Marblehead home each winter weekend. Though the boy had already displayed a somewhat alarming tendency to injure himself (broken leg, chin stitched up several times), Wildcat was a place where he learned to endure pain.

"I still rank those as my most painful days ever, bar none," he says. "But that's the way it was in my family—once you went outside you didn't come back in until the end of the day."

Bill and Lorna Hamilton had met skiing Tuckerman's Ravine, a famously gnarly hike-in descent in the White Mountains, and had essentially stayed outdoors ever since. If you were a Hamilton, it was a given: summers were spent sailing, winters skiing, in between were rafting trips to Alaska, climbs of Mount Washington. Craziness was permitted, even tacitly encouraged outdoors. Within the walls of the Hamilton house, however, another set of rules prevailed, mostly enforced by Bill, a computer consultant. Telephones were answered properly, meals attended punctually. And one of the most respected rules concerned boasting.

"It just was not done," Jennifer Linehan, Tyler's sister, remembered. "If you talked big about something you'd accomplished, they would listen politely and then move on."

Not that there weren't things to boast about. All three Hamilton kids were good athletes, and by his early teens, Tyler was one of the top downhill racers in New England. But that didn't mean he could act like it. After he won races, Hamilton's father required his son to congratulate the dejected losers. It was not particularly easy, but after a while Hamilton got good at it. He would make the rounds nodding and smiling—"I just got lucky this time, next time it'll be you"—and pretty soon the other kids would be nodding and smiling right along with him.

For high school, Hamilton attended Holderness School, a sports-minded boarding academy near Plymouth, New Hampshire, where Crazykid energy was funneled into a grid of old-fashioned Episcopalian discipline, and where Kaiter, the father of his roommate, first exposed him to the heady flavors of European-style bike racing. Hamilton attended mandatory church services, and was instructed by people like Phil Peck, a former Olympic Nordic coach who could recite the *Book of Common Prayer* and anaerobic threshold statistics with equal authority.

Poetically enough, it was an accident that brought Hamilton full-time to cycling, specifically an epic wipeout during his sophomore year at the University of Colorado, in which he broke two vertebrae, ending his budding downhill career and sending him to pedal off his frustrations in the Rocky Mountains. From that point, his cycling career took off with the steady upward tick that has marked it ever since: winning collegiate nationals in 1993, riding for the national team in 1994, turning pro in 1995, helping Armstrong win the Tour with U.S. Postal from 1999 to 2001, taking a pay cut to move to Bjarne Riis's talented CSC team for 2002 and 2003. "Baby steps," Hamilton called them.

"Tyler started later than most," said Jim Ochowicz, who coached him on the 1996 Olympic team. "He might be thirty-three, but his body isn't beat-up like the guys who've done the Tour since they were twenty-three. He's still got room to explore."

Hamilton's boldest exploration was taking place at the moment. After his sensational 2003 season, he opted out of his CSC contract to sign a high-six-figure deal with a formerly middling squad called Phonak, which had a new $9 million budget and equally large ambitions spurred by their cycling-mad owner, Swiss hearing-aid magnate Andy Rihs. The move caught many by surprise. Nice-guy

Hamilton breaking a contract? But as Hamilton patiently explained, there were reasons. At CSC, Hamilton had been one of several coleaders. At Phonak, he would be the unquestioned boss, supported completely at the Tour, given power over personnel and equipment issues. They would be his Crazykids. He would be their Lance Armstrong.

"I'm sad to leave CSC," Hamilton said. "But this is too good an opportunity to pass up."

Hamilton quickly helped recruit a passel of top talent, including Slovenian hard boys Tadej Valjavec and Uros Murn, along with three talented Spanish riders, Santos Gonzalez, Jose Gutierrez, and Oscar Sevilla—a group that bore more than a passing resemblance to the famed cadre of Spanish riders that had escorted Armstrong through the mountains in recent Tours.

With surprising speed, Phonak assembled itself as an alternative-universe version of Postal. While Postal held golf-and-strip-bar bonding sessions in Austin, Phonak held team-building exercises, including one where the team donned chefs' outfits and cooked gnocchi and bruschetta dinner together. While Postal deferred all big decisions to Armstrong and Bruyneel, Hamilton's Phonak tried to imitate a democracy, assembling a team phrasebook to enable clear communication. While the Postal bus thumped with Tupac and Limp Bizkit, Phonak had the peppy sounds of "Go for It!," the official team theme song performed by Chrissy, a Swiss pop star.

To win the competition is our dream
Communication is the spirit of the team
Friendship and emotion give us the drive
To feel integrated is the quality of life

Perhaps most important, Hamilton did it all while remaining reasonably integrated with his downstairs neighbor, at least on the surface. Hamilton was well practiced in this department. When Postal's Bruyneel urged then-*domestique* Hamilton to go after his first major victory at the 2000 Dauphiné Libéré, Hamilton would not ride ahead until he heard Armstrong give the verbal okay over the radio. When he decided to leave Postal for CSC, Hamilton did his best to keep things friendly. While others attributed his leaving to Armstrong's reneging on an alleged agreement they had made to let Hamilton win the 2001 Tour of Switzerland (an event Armstrong won), Hamilton said nothing, instead involving his team leader to the extent that by the end the move seemed almost like Armstrong's idea. When that Girona apartment became available in early 2001, Hamilton first called Armstrong, who'd already bought the second floor, to see if he'd be okay with the Hamiltons living above.

"Ty didn't want it to be weird," Haven said. "And of course Lance was happy about it."

Later, Haven expounded more on their relationship. "Lance can never go after Ty like he goes after everybody else," she said. "Ty is just too nice. It would be like hitting the kid with glasses."

Travel schedules being what they were, the two neighbors crossed paths mostly at races, but remained, in the estimation of Hamilton's brother Geoff, "professional friends," exchanging occasional e-mails, trading compliments in the press. When they arrived in Girona this winter, Armstrong and Crow had hosted the Hamiltons at a small dinner party. It was the sort of relationship that suited both riders, and which suited the sport's headline writers just as well: Lance and Tyler, the bold Texan and the quiet New Englander, two American archetypes.

"Lance and I have two different characters," Hamilton said. "Lance is good at talking, and he's got what it takes to back it up every step of the way. I'm quieter. What he does works for him, and what I do works for me."

What worked for him was to keep life simple. While Armstrong Lear-jetted to Tenerife, Hamilton remained in Girona, riding with his usual grab-bag assortment of American training partners—most often Levi Leipheimer of the Dutch Rabobank team, Christian Vande Velde of Liberty Seguros, and Landis of Postal. While Armstrong's bikes were kept and groomed in the bike vault, Hamilton's were leaned against the wall of his apartment. If he needed a part,

Hamilton visited the local bike shop; if his tires needed air, he pumped them up. For Hamilton's birthday in March, he and his wife celebrated with a small piece of chocolate cake.

The Hamiltons had held off having children until cycling was over, much to the chagrin of the older Spanish women who gestured at his wife's slim figure and asked, "Donde estan los bambinos?" For the time being, however, they had plenty of other irons in the fire. There was the new Tyler Hamilton Foundation to manage (which raised money to promote youth cycling and help fight multiple sclerosis, and which, though Hamilton had not suffered the disease himself, bore a passing resemblance to Armstrong's cancer foundation), their interest in Inside Track cycling tours, and the two houses in Colorado and one in Massachusetts. Not to mention the ever-present Tugboat, whom Hamilton doted on wildly, and with such unswerving devotion that it wasn't much of a stretch to see the dog as a symbol of home, children, and the shadow life of a normality long forsaken.

"People think this life is so glamorous, like we're in Europe, having fun, on vacation," Haven said. "They have no idea."*

"There's a lot of stuff we haven't done yet," Hamilton said. "We could go spend a day walking around Barcelona, seeing all the sights. But you spend a day doing that, and you know, there's a price to pay."

Most days the Hamiltons could be found in what they called "the office," namely a short, innocuous stretch of gently rolling two-lane blacktop a few miles north of Girona, known as the N-II Strip. Haven drove their Audi Quattro a few inches in front of Hamilton's

---

*Being married to a pro bike racer sounds a lot cooler than it actually is, which might help account for the oft-cited high divorce rate. Yes, there's travel; yes, there's Europe. But there's also the fact that you're dealing with a guy who's gone all the time (Hamiltons, who are together more than most, are separated two hundred days a year), who trains obsessively, who has idiosyncratic dietary requirements, who never wants to walk anywhere, and who requires a post-workout nap every afternoon. My wife, Jen, after meeting some of the Girona wives and girlfriends, pointed out that being partners with a pro bike racer, on the whole, wasn't that different from taking care of a toddler.

front wheel, shielding him from the wind, a training technique called motorpacing. She motorpaced him for one stretch, then he rode a lap alone, then they repeated, looping back and forth along the Strip for two or three hours, Tugboat's big blond head sticking out the car window.

"It's incredibly boring," Hamilton said. "But then again, boring can sometimes be good."

His cyclist friends saw the change as spring unfolded. In previous years, Hamilton had usually trained in groups; now he was alone more often. He was also involved with the team planning, making decisions about race lineups, equipment, and sponsorships. Not as much as Lance, of course, but certainly more than Tyler ever had been. They understood.

"This is a big year for Ty," said Vande Velde. "This is his shot."

Like any pro cyclist, Hamilton kept track of his power through a device called a powermeter. Riding the Strip during February and March, Hamilton gradually saw his numbers creep up. He was better than last year at this point; better, in fact, than he'd been any spring of his life.

He didn't tell anybody.

CHAPTER 5

DR. EVIL REVS THE MOTOR

You can have all the heart in the world, but it doesn't mean
anything unless you've got the legs.

—Lance Armstrong

Armstrong approached the 2004 season with the goal of correcting
every controllable problem that had marred his 2003 Tour de
France. The list looked like this:

1. Armstrong entered the race in subpar condition. His pre-Tour
   fitness tests showed that he was producing about 2 percent less
   power than in previous years.
2. His right hip had been injured in a June crash, an injury that
   was compounded by a misaligned cleat on his bike shoe.
3. Prior to stage 1, Armstrong picked up what was politely
   described as a "digestive ailment," which meant his initial racing was done mostly in the direction of a restroom.
4. On stage 12, in what Armstrong described as "the most important time trial of my life," he suffered from chronic dehydration,
   finishing the stage with a white ring of salt around his lips.
5. The race was marked by uncharacteristic mechanical screwups:
   During stage 8, Armstrong was slowed by a too-tight brake rubbing against his rear wheel. He also spent much of the race
   piloting a bike with a smaller model's front fork attached—a

hairsplittingly subtle mismatch, but significant enough to be noticed on television by Anderson, Armstrong's mechanic.

It wasn't as simple as that, of course. The problems interacted with each other, creating new ones. But if you wanted to make a list—and Armstrong did—the problems fell into three categories: fitness, health, and organization, and of these, the key was fitness.

Armstrong's fitness-testing facility was located a few miles north of Girona, on a hill near a golf course. It was a steep, anonymous stretch of pine-shaded road that began just past a culvert and ended at a small white surveyor's arrow. The road was 1,000 meters long and rose 98 meters. Ferrari knew this because he had measured it with his altimeter, just as he had measured other test climbs in St. Moritz, Arizona, Tenerife, Bologna, and on the Madone, a climb outside Nice, on which Ferrari had tested clients since the early nineties.

Armstrong's fitness was measured through a series of numbers. Both Armstrong and Ferrari loved numbers; their solidity, their doubtlessness. Both could effortlessly recite the results of past tests from memory. In their mouths, certain numbers were spoken with importance, as if they were the titles of great novels: Six point seven. Four point zero. Five hundred ten. Other numbers were less exciting, even scary. Some were unspoken.

The most important number, however, was the one they were searching for on this February morning, and no one yet knew whether it would be beautiful or frightening. It would arrive in the form of a half-inch-tall numeral on the small red-and-black monitor bolted onto Armstrong's handlebars, transmitted from tiny strain sensors built into the pedal crank that measured how much force Armstrong's legs could apply. It was such an important number, in fact, that they spoke of it not as a noun but as an adjective. It wasn't something that Armstrong reached, it was something that he *was*.

"He thinks he is 420, 430 perhaps," Ferrari said. "Last year he was 440 at this time. But sometimes he guesses low on purpose, I think."

That number, measured in watts, is called lactate threshold, and is referred to simply as "threshold." Threshold represents the sweet spot on a rider's tachometer: the amount of power an athlete can sustainably generate. "Sustainably" is the key word here. To ride at threshold means to not deplete the body's reserves—to avoid entering what's known in the parlance as "the red zone." For most pro cyclists, threshold plays the same role as the Dow Jones Industrial Average plays to stock market investors. They know it, they watch it, but they don't sweat the twenty- to forty-watt variations that can result from colds, a poor night's sleep, sometimes for no apparent reason at all. Armstrong, however, is not your average investor. He doesn't like market variability. In fact, it drives him nuts.

"If the number is good, then he is good. If it is bad . . ." Ferrari didn't finish his sentence, dismissing the thought with a wave. "It is very early, now. As long as we are near 500 watts by the Tour, and his weight is the same as always, then that should be sufficient."

Sufficiency consists of achieving a certain power-to-weight ratio, which is measured in watts per kilogram. This ratio is Ferrari's favorite measurement, not just for its elegance (determining, in essence, how much force each gram of a body can produce) but also because he knows exactly what the number must be for Armstrong or anyone else to win the Tour de France, a figure he pronounced slowly, as befitting the holiest of holies.

"Six point seven," he enunciated. "If you are near it, you can win. If not, you cannot. At the moment, for example, Lance is far, far too heavy for the Tour."

Ferrari would know, since he travels with a bathroom scale and a set of calipers, the latter of which he uses to measure Armstrong's body-fat percentage. Armstrong currently weighed in at 79.5 kilos (175 pounds); about 5.5 kilos (12 pounds) over his ideal Tour weight. To achieve the sacred 6.7 watts per kilo at his present weight, Armstrong would need to produce a titanic 532 watts at threshold—an unthinkable number, even for him.

"But as long as he loses the weight, and can produce the same power as is usual in July," Ferrari said, "6.7 should be possible."

He was quick to add that many other factors are needed—recovery, nutrition, team support, luck, and, of course, mental strength.

"But this ratio is a condition sine qua non," he said. "It is necessary."

Befitting its necessity, Ferrari and Armstrong used two kinds of threshold tests: short and long. Today was a short test, repeats of the one-kilometer climb. May and June would bring the longer tests, climbs of a half-hour or more that come closer to replicating the demands of the tour.

The mood had been light back in town as Armstrong, Landis, and Hincapie prepared themselves. They would go on an hourlong warm-up ride; Sheryl and Odessa, a former racer, would head off by themselves for some exploring.

"Did you tell Odessa to take it easy on her?" Floyd joked.

"Sheryl's a jock," Armstrong pointed out. "Ran track in high school."

This is reflected on.

"Have you tested her yet, Michele?" Hincapie asked.

"On the hills, she cannot yet go," Ferrari said, and illustrated his point by leaning over, sticking out his tongue and panting, a vivid pantomime that ceased abruptly when he caught a look on Armstrong's face. His tongue retracted as if it were spring-loaded.

"But it is clear, she is definitely an athlete," Ferrari added. "She has muscular *caaaaahhhhhlllllvves*."

Armstrong smiled, and why not? It was a beautiful day. Around them, the first spray of flowers would be blooming on the side of the road—yellow, his favorite color. Besides, Ferrari was right: Sheryl *did* have muscular calves, tan, taut, melony calves that gave a nice little shiver as she walked. That was one of the things that had attracted Armstrong right away, her athleticism, the way she was up for anything. In fact, that was her first line to him, back when they'd met in October, at Andre Agassi's charity benefit in Las Vegas: "Would you take me for a bike ride sometime?"

Well, she was going on a bike ride now, wasn't she? Out there in the freaking Pyrenees with Odessa, her taut rocker calves getting tanner and tauter on her new bike, with her new nickname. And here were George and Floyd, two of the boys, and they were shooting the shit, ragging on each other, having fun. Oh yes, it's a nice day, a damn nice day, filled with momentum and portent, not the least of which is his own good mood.

"The first sign of things going well is that he wants to be tested," Carmichael told me later. "Wanting to be tested, wanting to talk about it—hey, you're halfway there. If he's not going well, he won't go near the test."

While Armstrong and his teammates rode their hourlong warm-up, Ferrari set up shop at the top of the climb. The doctor's long fingers deftly unpeeled three steel lancets from their paper wrappers. On the tailgate, he laid out his graph paper and a blue box that resembled a handheld video game, and which would measure the amount of lactic acid in a drop of Armstrong's blood. He hung a stopwatch around his neck.

"This is all the technology I need," Ferrari said later. He was particularly pleased by the pencil, which he had pilfered from the hotel and now flourished like a symphony conductor. "Simplicity, simplicity, simplicity."

The test worked like this: Armstrong and his teammates would ride the hill incrementally harder and harder, making the first ascent at 300 watts and increasing power by 25 watts on each successive ascent until they moved into their red zone. Ferrari marked each effort on his graph paper, watts along the horizontal, heart rate and lactate on the vertical, creating a graph of power versus pain. He then would connect those points in a line, back-calculating the point of maximum efficiency—the threshold—defined as the power produced when blood lactate concentration starts to rise sharply, and which for most people occurs at 4.0 millimoles per liter (about a drop per liter).

"That has been established, through much experimentation, as the point where efficiency begins to be lost," Ferrari explained. "It is true for all endurance athletes, even for Lance."

The test began. The three rolled down to the bottom and began to ride up, one by one. Armstrong, as he usually does, went last. When they reached the top, they called out heart rate, watts, and time, and proffered their hand toward Ferrari as if they were inviting him to waltz. The doctor swiftly jabbed the lancet into the side of their index fingers, and wiped away the first drop of blood ("It contains sweat," Ferrari explained). The second drop of blood was dabbed onto a match-length absorptive tab that had been inserted into a slot in one of the blue boxes. The blue box flickered and delivered a number on its liquid-crystal display, the lactate concentration. Ferrari marked small, neat Xs on his graph paper, then linked the Xs. Lines began to form.

The three rode easily uphill, moving quickly one by one through the dappled light. At first the interaction was easy and flowing, the air echoing with catcalls and teases and the usual watercooler chat of athletes at work. But as they did their third and fourth ascents, the talk quieted.

Hincapie looked more elegant, his thoroughbred legs unfolding with each pedalstroke, his face tranquil, a skinny Buddha. Landis looked tighter, his face scrunching up, the veins rising in his muscular arms. Both riders had something to prove, having missed large portions of last spring—Hincapie to illness, Landis to a broken hip. They'd recovered in time to make the tour team, and both had ridden well. For them, this test marked a fresh start, a chance to hang up some big numbers, a chance that was underlined by the fact that Armstrong was keeping score. As they rode, he asked their numbers, tracking the lines in his mind, teasing and cajoling his teammates, and also himself.

Armstrong's natural position on the bike was not perfect. His right foot canted toward the bike and his left foot canted away, as if he were constantly making a left-hand turn, a natural imbalance that created tightness in his back and soreness in his left hip, and which required daily adjustments during the tour. A few years ago, some team doctors came up with the notion of adjusting Armstrong's position, a notion quickly quashed by the team chiropractor, Spencer. "It's an imbalance, yes, but it's also Lance Armstrong," he said. "What he does is working, as long as we stay on top of it."

They moved past 400 watts, then 425. Armstrong's efforts, still smooth, became visible. He stood more often, shoulders rocking in an easy, faintly circular motion, as if he were paddling a kayak. His legs fired out in the familiar high cadence that, on television, makes it look as if the film is being played at high speed. Here, however, one could sense the power of each downstroke, a burst of controlled, swift violence that was more like watching a middleweight champion work the heavy bag—boom, boom, boom. The chain whirred, the bike emitted tight popping sounds, like a house heating up in the sun. Armstrong began to sweat.

Ferrari watched. For him, the real drama was invisible. Armstrong's heart, which is one-third larger than the average male's (and slightly big for cyclists, whose hearts grow large), began to pump harder. At its maximum, around 185 beats per minute, it recycled his entire blood volume eight times a minute. Which meant that a single red blood cell made the loop from the heart out the arterial highways, into the muscle capillaries, then back into the veins and to the lungs and then back to the heart—every seven seconds. The power this created was not immense—cyclists routinely generated three times as much for short bursts. What was unique, what was beautiful in Ferrari's eyes, was its sustainability. Simply put, Armstrong could go harder for longer than anyone else.

At 450 watts, if Armstrong were lifting quarts of milk from the floor to a kitchen table, he would be lifting forty-five quarts of milk—two nearly full five-gallon buckets—once per second. A reasonably fit person might be able to sustain that effort for ten seconds. Armstrong can do it for half an hour or more. If he were to do it for an hour, as he does on some long climbs, that table would be filled with 162,000 quarts of milk.*

---

*Strictly for science's sake, I tested myself a few weeks later. (My profile: a thirty-nine-year-old weekend athlete who tries to ride his mountain bike at lunchtime three days a week, but who is, in fact, far more skilled at finding reasons not to.) My threshold came in at 195 watts, compared to Armstrong's customary 450–500. Which means, poetically enough, that he could beat me using just one leg. Or, to put it more accurately, one ventricle of his heart. When pitted against the likes of Juanita Cuervo, however, I fared better. Separately, we cycled Alpe d'Huez in May, and I beat her reported time, 85 minutes to 90 minutes, a result that gave me pathetically large amounts of satisfaction. Take *that*, rock star!

Armstrong is helped by a mysterious attribute—actually, it's something he doesn't have: lactic acid, aka the stuff that makes muscles burn and ultimately give out. Even when pushed into the red zone, Armstrong's body is able to process lactic acid far more efficiently than other cyclists. Under effort, most racers' blood lactate levels reach the teens or the twenties. In a decade of sincere attempts, Ferrari has never been able to push Armstrong above six. Whether it's a biochemical fluke or a genetic wonder is anyone's guess, but at bottom it is physiological proof of Armstrong's assertion that he was born to be an endurance athlete. As vividly illustrated on Ferrari's graph paper, his engine can produce more power with less pain.

"People have this impression that he's a regular guy who got cancer and then came back to win the Tour de France," Carmichael said. "That's not true. He was one in a million before, and he's one in a million now. He's got a card that other people can't play."

As coldly impressive as this may sound, it's important to note that even with that card, the performance gap between Armstrong and his rivals is on the order of 2 percent, or about one additional quart of milk per second. It's not a lot. In fact, it's a slender enough gap that he watches it, guards it, touches the number like a lucky stone. For here is the truth: the Tour de France is decided by many things—ability, concentration, teamwork, fate, and, most of all, by a fluctuating margin of physical strength equal to that of a three-year-old child.

Armstrong rose along the hill seeking that margin, in full flight. He stood and leaned forward. The vein on the right side of his head pulsed, his upper lip rising in the faintest hint of the Dead Elvis Grin. Hincapie and Landis, who had just finished, watched and waited. Ferrari stood poised, his pencil bobbing gently to Armstrong's cadence.

His teeth showing, Armstrong stood and crunched the last few pedal strokes to the line. His chest billowed in and out. His teammates watched in silence.

Armstrong swung over to Ferrari and held out his hand. Ferrari reached to squeeze a drop of blood from the puncture on the index finger, and when it rose, Armstrong didn't wait for Ferrari to wipe the sweat off; he stuck the finger in his mouth and licked off the blood, tasting it, wanting the number, now. He grabbed his finger with his free hand, Ferrari grabbed, too, and together they gently squeezed a jeweled drop, a tiny sun wobbling on its surface. It shone impossibly red. The number was inside.

"Come on," Armstrong said.

With a painterly dab, Ferrari touched the tab against the blood droplet and watched the blood slip inside, and a few seconds later the number came up. He marked it on his graph paper along with the wattage and time. He drew the line, and came up with the threshold Armstrong already guessed he was.

Four hundred and seventy watts.

The number had an immediate effect; it soaked into him, it vibrated in the soft spring air. He was 470, 40 watts higher than this time last year, the same number he was last June, just before the Tour. The same! It was a short test, which usually based higher, but still, it was promising news. To get to 6.7, he had to get 30 watts more powerful, and lose 5.5 kilos, and he had six months to do it.

Ferrari knew what would happen next. Armstrong would call Bruyneel, e-mail Carmichael. The number would be tapped into the BlackBerry and shoot out into the world. The new bike would be that much faster now; so would the mesh jersey and all the other secret stuff; the number would match up with the other numbers, push everything a little higher in the quivering energy of that info-chemical buzz.

It was good to enjoy it, because the feeling wouldn't last. In fact, it was disappearing even now, evaporating as Armstrong leaned over to look at Ferrari's graph paper.

"What did Floyd get?" Armstrong asked Ferrari. The doctor pointed a pencil tip toward a line: Landis had 420 watts but he only weighed sixty-nine kilos (152 pounds). Landis was faster.

Armstrong hawkeyed the numbers. He was too elated to be angry, but there it was, in black and white. He'd gotten beaten. Not by a lot, but still, there it was. Beaten. Second place. First loser.

"Well," Armstrong said, "it looks like Floyd's the leader for Portugal" (the team's first race). He said it lightly, so lightly that it seemed like nothing. So lightly, in fact, that it had the faint ring of a challenge.

Landis gave a halting laugh. It was what he wanted (Landis would go on to win the race in Portugal), but there was a suspended air of unease right now, as he waited to see what would happen.

Armstrong turned his attention to his bike, punching the buttons on his power meter, resetting it. The 493 blinked out. In its place stood a fat black zero.

Armstrong took a long drink, replaced his water bottle with a fresh one. He pointed his bike down the hill. He clicked his right cleat into the pedal, which made a sound like a gun being cocked. He rotated his foot to the top of the arc and looked across the road at Landis and Hincapie.

"You guys ready?" he asked.

Later that night, Ferrari met with Armstrong at his apartment, to discuss the results of the test. Johan Bruyneel flew in from his home in Madrid for the meeting; so did Dr. Pedro Celaya, the Postal team doctor. (To keep things simple, Bruyneel did not tell the other team members he was coming; but Girona being a small town, they found out anyway.) The four of them talked about Armstrong's condition and race schedule. The Dauphiné course had just been released, and it featured an uphill time-trial similar to the one that had been planned for the Tour at Alpe d'Huez. They decided to enter the Dauphiné, a decision that they would not reveal for several weeks.

In the meantime, Ferrari was trying to figure out why the test had gone better than either of them had expected.

"I think maybe it helps to have Sheryl around," he said. "He is happier. I think he wants to show off for her. You have a new girlfriend, eh? You want to be strong for her."

The flow of good feelings was interrupted that evening by sad news. Marco Pantani, the great Italian rider who'd won the Tour in 1998 and who had been the last man to crack Armstrong, was dead at thirty-four. Since 1999, Pantani's once-glorious career had disintegrated into a string of doping bans, rumored depressions, and unsuccessful comebacks. He'd checked into a hotel room in Rimini, Italy, a few days earlier, and hadn't emerged. A hotel manager found his body surrounded by cocaine, tranquilizers, and handwritten notes that ranted about betrayal and pain. An autopsy showed Pantani had ingested six times the lethal limit of cocaine. His death was later ruled an accidental overdose, but many viewed the ruling as a matter of semantics. Pantani's name would be listed alongside other Tour de France champions who had killed themselves—the final crack, as it were. Poor René Pottier, who won in 1906 and hanged himself from his bike hook in his garage a year later. The handsome Luis Ocaña, who won in 1973 and shot himself in 1994. Elegant Hugo Koblet, who won in 1951 and intentionally drove his car into a pear tree in 1961. Not to mention sad-eyed Thierry Claveyrolet, who won the king-of-the-mountains competition in 1990 and shot himself in 1999.

Armstrong expressed regret, and the desire that Pantani's family be treated with dignity through this difficult time. He said he would have gone to the funeral, but he could not. He had a race to get to. A race, as it happened, against the man whose talent scared and obsessed Armstrong more than that of any other rival, Jan Ullrich.

CHAPTER 6

ULLE AND VINO

The outcome [of the 2004 Tour de France] will determine how I will be remembered. Either as a gifted talent who made life difficult for himself, but always managed to succeed in the end, or as a sloppy genius who wasn't capable of using his exceptional talent.

—JAN ULLRICH IN HIS AUTOBIOGRAPHY, GANZ ODER GAR NICHT (ALL OR NOTHING AT ALL), 2004

While Armstrong was performing his first tests on a hill outside Girona, Jan Ullrich was enjoying the secret confidence that he'd aced his own tests. Characteristically, those tests did not take place on the bike, but on a nameless frozen lake on the steppes of Kazakhstan, three thousand miles from his home, where he'd gone to shoot boar with his teammate and friend, Kazakh rider Alexandre Vinokourov.

Specifically, the test was this: First Ullrich took off all his clothes. Then he jumped through a hole in the ice. Those who might say that this test was unorthodox—well, they didn't know Ullrich, and they certainly didn't know what he'd been through over the last eight years.

Jan Ullrich was a sweet-tempered, russet-haired East German whose career had thus far been a parable of unfulfilled promise. When the baby-faced twenty-three-year-old had won the 1997 Tour, he did so with such cool, godlike dominance that no less an eminence than Bernard Hinault had predicted he'd win five or six Tours at least. But it hadn't happened. Ullrich had spent most of his career in the shadow of Armstrong, beset by problems with conditioning and injury. He'd finished second five times, but it was this latest second place in the 2003 Tour, crowning a dramatic comeback from injury and exile, that gave him new optimism. Ullrich was different; he had changed. He could prove it, and that's why he had journeyed to this icy corner of one of the world's most godforsaken places.

"I turned around and heard a splash, and he had gone in," Vinokourov said later. "I couldn't believe it."

The exact location of this baptismal event is difficult to ascertain, even for Vino. The former Soviet state of Kazakhstan is the size of Western Europe, and is not so much its own country as its own planet, a vast sameness of boreal forests and grasslands, boiling in summer and frozen in winter, a land the Soviets found ideal for growing wheat and testing nuclear bombs—470 tests between 1949 and 1989, most of them thoughtfully done on Sundays, so as to not disrupt the happy productivity of the proletariat. The ensuing years have only added to its charms: the rivers are so syrupy with toxins that they can't manage the trick of freezing; the rails of the trans-Siberian railroad are so elaborately twisted by frost that passenger trains cannot excede thirteen mph. Kazakhstan, in short, is the perfect hothouse in which young cyclists may bloom.

Alexandre Vinokourov, in many minds, is that perfect cyclist. He showed up at the French amateur team EC Saint Etienne Loire in 1997 with a rucksack on his shoulder and a coach's note in his pocket that sketched out the outline of his story. The wall had come down, and Vino had come to race bikes.

Vino was not taken seriously. For starters, he looked like he was nine, with bright blond hair, pink ears, and a penchant for tight, shiny shirts and fat gold necklaces. He resembled a cross between a mafioso and an elf, and he hardly ever spoke. At first people assumed it was because he didn't know French, but that wasn't so. He knew it fine. He just didn't talk. His background was, and remained, a blank slate. His parents were reported to have been chicken farmers in Petropavlovsk, but he would not speak of it. When he did speak, which was about once a week, it was in short, pointed sentences, so simple that it was like listening to Japanese poetry:

I will ride hard today.
The hill is not steep.
I will attack them.

Then Vino rode. He didn't look any prettier. His form was squashed, his ears even pinker. But it was the way he rode: fearless, attacking on flats, steeps, descents, everything, always with that same titanically unimpressed look on his elfin face, which wasn't really a look at all as much as the absence of any look, a depthless Siberian-wasteland gaze that said, "I've seen worse."

Racing as a neo-pro in 1998—cycling's version of a single-A minor league baseball player—Vino achieved the unthinkable, winning two professional events, the Four Days of Dunkirk and the Circuit des Mines. In 2000 he won the silver medal at the Sydney Olympics and ascended to national-hero status, which in Kazakhstan qualified him for a state pension and a regular supply of honorary horse-meat dinners.

Vino became known as one of the hardest of cycling's hard breed: the Eastern Bloc goombahs; riders like Jens Voigt, Andrei Kivilev, and Viatcheslav Ekimov, who had been selected as children, their growth plates and femurs carefully measured by state examiners, their biotype profiles matched against that of a "superior child," and who were duly whisked away to the barracks of various sports schools throughout the Soviet empire. Once there, their life became an endless series of training exercises, the governing philosophy of which was summed up by a former coach: "You throw a carton of eggs against the wall, then keep the ones which do not break."

Life inside the carton contained a few simple elements. Mandatory six a.m. rides on ancient forty-pound bikes. Megaphone-wielding coaches who forced them to race a hundred miles for a prize of canned fruit and a half-pound of butter, or, later, for the state-sanctioned bribe of a slightly less bleak apartment for the family. When one of Ekimov's teammates broke both collarbones in a crash, his coach thoughtfully rigged a body-harness from the gym ceiling so the injured rider could complete the following day's assigned mileage. Vino and the rest were the unbreakable eggs. When the Berlin Wall came down, they left in droves to join the rest of Europe's hard boys in the professional peloton, and quickly became identifiable by their willingness to take any and all risks.

"It's very understood in the peloton—they don't have anything to go home to," said Jonathan Vaughters, who rode with the U.S. Postal team and Credit Agricole. "Sprints, climbs, descents—they are never going to give up, and they will go all the way to the edge, because they just don't care."

To be a goombah was to be loosed into a new world of creamy possibility, where risk and reward were intoxicatingly linked. Crashing on a bike was a *privilege*, of which they took full advantage. Riders like Djamolidine Abdoujaparov, the Tashkent Terror, invented new ways of crashing, a kind of exploding human pinwheel display that resulted from his riding straight into the barriers during a sprint on the Champs Élysées. He didn't care!

Professional teams were quick to perceive the intimidatory value of this new species. Goombah-looking guys with tight, shiny shirts and gold chains started popping up everywhere. Names cluttered with v's and z's appeared incongruously on French and Italian team rosters, usually no more than one or two to a team (who knew what Stalinesque madness might ensue if you got too many of them?).

Of course, not all of the former Eastern Bloc riders handled the transition so well. In fact, many of them did not survive their first sugary taste of Western temptation, either abandoning the sport immediately or riding a few years and cashing in early, like Russian rider Eugeni Berzin, who won some big races and retired at age thirty to pursue his true dream of owning a car dealership.

"It is like getting off a ship," Ekimov explained. "At first all you can see is the freedom. You say, what the fuck, I do not need to train, I feel good! And then, of course, you might never come back on."

Which is precisely the wobbling gangplank upon which Jan Ullrich had spent most of his career. The thirty-year-old German had a letter-perfect Eastern Bloc hard-boy pedigree: he was raised amid the soot and squalor of Rostock, East Germany; his mother, Marianne, worked at a collective farm and drove a rusting, roaring Trabant; his alcoholic father, Werner, disappeared when Jan was three, reappearing only often enough to terrorize Marianne and beat Jan and his brothers. At thirteen, Ullrich was identified as an athletic talent and spirited away to East Berlin's famed Dynamo sports school, where he was serenaded by the famously brutal voice of the despotic cycling coach Peter Becker, who found in young, fatherless Jan a pliant spirit, a body ready to be molded for the good of the collective will.

Ullrich grew to six feet, 160 pounds, a broad-shouldered, narrow-waisted engine of the state. His legs alone inspired awe: they were slabbed, majestic columns entwined by a Gothic rigging of hawsers and cords, topped by quads the size of Christmas hams. In size, shape, and definition they did not resemble cyclists' legs so much as the sort of legs comic-book artists gave Superman. Such was their tinge of unreality that other cyclists would stare at them before races, leading the shy Ullrich to keep his sweats on until the last moment.

When the wall came down, those legs were ready to take center stage. Ullrich won the world amateur road racing championship in 1993, then signed a professional contract with Telekom in 1994. He finished an unthinkable second in his first Tour, in 1996, and the following year he won. He was only twenty-three years old. His future, and that of the sport, seemed guaranteed. Yet it had not come to pass, and the arrival of Lance Armstrong was only part of the reason. Ullrich's story since 1997 was a tale of softness, both metaphorical and actual. He ate too much, trained too little and too late. He was magnificent at times, terrible other times. He had never finished lower than second in the Tour—five times in all—but he had never finished higher, either.

But, most crippling, Ullrich was simply too nice. "My little teddy bear," his mother used to call him, and it was true. He was too sweet, too willing to please. When critics called him "Fat Boy," Ullrich agreed with them, explaining how big thighs ran in the family, and how he loved gummy bears and chocolate, even coming up with a name for his appetite: "The internal pig-dog."*

The press called him "Calamity Jan," a name that took on literal meaning in the summer of 2002 when, after yet another Tour lost to knee injury, Ullrich brought fresh diligence to a new project: destroying his career. In May, he drunkenly crashed his Porsche 911 into a bicycle rack in Freiburg and then, a month later, tested positive for amphetamines he said he'd taken from a stranger at a nightclub. It was a clinical meltdown: the Eastern Bloc boy run amok. Armstrong wasn't just a competitor who had beaten him in two Tours. He was the symbol of everything Ullrich was not: organized, disciplined, relentless—a fact that was not-so-subtly underlined when Telekom loosely offered Ullrich to Postal to ride in support of Armstrong—and Postal turned them down.

Ullrich's $2.5 million contract with Telekom was torn up, and he received a six-month suspension from the German cycling federation. His career was assumed to be over. He traveled to America, "reaching the bottom and finding what is there." In the spring of 2003, word started trickling out: Ullrich was thinking about a comeback. He had sworn off drinking. He was looking for a team. He was

---

*It would be possible to write an entire chapter on the subject of bike racers and their food obsessions, but the bottom line is that they are skinny guys who eat like fat guys. Eating with a group of bike racers is like being in an aquarium during feeding time: they gather frenziedly, open their mouths, inhale, and the food vanishes. This ability, plus associated digestive efficiencies farther down the line, are key to their success.

"Look at Eddy Merckx," Jonathan Vaughters said, pointing to the legend, still portly despite recently losing forty pounds. "The thing that made him great at the Tour—recovering energy, absorbing huge quantities of calories—is exactly what turned him into a fat tub of goo when he retired. I bet Lance gets fat when he retires, too. Or he would, if he ever let himself go. Which he won't."

working with his old coach, Rudy Pevenage. He was seen riding in Tuscany, and the rumor was that he was training with the brilliant Cecchini—the notorious Cecchini!

Later, in the spring of 2003, Ullrich emerged from exile with a makeshift team called Coast, which promptly folded and was replaced by the bike manufacturer Bianchi just before the 2003 Tour de France. He showed up in Paris tanned and slim. Comrade Becker had been banished, replaced by the slender, blond Birgit Krohme, a soulful-eyed physiotherapist who played Indian music during massage. Rigid sports-school regimens had been replaced by Cecchini's targeted training and organic food. Moreover, Ullrich had new family stability with longtime girlfriend, Gaby: a baby girl named Sarah Marie, who arrived a few hours before the Tour. Ullrich even sounded different, speaking of following his instincts, of doing things his way, of living outside a system, of racing for himself, not to please anyone else. When he came within a hairsbreadth of knocking off Armstrong in the Tour, the cycling world was turned fairly on its ear. Calamity Jan was gone, the internal pig-dog had been brought to heel! In his place was this new sunlit Tuscan version, loose and independent.

After the season, Ullrich reunited with his old team Telekom— newly rechristened T-Mobile—to the tune of $3 million per year. The move worried some, who feared Ullrich would slip back to his old habits. But it made sense to others. It was a German-owned team, it had unquestionable quality and depth, and best of all, it would be a way for Ullrich to reunite with his friend Vino, who had just finished third in the 2003 tour. Vino plus Ullrich—it was exactly what Calamity Jan needed to put him over the top! A high-octane dose of the goombah Communist juice. Vino, it turned out, had called Ullrich to persuade him to sign (an incident as notable for its effect as for the fact that Vino had apparently actually spoken). Adding to the alliance's poetry was the fact that Vino's best friend, fellow Kazakh rider Kivilev, had died in a crash in the previous year's Paris-Nice stage race.

The potential chemistry was evident already in October, when

Vino and Ullrich took their appointed places next to Armstrong in the front row at the Palais de Congrès in Paris for the 2004 course presentation. There they were, sitting uneasily in red plush chairs with tissue-like swatches of yellow fabric on the headrests, looking for all the world as if they were seated in a monstrous, questionably built airplane. On the left sat Armstrong in an open-collared shirt and jacket, a vein protruding from his temple as he beamed The Look at the course map. In the center was Ullrich, casual and smiley. When the two of them sat together like that, the dynamic of their relationship was immediately evident. Armstrong attacks; Ullrich responds.

But there, on Ullrich's left, sat the new element in the equation. Vino's head was tipped back, his legs were spread wide, his feet flat on the floor. He was wearing shiny sharkskin pants, a massive silver bracelet, and a shirt with fluorescent red piping that had been stretched so tight that each button-space opened up, a series of tiny mouths echoing his own, which was partly open in that sleepy, lethal face favored by hitmen. His shoes were tango-dancer pointy and blood-red. Afterward, as the endless flow of predictions, hopes, and advice began, Vino stirred himself awake long enough to utter only five words: "A great Tour for attacking."

Ullrich fans around the world thrilled at those words: this was the pairing they wanted, Vino's unbreakable mind and Ullrich's unbreakable body, a kind of Eastern Bloc cycling monster that would match the Texan, hardness for hardness. Tactically, the combination set up the classic one-two punch: Vino could attack and Armstrong would be forced to spend energy chasing, giving the new Ullrich opportunity to follow him and, when the champion tired, to show the true talent that lay within him to seize his destiny, to finally beat Armstrong.

Which brings us back to that nameless freezing lake in Kazakhstan. Vino and Ullrich had spent a few days on the steppes by now, hunting birds and boars, staying in remote cabins and dachas. Vino, being a Kazakh hero, could order military helicopters to take them wherever they wanted, and so they flew over, landing and hunting as they chose, kings of a wilderness too vast for even nuclear bombs to touch. Vino didn't say much; rather he showed Ullrich how to hunt. Kazakhs are storied hunters—they have hunted for centuries on horseback, with trained eagles and dogs. And now Vino showed Ullrich how to hunt like an eagle. They watched how silently the boars moved, how quickly they could turn, how sharp those razor tusks were. How you must wait patiently for the moment the animal turned to the side, and how you struck once, at the heart.

Later, in the evening, during sauna time, Ullrich decided to go on a journey of his own. He walked down to the lake and looked out, the mirror of the water beneath the sky, in a place that seemed as far from the smoke and stink of Rostock as you could get. And when he felt the urge to leap he did so without thinking.

Vino watched that pale body disappear into the dark water, and Ullrich rose up, big muscles smoking, mouth gasping, his eyes wide with cold and surprise, learning a hopeful truth that his silent friend already knew: that the word "Kazakh" means "free man."

CHAPTER 7

THE Q FACTOR

Strange people, bike riders. They imagine a racing bike is made for going quickly. They're wrong. A racing bike is made solely for winning races.

—JACQUES ANQUETIL, FIVE-TIME
TOUR DE FRANCE WINNER

The European professional road-racing circuit starts in February and runs until October. Its structure is partly provided by the every-other-month rhythm of the three grand tours: May's Giro d'Italia, July's Tour de France, and September's Vuelta a España. In additon, April holds a passel of one-day classics (Tour of Flanders, Paris-Roubaix, Liege-Bastogne-Liege), and every so often there are moderately big stage races (Paris-Nice in March, the Dauphiné Libéré in June). But mostly, the pattern is that there's no discernible pattern. There are just races, whole mapfuls of races, races in Spain and Belgium and Switzerland and France and all points in between, races that come and go according to sponsorship and politics, and whose only common bonds are that they are all sanctioned by the Union Cycliste Internationale, and that if you added up all the money and passion behind each one, it wouldn't come close to the money and passion generated by the race that towers over all, the Tour de France.

Fittingly, every Tour de France contender constructs his race schedule around July, resolutely insisting that every pre-Tour race is strictly for training. This is manifestly untrue. The link between

Tour potential and pre-Tour performance, while subtle, is substantial. To claim that the pre-Tour races are merely training for the Tour is akin to a baseball team claiming that the regular season and playoffs are merely training for the World Series. In fact, all the contenders are shadowboxing; scouting each other all the time, either playing head games or ignoring head games—which is, of course, another level of head game. But the strictly-for-training fiction serves riders' purposes, so they stick to the story with the numbing tenacity of presidential candidates.

Today, however, was a day whose importance no one could deny. It was March 3, the first significant gathering of Tour contenders at the Tour of Murcia, a weeklong stage race in eastern Spain. Armstrong, Ullrich, and Mayo had come to these sunbleached plains to begin their seasons in earnest. This morning they were taking the first steps toward Paris by engaging in the age-old and indispensable early-season ritual of their profession: the belly pinch and the ass check.

The belly pinch usually comes first, and it is often employed under the guise of a handshake delivered by a rival, a teammate, or a coach. The purpose is to measure body fat. The preferred technique is to smile broadly—*hey there, you old so-and-so*—grasp their target's hand, and tug them forward in a teasing manner, twisting their bodies slightly to grant access to their unprotected midsection, on the side, just above the waistline. The French are particularly known for their vigorousness of technique; on encountering Gallic teams, several American cyclists reported finding their midsections covered in red marks, as if they'd been attacked by a pack of lobsters.

The ass check is a more unobtrusive art. It is practiced from a distance, and requires not only a keen eye but also experience. An ass, properly examined, is one of the best available calibrations of potential. Ass checking is not a pastime, it is part of the race, as sure a measure of a rival's ability as timing a baseball pitcher's warm-up with a radar gun. When most riders reach top form, their asses become small and vaguely feminine, as if grafted from a disciplined teenage gymnast.

"It's not written down, but it may as well be," says former Postal rider and OLN commentator Frankie Andreu. "After a while, you get everybody memorized, what's big for them, what's small for them, what they look like when they're going to tear it up."

"First, you have to know the guy. You have to know the ass," Bruyneel says. "After you know it, it tells as much as [powermeter] numbers."

With the possible exception of supermodels, is there a more body-discerning group on the planet than professional bike racers? Their vocabulary has as many words for "fat" as Eskimos have for "snow": puppy fat, chicken skin, baby fat, cheese, despite the fact that none of them is remotely fat. In fact, 10 percent of men and 30 percent of professional women cyclists are estimated to suffer from eating disorders, according to Dr. Arnaud Megret of the French Cycling Federation.

But the obsession is bent toward strategic purpose, because within the society of riders, fat is not fat, nor is an ass merely an ass— it is time. It's a simple idea: the more you weigh, the slower you go uphill. An extra ounce here or there sounds meaningless, but it can make a huge difference, especially on a long climb. Of course, trainers like Ferrari have figured it out: each kilogram (2.2 pounds) adds about 1.25 percent to a rider's time on a climb. On a typical eight-mile climb, that works out to just over a second per additional ounce.

"Losing weight is the single most important thing you can do," Armstrong says. "You have to train. You have to be strong, of course. But if you're too heavy, it's all over."

At this particular moment in eastern Spain, the peloton was pinching and eyeing one another with carefully disguised abandon. They were gathered on the street in loose circles by nationality, clutching plastic cups of espresso, eyes quick behind sunglasses. There, pixielike, stood Damiano Cunego, the promising twenty-two-year-old. There was Spanish phenom Alejandro Valverde, who'd finished third in the 2003 Vuelta a España and had been widely con-secrated as a future Tour winner. There was Eric Zabel, the elegant German veteran. There, skinny-assed and relaxed, stood Iban Mayo, chatting in indecipherable Basque. Armstrong was nowhere to be seen—according to custom, he'd signed in early and retreated to the team bus, to avoid the crowd. But what of the ass everybody wanted to see? What of Ullrich? The clock ticked forward. Five minutes to go before the start. Four minutes. The crowd, which included a sizable contingent of Germany's sporting press, shifted anxiously.

With two minutes to go before the start, a T-Mobile sedan pulled up, the door swung open, and out stepped Der Jan himself, striding purposefully toward the stage in his pink racing kit, hat pulled low.

The crowd pressed forward, craning its collective neck. It saw the slightly rounded face, the giant Duran Duran sunglasses, the hoop earring, the muscular thighs heaving beneath black Lycra, the gently amused smile. It was all there, along with—yes—a big ass. Not the biggest anyone had ever seen, no, that would have to be 2000, when he showed up twenty-five pounds overweight. No, the 2004 vintage was looking decidedly mid-range. Not huge. But not small, either. Depending on how you looked at it, he was either a little bit fat, or a little bit more muscular.

Then, as their eyes roved eagerly over the rest of his body, the onlookers saw something else. Ullrich appeared to be walking stiffly, his abdomen unnaturally rigid beneath an arch of rib. It was a subtle adjustment, which would not have garnered any attention, except for the fact that dozens of eyes were staring at that precise spot, a spot that, as he strode to sign in, revealed the truth: Ullrich was holding his belly in. Not just a little, either. He was hoovering that baby, sucking his bellybutton spineward, expanding his upper chest in the ageless, hopeless Charles Atlas–wannabe manner of suburban dads at the beach. Reporters scribbled and photographers fumbled for zoom lenses as the old Ullrich equation began to crystallize: Ass plus belly equaled Jan was big again.

In the days afterward, Ullrich and his cortege would make considerable efforts to some lengths to enlighten the media on the subtle yet vital distinction between being big and being powerful. The training he had done had added some muscle, yes. But not fat. This subtlety was apparently lost on the marketing department for team sponsor Giant bicycles, which postponed a planned photo shoot until such time as its star could look a little less, well, fat.

Ullrich took his place in the rear of the start area amid the mostly Spanish riders, standing out like a bull in a pen of greyhounds. Armstrong (whose ass, while not near its Tour conformation, was looking pretty standard for this time of year, everyone agreed) emerged from his bus and proceeded directly to the front row of riders. Then the photographers alertly spotted Ullrich and started baying for him to come up front so they could get the money shot: Armstrong and Ullrich, the two rivals together.

"Jan! Jan!" the photogs screamed, and after pretending not to hear them for a moment, Ullrich gave a resigned smile and began to pick his way up to the front, parting a mentholated sea of skinny bodies. Wheeling his bike, Ullrich moved in the manner of a businessman on a crowded train—pardon me, excuse me, sorry about that. Armstrong turned to watch. Ullrich might have been embarrassed, but he did not show it one iota. He smiled that gently amused smile behind his sunglasses. Armstrong, meanwhile, adjusted his helmet, checked his earpiece radio, straightened his sleeve. As Ullrich approached, Armstrong exchanged a word with Valverde, who stood to Armstrong's left.

The photographers readied themselves. When Ullrich finally arrived next to Valverde, he smiled and stuck his hand out toward the American—except that Armstrong didn't seem to notice, still engrossed in conversation with Valverde; so engrossed, in fact, that he seemingly failed to notice the large man dressed in pink standing six inches farther away. An awkward second or two passed, Ullrich smiled patiently and waited, hanging in the breeze. The photographers waited. Then Armstrong looked up—hey, who's there?

"Hey, Jan!" he said, flashing his big-weekend grin.

"Hullo, Lance," Ullrich said.

Ullrich nodded his head slightly, his smile remaining fixed. It was the German's answer to Lance's squint, a look of pleasant impassiveness, letting us know that this—all this, the gamesmanship with the handshake—didn't bother him in the least.

The handshake lasted about two seconds before it was broken up by a highly excited red-faced man: Maximo, the race director. Maximo was nervous, because it was time for the race to start.

"VENGA VENGA VENGA!" Maximo screamed, and the photographers yowled in protest. They hadn't gotten their shot yet! But Maximo was insistent that the race begin on time, and so he stepped in and purposely blocked the shot, sending the photographers into operatic paroxysms of rage. Ullrich looked around nervously—what to do? Armstrong surveyed the chaos and raised his palm.

"TREINTA SEGUNDOS!" he announced. At the sound of his voice, Maximo turned.

"Treinta segundos," Armstrong repeated, with a smile of perfect American cool. It worked. Maximo stepped back and simmered down. Armstrong reached over and grasped Ullrich's hand again, and the photographers snapped the image that would go around the world: the confidently smiling Armstrong (who's so happy, so content) and the uneasily smiling Ullrich (who's fat again!), with Valverde back one step and in between, his eyes shifting between two Tour-winning asses as if he were watching a tennis match.

The Tour of Murcia's opening stage followed a similar pattern. Armstrong asserted, Ullrich impassively went his own way. At kilometer 90, when the race reached its first climbs, Armstrong and Bruyneel had Postal push the pace, leaving Ullrich behind as the peloton passed a swanky golf resort. Perhaps, one of the German press hopefully theorized, Ullrich just wanted to play a few rounds.

The riders' bodies weren't the only items being eyeballed in Murcia. There was also the crucial matter of the riders' faithful steeds, their alter egos: the bikes. The following morning, as the riders prepared for the stage 2 time trial, bikes were everywhere: millions of dollars of tropical candy-colored frames stacked in casual piles next to buses, antlering team cars, whirring atop stationary trainers. The cycling press strolled among them, lofting the ritual questions: "How's the new bike? How's it feel? How's it ride?

This year's plot was particularly thick, focusing mostly on the secret black bike that was now in some undisclosed location within the Postal compound, and whose attributes Armstrong was now discussing with journalists in front of the bus—or, rather, not discussing.

"You'll see," he told the breathless crew, which was clamoring for detail. "You'll see."

"Secret" was not quite the right word. A multimillion-dollar industry had been built around Armstrong's equipment selection, an industry that feeds on the tideline between telling enough to sustain interest and not telling enough to give away competitive advantages. Over the past five years, Trek and Armstrong had become quite deft at this process, to the point where this particular bike, the construction of which had begun back in August, was the best-publicized secret bike in history. The bike had been created by a task force of companies that called themselves F-One, and that consisted of whiz-bang experts from Trek, Giro, Hed Cycling, and Nike, among others. Numbers were being thrown around—it was one minute faster over fifty kilometers. Two minutes! After his first race in Portugal, two weeks before Murcia, Armstrong pronounced it "the fastest bike I've ever ridden."

Exactly why it was so fast—well, that was the secret. The cycling media was abuzz with speculation—it was a new hand position, it was a new front fork—and each time somebody guessed, Armstrong would smile knowingly.

"It's something pretty radical, pretty deep," he said. "Let's just say that the bike's fast and leave it at that."

While Armstrong was being interviewed, two men were picking their way discreetly through a crowd, moving toward a stack of bikes. One had long gray hair; the other was younger, with a shaved head. They wore sunglasses and baseball caps and dark, rumpled T-shirts chosen because they lacked any betraying logos. The long-haired one toted a backpack and a dated, clunky 35-mm Olympus camera that any self-respecting bike geek would refuse to carry.

But they were more than bike geeks; they were high gods of bike geekdom, handpicked members of Armstrong's F-One project. Their names were Steve Hed and Scott Daubert. Hed, a forty-eight-year-old Minnesotan, was founder and owner of his eponymous wheel-manufacturing company and was known as one of the foremost aerodynamics gurus in America. Daubert, a thirty-five-year-old Coloradan, was Trek's liaison to the Postal team. They had come to Murcia for a variety of reasons, one of which was to spy on the other teams and report back to Armstrong. And like any respectable spies, they were worried.

Specifically, they were worried that some of the other teams might have caught on to F-One's big secret—or worse, have come up with some new fast design of their own. This was the season's prime information gathering time, after all. With four months to go before the Tour, teams still had plenty of time to make adjustments. Spies were everywhere. Two weeks ago, in Portugal, the F-One boys had a scare when they noticed some German guys with a camera skulking around the Postal bus, and they quickly covered up the secret bike with a black tarp. The Germans had turned out to be bored magazine photographers, but still, you never knew.

The F-One boys moved from team bus to team bus, mixing innocuously with the crowd, sauntering touristically up to the various bikes along with the rest of the curious masses. Hed carried a tiny tape measure in his fist; occasionally he would reach toward a bike, capture a measure, and let the tape snake noiselessly back into his palm. But mostly the two of them just looked, eyes blank as camera lenses as they roved over forks, seat posts, and cables. So precisely attuned were their minds that bikes registered not as shapes but as time—specifically as time savings per kilometer. "This bike looks like two seconds," Daubert said. "That bike looks like one, maybe one and a half."

The place Hed and Daubert gazed at most, however, was a small area called the bottom bracket, where the pedal cranks insert into the frame. The bottom-bracket width was an indicator of what was called the Q Factor—the distance between the pedals—and this distance held the key to Armstrong's and the F-One project's big secret.

Here was the secret: Armstrong's new bike was narrower. Its bottom bracket was eighteen millimeters narrower than a standard bike's. It wasn't much—about the width of a pinky finger—but the change pulled the pedals closer together, creating a slimmer profile to cut through the wind. It was dead simple, and that was part of what made it such a pleasure for Armstrong to see the finest minds of the cycling world puzzling over it, focusing wrongly on the bars and the fork and all the extras when the truth hovered right in front of their noses—it was narrower! The narrow bike combined with the smaller changes (new helmet, new bars) had been measured as thirty-six seconds faster over fifty kilometers than Armstrong's previous setup.

The competitive advantage of this advance was complicated slightly by the fact that the F-One boys most assuredly weren't the only ones with the idea. Bikes with narrow Q Factors had been ridden on and off in track and road cycling for years. In fact, as the F-One boys would tell me a few weeks after Murcia, a handful of riders in last year's Tour rode them, including Ullrich himself.

The reason that the F-One boys played those facts down undoubtedly had something to do with corporate spin, and the fact that it wouldn't do to be seen as cribbing from a competitor's approach. But there was something else in play here as well. The F-One project, as with so many of Armstrong's endeavors, had confidence in its own supremacy. CS&E's Bart Knaggs, who played a key role in putting the F-One project together, called this Armstrong's "we can conquer the world" feeling.

"He sees all the facts, figures them in, but he doesn't get hung up on them like you or I would, because he's got faith in his decision-making process. That's the engine that drives this thing. He knows—we all know—it's going to be better because it's going to be better."

The F-One project had been born in a conference room in Armstrong's agent's office in Austin, Texas, on August 26, 2003. It was not an auspicious birth; in fact it was rather tense. In attendance were the brass from Trek: Ed Burke, Dick Moran, Doug Cusack, and Scott Daubert, along with Armstrong's agents, his mechanic, Mike Anderson, and Johan Bruyneel.

"On the ride from the airport, we knew we were in for it," Daubert said.

Bruyneel kicked off the meeting by pointing a long finger at Burke and telling him that the time-trial bike was too slow—it was old technology. It hadn't been redesigned since when, 2000? Then there were the other problems: Armstrong hadn't liked the last road bike, the Madone. And then the mixup with the fork, which had been caused, it turned out, by a human assembly error at the factory. Bruyneel laid it all out while Armstrong sat simmering.

Burke apologized. It was their fault, they would fix it, all of it. First and foremost, however, they would build Armstrong the fastest time-trial bike on the planet. Various ideas were thrown around, all of them limited by the fact that the size and shape of time-trial bikes are tyrannically constrained by the Union Cycliste Internationale. The narrow Q factor was settled on as a likely path, particularly given Ullrich's success.

The next step was obtaining a copy of Ullrich's bike. Unfortunately, that bike was made by Andy Walser, the famed Swiss designer who produced a handful of frames each year for pros and recreational athletes. Figuring Walser would naturally balk at selling a frame to Trek, the company dispatched one of their European salespeople to Walser's shop, posing as a wealthy triathlete—a perfectly legal subterfuge. The ruse worked. By the time Walser discovered the triathlete's true identity, the bike was en route to Trek's headquarters in Waterloo, Wisconsin, being prepared for dissection and testing.

Meanwhile, the industrial design process revved up, each detail flowing through the window of Armstrong's BlackBerry. Mannequins were built, Nike's skinsuit people were summoned, body doubles were hired, a new wind tunnel was found. The vivid spectacle of intercorporate effort helped persuade Armstrong to participate in "The Lance Chronicles," an eight-episode OLN series whose first few episodes were devoted to the narrow bike's development, and which was, in Knaggs's words, "a win-win-win-win proposition. A thousand images of Trek and Nike and Giro at work making Lance go faster—what's not to love?"

Viewers got a taste of the hours spent analyzing such seemingly tiny issues as that of the race number, which had an unkindly tendency to balloon out like a parachute and add thirty-six grams of drag, or about 1 percent of the total. Could they make a sleeve for it? Could they integrate it into the jersey? Tape down the leading edge?

"We had long conversations over who would be the number pinner-onner," Giro's Toshi Corbett recalls. "It was like being at NASA or something."

The beautiful part was, the exact same process was happening everywhere else in Armstrong's world, a flurry of Cape Canaveral–like activity designed to fix what were regarded as the series of problems that had caused 2003's near miss. Since Armstrong had been dehydrated, the Postal team started adding salt to its water bottles. Since heat had caused the dehydration, Carmichael started researching methods of staying cool, including heat-dissipating vests and tiny refrigerator-like devices that worked by cooling the hand. Corbett briefly looked into a helmet with a battery-powered refrigeration system built in, strong enough to give the wearer an ice-cream headache.

There was more. For the uphill Alpe d'Huez time trial, chief mechanic Julien DeVriese suggested using silk tires, which weighed a fraction of what conventional tires weighed. Hed and Daubert came up with the idea of profiling the Besançon time-trial course, mapping it with GPS, a digital level, and a wind indicator; examining historical weather patterns; and locating hedges and walls that might provide shelter. Anderson found an aluminum frame that allowed mechanics to replicate Armstrong's preferred position on any bike with 3-D precision.

Here was the interesting thing: most of these ideas failed utterly. The salt solution tasted awful. The UCI was not likely to allow the ice cream–headache helmet. The silk tires were deemed too prone to puncturing. The course mapping turned out to be too complex to be useful, and the Belgian mechanics summarily refused to use the Dutch-built bike frame on point of national pride. ("They won't budge," Daubert said. "Not even Lance could convince them, I think.")

Here was the other interesting thing: none of the failures mattered. The point was the process itself, in the way Armstrong transmitted his gaze through other people who hawkeyed the world to find the new Shit That Will Kill Them. The failures were banished, the rare successes embraced.

"We cannot have a feeling like we are standing still," Bruyneel said. "For every ten ideas, perhaps one or two will be used. What it's about is knowing that we have all the options on our side."

"At some level, the science of it disappears," Daubert said. "The important thing is that we get Lance something new and cool that he loves, and that's what makes him faster."

To be sure, he was getting faster. The new wheels were light. The new skinsuit was fast. Best of all, the narrow bike itself was looking quite promising, which was underlined in January, when Armstrong road-tested it for the first time.

"What we want is for him to go 'wow,'" Daubert said. "We try to catch him at a good time, or we'll give it to an impressionable person, so they can say 'wow' and talk about it with him, warm him up.

"It's a game," he continued. "We have to be careful not to show him everything, or he'd be like a kid at Christmastime, and we'd be left with nothing. So we unveil things slowly, and we always keep an ace in the hole, something really cool we'll give him right before the Tour. It's kind of strange, but it seems to work."

Armstrong didn't like the narrow bike—he loved it. He tested it in Austin in December and again at the team's California training camp in January, most memorably on a training ride where he started out on his regular road bike and switched partway through, letting the team go ahead. Armstrong powered up to them on the narrow bike and blazed past, a big smile on his face.

"How much did this cost?" he yelled as he rode. Hed and

Daubert quickly ran the numbers: $250,000 so far, which made him even happier. Thirty-six seconds! It was beautiful!

By the time Armstrong had come to Murcia, enthusiasm was reaching a new peak. He'd ridden the narrow bike two weeks ago, at a small race in Portugal, and had performed well enough. He had noticed a slight drop-off in his power toward the end of the time trial, but it wasn't much—something to investigate. The morning of the time trial, Armstrong called for a quick meeting with Hed and Daubert on the street outside the hotel lobby.

Armstrong walked out of the hotel into a blast of sunshine, CrackBerry in hand, the field-trip vibe on full throttle. The Postal bus was thrumming at curbside, busy Belgians prepping cars. Miguel Induráin was supposedly in town. The sun had drawn a couple of Spanish lovelies into the open, marking the first official groupie-sightings of the spring: a brunette and a blonde in spectacularly white pants, the contours of which Armstrong took a half-second to appreciate just before he examined a new tri-spoke wheel Hed handed him.

Armstrong held the wheel to the light, sighted down it.

"This is wider here," he said, pointing to a spoke.

Yes, Hed said, just a hair.

"And narrower up here."

Right-o, Hed affirmed.

"Hmm," Armstrong said.

"And oh," Hed said casually, "we might have Boone Lennon take a peek at the aero bars."

Armstrong perked up. Boone Lennon! Lennon was the cycling world's equivalent of J. D. Salinger, a genius recluse who had invented aero bars in the 1980s and had last been sighted living in some cabin in Idaho.

Armstrong smiled broadly—Boone Lennon! No way! He glanced over to the groupies, to Daubert, to the Belgians loading bikes, sharing the moment. "I thought he was dead or something."

"He's back," Daubert said. "He's on board."

"You going to get some video today?"

Hed nodded. One of F-One's changes was to alter Armstrong's position on the time-trial bike, moving his hands lower and his elbows closer together.

"We'll have some profile shots and head-on stuff," Hed said. "We'll check them out tonight."

Armstrong smiled. This was the kind of thing that made him happy, proof that things were clicking, dead geniuses were rising from the grave, videos were being dissected, the engine was revving. As if to confirm that feeling, up strolled the tall, dark figure of five-time tour champion Miguel Induráin.

"*Un momento,*" Armstrong told Induráin with a smile, asking Daubert about some new Shimano brakes.

"You want me to call them?" Daubert asked.

"I'll call them," Armstrong said, absently caressing the Black-Berry. "We set?"

Hed and Daubert drew back. Armstrong warmly greeted Induráin, who was looking shy and suburban-daddish in cable-knit sweater and corduroy pants. Armstrong and Induráin stood together on the sidewalk in the Spanish sunlight, morning traffic going past, white-panted groupies agog at seeing a combined ten Tour de France victories chatting it up.

"*Que tal?*" Armstrong asked.

Induráin gravely considered the question. "*Bien,*" he decided. "*Muy bien.*"

Compared to most Tour champions—indeed, most athletes—Induráin was an enigma: a quiet, unassertive sort who gave so many favors to opponents that late in his career it was joked within the peloton that he needed no team, since they all were his team. He had won five Tours almost quietly, following a simple strategy of keeping up in the mountains and dominating the time trials. He was famously uninterested in bike technology. The former farmboy lived in Pamplona, keeping busy living out the life of an ex-god: vacation home in Benidorm, occasional television work, charity dinners, and the like.

Armstrong and Induráin chatted quietly for five minutes. Then

Armstrong moved toward his bus to talk with Bruyneel, and Induráin sauntered idly over to where the F-One boys were standing in front of the hotel. Hed was shifting from foot to foot, excited at the chance to gather a rare and singular piece of data.

"Ask him what he thinks," Hed whispered to his Spanish-speaking colleague, José Navarro Cases, aka Pepe.

Reverently, Pepe asked, had Induráin seen Armstrong's new position on the time-trial bike?

Induráin nodded—he had seen some photos, yes.

What did he think of it?

Hed swallowed hard. Induráin gazed into the distance, his eyes black and still. Then he opened his mouth and emitted a kernel of wisdom: *"No se olvide de las piernas."* Don't forget about the legs.

Hed puzzled.

"Does he not like it?" Hed asked. "Does he think it's too low? Too far forward?"

Pepe shook his head. "I think he means do not change too much from normal position, or it will cost the next day."

"Ahhh," Hed said, unsatisfied.

"Ahhh," Induráin echoed helpfully.

"Don't forget about the legs," Hed repeated slowly.

"The legs," Induráin said in English, pointing to his own, plucking the corduroy for emphasis.

"Ahhh," everybody said. Then they turned to watch Armstrong walk on to his bus amid a crowd of busy Belgians. The door hissed shut, the engine revved, and they pulled away into the sun dazzle.

CHAPTER 8

THE SPACESHIP VERSUS
THE WINNEBAGO

Postal's race strategy—which is to say Armstrong's race strategy—started with the parking job. Two hours before start time, the gleaming blue capsule of the team bus would rumble in, staking out a prime location, preferably facing the exit, alongside a hedge or fence. The bus was then docked parallel to the barrier, about fifteen feet back, and two team cars were deployed on either end to form a private area, a walled kingdom. A mini-Belgium, to be precise, populated by that distinctive species that dominates the culture of the U.S. Postal team: Europe's answer to the Windy City tough-guy—the Belgian male.

They were easy to spot. They wore their hair longish, with a hint of pompadour. They walked in a rolling bad-ass saunter. They laughed in booming *ha ha has*. Most distinctively, however, they whoof-shrugged. The whoof-shrug is the Belgian national gesture, and is executed by contorting one's face into an expression of supreme disdain, lifting one's shoulders until they almost touch the ears, and blowing air through loose lips, as if imitating a horse. We shall leave it to anthropologists to determine the whoof-shrug's origins—is it a visceral response to the near-ceaseless wind and rain? A result of their doormat-flat nation's having been conquered and reconquered a dozen times in the last few hundred years? For

Postal's purposes, it's enough to say that the gesture worked because it conveyed complete imperviousness. It was a full stop, a conversation-ender that rendered the very idea of conversation obsolete.

"Of course life in cycling is hard," Dirk Demol, Postal's assistant director, told me, whoof-shrugging. "What you gonna do, complain?"

Armstrong loved Belgies, and that is why his Postal team was built around them. He admired their loyalty, toughness, and savvy, even when they were shamelessly stripping the team bus of jerseys, hats, and spare bikes to be resold in the smoky backrooms of their hometown bars. He loved them because they were working-class guys accustomed to playing an angle, usually several at once. They understood that the most important thing about having The Shit is showing that you have it.

For example, take the conversation between Scott Coady, an aspiring American filmmaker, and Freddy Viane, a Postal *soigneur,* during the team's California training camp. Coady was hatching a plan to film the famous Paris-Roubaix one-day race in April. It was a difficult problem—the race takes place on narrow country roads, which are mobbed with people. Coady, an optimistic, can-do sort, was considering hiring a helicopter so he could shoot footage from several vantages.

"Helicopter?" Viane said incredulously, whoofing and shrugging. "No no no. I will set you up with a car, a driver. I know every road, every shortcut."

"There'll be certain guys I want to film," Coady said, not yet warming to the idea. "It'll be muddy or dusty. We'll need to be flexible."

"No problem, I will show you." Viane shrugged again and leaned in confidentially. "Besides, I can see through the dust."

"You can see through the dust," Coady repeated slowly, squinting as his optimistic American brain grappled with the sheer impossibility of this notion. To see through the legendary Paris-Roubaix dust, the billowing stormcloud of Ice Age silt loosed by the force of several hundred bikes, cars, motorcycles, and screaming fans. "You can see through the dust—at *Paris-Roubaix*?"

Coady could not hide his raw skepticism, which was exactly the reaction Viane wanted, skepticism being the mother's milk of every Belgian boy. Viane waited, a foxlike smile on his face.

"How in living hell can you see through the dust?" Coady finally asked.

"Ahh," Viane said, leaning in still further and taking a long, covert look around before whispering his secret: *"Night-vision goggles."*

Belgium, or, more specifically, the five million people who live in the Flemish/Catholic half of it, love cycling. They devote the same degree of national attention to cycling that America devotes to professional football. Quaint provincial enthusiasm, perhaps, but when it's filtered through the genome of the Belgian male, the result is people like Viane, Bruyneel, and head mechanic DeVriese (who worked for the legendary Merckx), men who dedicate their lives to cycling the way their forebearers might have devoted their lives to the priesthood. Postal's Belgians distinguish themselves, like most underdogs, by what they are not. They are not dreamy (like those Italians), or cynical (like those French), or casual and chatty (like those Spaniards). No, they are Belgians, which means they are watchful, believers in secrets, seekers of what they call "correctness."

Take a tire, for instance. Most teams bought tires that clinched onto the wheel rim by wires—the same style as you or I might use. But Postal's Belgians looked at those tires and shrugged. Instead, they did it the old-fashioned way, buying tires called sew-ups, which had to be glued to the rim. But first they had to be aged in the sacred darkness of DeVriese's basement—two years at least, which added to their suppleness and strength. Then they had to be sorted and selected to be attached to the rim of a wheel, a process that took four days and four coats of a gluelike varnish applied with a special brush, the last a double coat. Then, and only then, was the tire worthy of sitting beneath a Postal bike.

Or take breakfast. Other teams might deploy themselves casually for the morning fuel-up, but Postal's directors arrived early and chose seats in the corner of the dining room, so that they could better watch their riders eat, and thus gauge their capabilities for the coming race. So that they may look for a slow laugh, a weary tilt to the fork, a strained swallow, all of which would be noted, measured, and calibrated within several Belgian brains.

"You can tell things at the meal," Demol said. "How they lean toward the plate, how they walk down the stairs."

"I can tell how Lance will ride by when he comes down to breakfast," Viane said. "If he is there first, getting coffee, then it will be a good day."

Such fortune-telling doesn't always sit well with the team's more scientifically minded riders. "It's crazy," Landis said. "They're always acting like they know exactly what you are going to do that day. If you do well, they say it's because you looked good at breakfast. If you suck, they say you looked bad. It's complete bullshit! They might be right some of the time, but they always forget about all the times they're wrong."

But that's not the point. Belgians—and thus the Postal team— are all about the knowing and the underlying assumption that there is something out there worth knowing, a secret truth waiting to be discovered and unleashed on an unsuspecting world.

Now, stretched before Armstrong's gaze, the Postal team area was a terrarium of correctness, a cadre of black-T-shirted, sunglasses-wearing tough guys whoof-shrugging at each other so frequently that it sounded like the starting gate of the Kentucky Derby. They were a step ahead, as usual, having procured a suite at a nearby hotel so the riders could relax in comfort. Not to mention having executed the usual setup: poised the bikes on the stationary trainers, laid out the various amino gels and recovery drinks and salves and Clif Bars, washed the cars, stacked the fussy white plastic cups for the espresso machine, and tightened the lugs on their tightly run world—no fruit at night, no Cokes during the race—which accomplished the dual goal of affirming the Postal team as the most correct team bar none, and doing it with such whoofing Belgian insouciance that it seemed like nothing at all.

In fact, Armstrong was doing the Belgie shrug himself, working the shoulders to his ears, his cheeks puffed with air aimed to dispatch a persistent question.

"I'm strictly here for the training," Armstrong said.

The reporters nodded like bobbleheads.

"It's just another race," Armstrong repeated. "Jan might happen to be here, I might happen to be here, but this isn't July. It has no significance for either of us."

Meanwhile, across the parking lot, Ullrich's T-Mobile team was also preparing for the race. They were parked far from the center, having arrived late. Their encampment was identifiable at a distance by a set of sounds: a mix of laughter and a crackly stereo, the distinctive pop-hiss of beverage cans opening. Drawing closer, the song clarified itself: "Stuck in the Middle with You," by Stealers Wheel, accompanied by several leathery Teutonic voices.

Then, rounding a corner, one caught sight of a smallish Winnebago painted in the pink T-Mobile colors, outfitted with the requisite banging screen door and rickety foldout stairs. Surrounding the Winnebago stood a loose assemblage of mechanics, *soigneurs*, and riders, a few bikes and lawn chairs beneath a flimsy white tent. A big man in shorts was handing out Cokes from a large blue cooler. On the Winnnebago's front dash lay a banana peel.

And now the Winnebago was creaking and tilting mightily as here came Ullrich himself, unshaven, sweatsuited, and looking rather imposing, at least until he waved his hellos. He didn't say hello, he sang it—*Haloooooo*, he said, greeting his ponytailed physiotherapist and his teammates and some fans. He waved to his personal coach, Rudy Pevenage, a Mickey Rooney–looking Belgian standing nearby, who was now having a bitter feud with T-Mobile boss Walter Godefroot (another Belgian, of course) and who had been banned from riding in T-Mobile's car. It was dramatic, soap-operatic stuff that had been played to death in the German media, but it didn't seem to affect the picnicking mood. Ullrich flipped Rudy a Coke. They chatted.

Everybody chatted; chatting seemed to be the order of the day. Ullrich's friend Vino was attending another race, having been spiritually replaced by the sweating, burly, shaven-headed Stefan, Jan's brother and mechanic. Stefan, too, was a product of the Eastern

Bloc sports-school system, a former eight hundred-meter runner, and,. judging by the size of his belly, seemed to have fully adapted to the challenges of Western life. Stefan cut a Falstaffian figure, his eyes gleaming with roguish humor behind a cloud of cigarette smoke as he handed out Cokes and slapped wheels onto bikes. A few minutes later, while he loaded the bikes on top of the team car, Stefan began to sing in heavily accented English.

> Regrets, I've had a few. But then again, hmmm hmmm
>   humhumhum
> I did what I had to do, and saw it through hmmm hmmm
>   humhumhum
> To think I did all that, and may I humm, sha-boom-de-boom
>   bay

Stefan took a drag on his Marlboro, slapped the last bike in place for the big finish.

> Nooooo, oh no not me. I did it myyy wayyyyy.

Stefan smiled. Jan smiled. Birgit smiled. Everybody smiled—big, toothy, life-affirming smiles that sent the message that this was just a game, mere sport, and sport was about simple things: talent, timing, luck. The Spanish sky was blue and the wind was warm and the Cokes were sweet and cold and everything was going to be fine, right?

And yet neither T-Mobile nor Ullrich was quite so casual as they appeared to be. They were the richest team in cycling history, and no slouch in the technology department. T-Mobile was sponsored by Trek's rival Giant, the famed $500 million Taiwanese company that had pioneered superlight carbon frames. Perhaps more impressive, Giant's lead engineer was none other than Dr. Kuan Chun Weng, the same Dr. Weng whose previous project was designing 2,800-mph air-to-air missiles for the Taiwanese government. Who knew what sort of Sino-Germanic ammunition the good doctor might be cooking up? The T-Mobile *soigneurs* were nearly as efficient as their shrugging Belgian counterparts at setting up for the race. Moreover, behind it all lay the imposing shadow of the brilliant and notorious Cecchini, with whom Ullrich was said to have been training these past few weeks, not at his still-wintry Switzerland home, but in sunny Tuscany, the proof being a fresh crop of freckles on the Superman legs.

But just as Postal preferred to hide any hint of disorganization behind a steely facade, so T-Mobile liked to hide its organization behind a casual facade. It was a classic bit of Darwinism, a sibling rivalry where the two teams instinctively developed opposing characteristics. Armstrong relied on certainty, so Ullrich and his team relied on mystery, a tool they hoped would prove to be the kryptonite for which Armstrong had no defenses. The kryptonite was simple: Ullrich did not know how strong he was. As Pevenage put it, "There comes a time in each race where Jan trusts in his talent."

If this sounds foolish, it is because most of the time, it was foolish. Most of the time, in a modern endurance sport, it's better to know how strong you are so that you may gauge your effort for maximum efficiency. Not knowing leads to wasted energy, to wasted opportunities.

However, as Ullrich was fond of pointing out, bike races were not held in a lab. Out on the road, in weather, amid the storms of exhaustion and tactics, there were times when it was smarter— more efficient, even—to do what riders used to do before the days of power meters and heart-rate monitors: to simply, stubbornly, ride like hell until the answer was revealed. Because as all bike racers will testify, there are times when the numbers stop working, moments when strength unexpectedly arrives.

As a young rider in his first Tour, Ullrich was put on the team at the last minute, and nearly won. In his second Tour, he did win, even though he was not the team leader going into the race. In subsequent years, he would struggle through the early season and into June, seemingly in need of a miracle. One year, in late May, the British cyclist Chris Boardman listened as Ullrich gasped his way up a short climb, and turned to a fellow rider.

"If that guy does well in the Tour," Boardman said, "I quit."

Ullrich finished second in the Tour. Boardman quit.

"His middle name should be Phoenix," said fellow East German Jens Voigt.

"Lucky," was how Ullrich described his feats, a word which seemed inane until one realized the sheer intimidatory power of it. To ride next to a powerful, controlled rider was one thing. To ride next to one so powerful that even he had no control was intimidation of another order.

Ullrich's world, then, was designed to be an unpressurized biosphere in which such miracles could freely bloom. He did not test himself very often (three times a year on a stationary roller). Like Induráin, he steered clear of technology, preferring to let the team handle it; indeed, he rarely went near a computer. Instead of a large staff, he preferred a tiny, family-like support crew of Pevenage, Krohme, and brother Stefan. He famously did not focus on cycling in the off-season—his winter sleep, his coach called it. This winter, Ullrich forwent the option of attending a wind tunnel, a choice that was widely interpreted as laziness and yet perfectly in keeping with his approach. A wind tunnel? What was he, a machine? (Exactly, Armstrong would say.) Ullrich, who was just that for so much of his life, seemed bent not just on winning, but on proving the validity of his old-fashioned, soulful methods. His fans saw him—and he saw himself—as a kind of John Henry, slinging the heavy hammer into the mountain, trying to outdo Armstrong's modern steam-drill.

The belief around the Winnebago was that Armstrong, like that powerful steam-drill—like America itself, they intimated—was strong but brittle, too reliant on technology and gamesmanship. This belief was given voice by the German press, which focused on what it saw as evidence of Armstrong's nervousness, shown most vividly in the dispute that arose in the weeks after the 2003 Tour, the dispute titled "Did Ullrich Wait?"

Background: On stage 15, Armstrong crashed on a climb called Luz Ardiden when a spectator's bag snagged his handlebar. Ullrich, riding just behind, avoided the crash and kept going. Cycling's rules of chivalry dictate that rivals do not attack when the yellow jersey is down, a rule that Armstrong and Ullrich had observed on two previous occasions. Indeed, immediately after Luz Ardiden (which Armstrong won, in dramatic fashion), the American expressed gratitude to his rival for not attacking.

However, in the weeks afterward, Armstrong changed his tune, wondering archly and publicly if Ullrich had waited, and the issue duly blew up into a controversy of Rashomonic proportions. Sides were taken; tapes were reviewed. Armstrong pointed to the fact that Ullrich seemed to be maintaining the same tempo, and had his "race face" on, and only slowed down when Tyler Hamilton rode to the front of the group and waved him down. Ullrich countered with the less subjective evidence that Hamilton, who had been decisively dropped, would never have caught up if the German hadn't eased off. But to the Ullrich camp the true revelation was that this so-called controversy existed at all. Armstrong had won, hadn't he? Why on earth would he start in on this, unless he needed to, unless his confidence was so meager as to require this sort of motivation?

"There is no controversy here, but he started one anyway," Rudy Pevenage said. "I think Armstrong will have a very good career in Hollywood when he is finished cycling."

Ullrich, to the Germans' pride, needed no such artificial fuel. He had proved himself stoic and sportsmanlike in each loss, able to return and try again. Ullrich might lose, the thinking went, but he was a more complete man because of it. There was a widely held assumption among the German press that Armstrong would never finish second in the Tour; that he would find some excuse to quit: an injury, an illness, anything but the task of finishing a race second best. It was the old transatlantic divide, the way Europe viewed America: winning is easy; what's hard is accepting fate.

It was an article of faith among seasoned Tour observers that Ullrich had lost the 2003 Tour in the stage to Luz Ardiden—not after Armstrong's crash, but long before, when the German had embarked on a solo attack on the Col de Tourmalet with forty kilometers to go. Armstrong expressed incredulity—what was Ullrich thinking? The odds of getting away were slim and, as it turned out, nil. Armstrong played by the book, remaining within striking distance, allowing Ullrich to tire himself. And yet after the Tour, when Ullrich was asked about his proudest moment of the Tour, he went out of his way to mention his Tourmalet adventure. To most ears, it sounded absurd, like hearing Napoleon boast about Waterloo. And yet Ullrich was sincere. The Tourmalet attack was idiotic—and that was precisely the unscientific, romantic point. For a moment, he had caught Armstrong unawares; he had rolled the dice. Ullrich may not have been a tactical genius, but he was firmly in grasp of a singular truth that seemed to elude much of the peloton: one did not beat Armstrong by trying to be like Armstrong.

"Simply waiting and attacking on the last climb is not that great of a strategy," Ullrich said. "When luck smiles on me, I have to be ready."

While Ullrich readied himself for the time trial, Armstrong's F-One boys happened on T-Mobile's Winnebago. They'd come to do their spying, to see what Ullrich was riding. In their eyes, all the casualness appeared a tad theatrical, as if some hidden door might accidentally slip open, revealing a smoking laboratory in which Dr. Weng was building some missile-like bike. But it didn't, and gradually, Hed and Daubert sidled toward the bikes mounted on the team car. Nobody stopped them. They eyeballed the Q Factors, confirming what they would report later to their boss. Giant wasn't showing anything too special in their time-trial bikes, and certainly nothing taking the narrow bike's approach. Ullrich could ride his Walser narrow bike, of course, but that would be status quo; nothing new.* In other words, it looked like Armstrong still had The Shit.

---

*To the frustration of sponsoring bike manufacturers, racers sometimes prefer a rival brand over the official team bike. The more notable examples include 2003, when Ullrich rode his Walser instead of a Bianchi, and 1999, when Armstrong rode a Litespeed instead of a Trek. To preserve appearances, the contraband bike is disguised with paint and stickers to match the official team bike, a tactic that keeps sponsors happy, but can confuse legions of potential bike buyers.

Had Hed and Daubert lingered a few minutes longer, they would have witnessed something that would have made them feel even more comfortable: the sight of Pevenage carefully extracting a piece of white paper from his coat pocket and handing it to T-Mobile director Mario Kummer. It was a blueprint for a bike, a simple drawing on graph paper with the angles and lengths labeled, all of it encased in a flexible clear plastic sleeve, the kind elementary-school students use for book reports. It was the road bike Jan used last year, and which he would like again, since he's not that fond of the bike he's riding now. Could they make one for him for the Tour, please?

Of course, Kummer politely told Pevenage. He would make sure the drawing was passed on to the proper people.

So, the situation was this: Armstrong had the F-One Project. Ullrich had a drawing on a sheet of paper. It was four months before the Tour de France. Both sides were convinced they held the upper hand.

A couple of hours later, in Murcia's much-anticipated time trial, Armstrong and his narrow bike finished fifth, while Ullrich and the Walser finished thirty-first and Mayo eleventh. Armstrong professed to be pleased, but in private he was dissatisfied with his performance: he'd experienced some power loss near the finish as he had experienced two weeks earlier in Portugal. It could have been the warm-up, could have been something else. But as for the overall race result, everyone agreed it was totally insignificant, since, after all, they were here strictly for the training.

Amid all the strenuously declaimed insignificance lay two unusual occurrences.

The first was political. On March 4, the day after the time trial, Armstrong's agent released an open letter that Armstrong had written to Dick Pound, the president of the World Anti-Doping Association. Pound had been quoted in the January 27 edition of *Le Monde* saying, among other things, "the public knows the riders of the Tour de France and the others take banned substances," a statement to which Armstrong took strong exception.

In his letter, which received prominent play in the world's sports pages, Armstrong wrote that he was "stunned and saddened" by Pound's comments. "Should a person having such a conviction direct the biggest anti-doping agency the world? I reply, 'No.'" He went on to write, "I've said it before and I will repeat it: I believe that I am the most tested athlete on this planet, I have never had a single positive doping test, and I do not take performance-enhancing drugs."

The second event was athletic, and uncoincidentally occurred on Friday, the day Armstrong's letter was released.

"Lance definitely knows that when he says something strong, it has to go together with some strong results," Bruyneel said. "You cannot make a big stand and then be Mr. Nobody on the bike."

On that day the Tour of Murcia's stage 3 was moving toward a drab and dusty burg called Yecla, toward the end of a 156-kilometer stage. An Italian, Danilo di Luca, had broken away from the group with another rider, and Armstrong saw his teammate Max van Heeswijk shake his head and sigh. Which made Armstrong angry.

"You're going to fucking win today," Armstrong told him, and ordered the team to chase down the break.

Within twenty kilometers the break had been reeled in, and there were seventy-six riders together. Van Heeswijk—a shy and amiable man known ironically as Mad Max—did something slightly out of character. Van Heeswijk asked if Armstrong would be his lead-out man in the finishing sprint. An innocent enough question, but one that ranked as nearly bizarre within the Postal team. Since becoming a Tour rider, Armstrong had made a wholly sensible policy of steering clear of dangerous finishing sprints, those chaotic and often violent dashes to the line that produce most of the highlight-reel crashes. Armstrong, like most Tour contenders, preferred to roll in amid the relative calm of the peloton (according to custom, everyone who finishes together is given the same time). Asking Armstrong to do a lead-out? It was like asking a star quarterback if he wouldn't mind throwing a block on a linebacker: it simply wasn't done.

"I thought, oh shit," Armstrong said afterward. "Nobody's ever asked me that."

But there he was, nevertheless, leading his teammate down the Avenida Juan Carlos I and through a series of tight turns—left, right, left—diving into them, head up, letting his teammate save energy until the last crucial moment.

Somehow it was all present: the new bike, the media, Ullrich, the letter to Dick Pound, all combining to form a question that demanded an answer. So he gave it: legs blasting, jaw tight, knifing through the sunshine. Finding a new spot on the map and showing everybody. *Guess where I am right now?* When the quiet Dutchman pulled out of Armstrong's draft and broke free for the win, Armstrong celebrated as if he'd won, clapping his hands, pumping the air with a fist, and the photographers were squinting to make sure their eyes weren't fooling them—Armstrong doing a lead-out?

The rest of the weeklong race turned out as expected: Armstrong finished twenty-third; Ullrich a full twenty minutes back at seventy-first. But afterward, it was the thrill of that sprint that lingered.

"If I could do that tomorrow, I would," Armstrong told Bruyneel. "It was cool."

They both assumed, of course, that Armstrong would not do it tomorrow and perhaps not ever again. It was fun, this sprinting thing. But it was a one-off; a fluke. Sprinting, any rider can tell you, has never won a tour.

CHAPTER 9

ISLES OF THE DOGS

On Sunday, March 7, Armstrong and Crow returned to Girona from Murcia. At four p.m. Tuesday, with a stretch of stormy weather bearing down on Spain, a quick decision was made to decamp to one of Armstrong's favorite training locations, the volcanic island of Tenerife, one hundred miles off the Sahara Desert on the northwest coast of Africa. By seven p.m. the plane took off.

Tenerife consists of two landscapes. Its lower reaches are clustered with resorts built around postcard beaches. Its upper portions are a lifeless, baking lump of twisted rock rising twelve thousand feet to a sulfur-coated crater otherworldly enough to have served as the backdrop for a *Star Wars* movie. Tenerife is part of the Canary Islands, named not after the sprightly bird but for *canis*, the giant, ferocious hunting dogs kept by the island's aboriginal people.

Armstrong and Crow were joined by Dr. Ferrari, who flew in from Italy, as well as by Scott Daubert. The plan was to hold a weeklong training camp and to do more testing of the narrow bike before Armstong's next race, which was Milan–San Remo, on the twentieth.

On Tenerife, Armstrong fell into his routine. They stayed at the Parador Nacional Hotel on the crater, following the customary regimen of sleeping high and training low, which naturally boosts red blood-cell counts. Ferrari took his measures: Armstrong weighed 169 pounds (77 kilos) now; his wattages were unchanged from February's measurements. Training days started early, and consisted of a series of steady climbs. Afternoons were reserved for the usual routine of naps, massage, and tracking his tour rivals, many of whom were taking part in this week's big stage race, Paris-Nice. The weather in France was comfortingly horrific—blowing snow, ice storms—but the competitors looked strong.

There was Team CSC in their red-and-black kit dominating the race, taking three of the top four spots. Armstrong had heard rumors about CSC—they'd participated in a survival camp near Tenerife before the season, led by a former Danish Special Services soldier—and now they were a tight, lean troop directed by the bald, imposing Viking himself, Bjarne Riis, the former tour winner, who had scuttled Induráin's try for a sixth tour in 1996. Riis was regarded as a motivational artist; he was good friends with the brilliant and notorious Cecchini, and he had a young rider in his charge named Ivan Basso, whom Armstrong admired and had, in fact, tried to sign for Postal.

Furthermore, there was the sight of Vino winning three stages in his signature fashion, heading off alone at the hardest possible moment. In stage 5 he rode off on a steep climb with eight kilometers remaining. In stage 7 he broke away to ride alone into a gale-force wind in Cannes. It was quite a sight: the wind screaming, the sand flying, the palm trees whipping around, the French running for cover—a ruined landscape of bourgeois apocalypse—and here, right on cue, came the Kazakh horseman riding away from the pack, his ears radioactive pink, his elfin face set in stoic grimace. The next day, he did it again. It was a calculated display of Eastern Bloc fury, and it made its impression on the peloton.

For Armstrong, those images took on a bit of extra significance, given a change that took place a few days into his stay on Tenerife: the narrow bike was dead, finished.

It happened in about thirty minutes, the time it took Ferrari and Armstrong to do two thirteen-kilometer tests, first with the narrow bike, next with the old time-trial bike, measuring the maximum power produced with each. But when the tests came in, Armstrong could produce about twelve watts less power on the narrow bike, and, perhaps more disturbing, his power diminished steadily as the ride went on.

Twelve watts was not a lot of power. But it was enough, especially considering Ferrari hadn't been optimistic going into the test.

"He said, 'Ehhh, why didn't you tell me about this bike? This bike, it is a bullshit bike,'" Armstrong later said, imitating Ferrari's voice. "He was right. The power went off the table, and I'm the pilot, at the end of the day. My decision."

The narrow bike was disassembled; a few days later it was seen hanging in parts, tossed atop the great slag heap of equipment not good enough to be The Shit. The news trickled out to the F-One group as if it were a particularly uninteresting piece of history. Because that's exactly what it became, starting one second after the power numbers came in. It didn't work, so it was out. No regrets, no dithering, no second test. He was now thirty-six seconds slower.

"Part of me wishes that he would have given it more of a chance," Daubert said. "The narrow bike, even with the power loss, was still faster. But that's the way Lance works. On or off. Yes or no."

The problem was clear enough: the slight realignment of the hips, caused by the eighteen-millimeter change, made Armstrong lose power. What the problem *meant*—well, that was a different sort of question, the kind that Armstrong's software didn't deal with so well.

The questions were these: If Ullrich (and later, Armstrong's teammate Ekimov) could ride the narrow bike so effectively, then why couldn't Armstrong? What if Armstrong's hips were thrown ever so slightly out of alignment by some other factor; say, a crash? Was the margin really so slight?

"Lance did have some tightness in his hips, particularly the next day," Ferrari said later.

Click. From the moment the test ended, it was determined: Armstrong would ride the old bike, and everybody who knew Armstrong knew what would happen next.

"When things aren't going right, you can always tell," says Korioth. "Lance gets quiet and grouchy and the schedule gets shot to hell."

Shortly after the narrow bike was abandoned, Armstrong awoke

early and drove down the volcano with Ferrari. They threaded their
way through the Legoland resorts and faux-English pubs, past the
drowsy, broiled legions of German tourists.

Armstrong climbed aboard and rode up, back toward the crater.
Past the cacti and the yucca plants, the road cutting up, through
windblown fields of gray pumice stones that sounded like broken
pottery. There were no animals here, only the purr of bees.

"On this climb it goes up and up and up," Ferrari said later. "It
is different from what you can do most places in Europe."

On and on. Past frozen rivers of lava, past houselike basalt boulders flung from eruptions, past the fissured rock where the aborigi-
nals had placed their mummified dead, up through the graceful
fleet of clouds that encircled the peak. Nobody was here. Not Ullrich, not Hamilton, not Vino or Mayo or anybody. He had lost the
narrow bike, but he had something they didn't: this feeling, right
now, on the Isles of the Dogs.

Armstrong climbed for six hours.

Back in Girona, of course, none of Armstrong's teammates or rivals
knew of the drama about the narrow bike. Cycling being cycling,
however, this did not prevent any of them from speculating about it,
just as they did about any other news related to Armstrong.

Girona was good for gossip—it was built for it, in fact, the stone
houses set close enough that you could whisper from one balcony
to the next. At the moment, in mid-March, there was a lot of whispering going on in Girona's ever-growing community of American
riders, girlfriends, and wives, and a lot of it was about Armstrong.

Most of the gossip followed fairly predictable lines, addressing
Armstrong's fitness (he was in fantastic form or he was surprisingly
out of shape); his location (he was in northern France or he was in
Italy); and his relationship (he and Sheryl had an angry breakup or
they were madly happy). Cyclists, perhaps because of the nature of
their jobs, are peerless when it comes to chatting, and the doings of
Lance and Sheryl provided regular fodder, even more so since the
rumors could flourish in an atmosphere almost entirely free of hard

facts. Armstrong and Crow came and went like ghosts—when they were in town, word would flash around, sightings would be compared. While Landis and Hincapie rode with Armstrong on a semi-regular basis, the five other Postal riders who lived in Girona—Mike Creed, Pat McCarty, Dave Zabriskie, Michael Barry, and Tony Cruz—didn't. Their running joke was that the easiest place to find Armstrong was on television.

In all of Girona's cycling community, however, it would be difficult to find someone who gossiped less than Mike Anderson. This was partly because of his reserved nature, but mostly because he had no need to. After all, he knew what Armstrong was doing most of the time, living as Anderson did, with his wife, Allison, and one-year-old son, Soren, in a small apartment that connected to Armstrong's.

As it happened, my wife had become friends with Allison, who overheard Jen speaking English to our daughters in a toy store and quickly bonded with her, two mothers far from home. Before long, we invited the Andersons to our apartment for dinner. They proved good company: Allison was a massage therapist who'd studied in France; Mike was the kind of sharp, overqualified guy often found in bike shops, the son of a military family, who spoke four languages, who had majored in anthropology, and pursued a graduate degree in Middle Eastern studies before leaving to be a bike mechanic.

Jen asked, Was it tough working for Armstrong?

"Like learning Arabic all over again," Mike said with a smile.

The following week, Anderson and I sat down at the café outside Armstrong's apartment, and he told me his story: how he'd met Armstrong back in Austin in 2000, and had ridden mountain bikes with him as a friend. How, in 2002, Armstrong had offered him a job as a personal mechanic, and how it had grown to be more than that—trailbuilding, maintaining vehicles, accompanying Armstrong on training rides, shopping for groceries, changing lightbulbs, assembling the kids' Christmas presents. Armstrong and Kristin had called him H-2, for "husband number two." Last year's divorce, he said, caught him by surprise.

"Total shock," Anderson said. "They seemed completely happy, and I saw them very often, almost daily. Then, boom, they're splitting up. It's like there was this level on the surface, and then, underneath it, another level that nobody saw, or at least I didn't. It really burst my bubble."

Anderson spoke of the day in January 2003 when Armstrong and his wife split, how he stayed with Armstrong that night in Santa Barbara after she packed up the kids to leave. They were alone.

"Lance and I talked about a lot that night," he said, plainly affected by the memory. "We talked about everything, stuff I'll never forget."

Following the divorce, Armstrong seemed to lean heavily on Mike and Allison. He asked Allison to accompany Mike to Girona and work as his personal cook. That season, the Andersons and Lance lived as a makeshift family, taking most meals together, filling the empty apartment.

"He's like a little kid in some ways," Anderson said. "If there are cookies around, he tells us not to leave the bag because if it's there, he'll eat the whole thing. Or when he makes a sandwich, he leaves everything all over the place.

"Funny, last year he was so organized about his training," Anderson continued. "He never missed a day, always on time. This year, things are a lot more casual—staying up late, having an occasional bottle of wine with dinner, sleeping in, starting late. It's not time to get real serious yet—and when he does get serious, he will, you can believe that, 1,000 percent. But this year compared to last year, it's night and day."

At one point in our conversation, I proposed that most bike mechanics would say Anderson had the ultimate dream job.

"Well, yeah," Anderson said carefully. "It sure sounds that way. The reality of it is different, of course."

Anderson expressed this kind of sentiment several times during the conversation. When I asked him why, he told stories of how he had to serve as a buffer between Armstrong and Texas motorists, with whom he tended to have occasional run-ins while training. Or how

Armstrong would change schedules at the last minute, over and over. He told how he and Allison had been celebrating this past Christmas Eve at home in Austin when the phone rang—they needed to get themselves to Los Angeles, to Sheryl Crow's house, immediately.

"He calls, we jump," Anderson said. "It's pretty simple."

Anderson was circumspect when I asked him to comment on the never-ending flow of rumors surrounding his boss. No, Armstrong wasn't selling the place in Girona, so far as he knew. Yes, he was probably a bit heavy, but it was still early and he was on track. No, he and Sheryl hadn't broken up. They seemed happy to him.

"All the same," he said. "It's not like I would know if they weren't. After what happened with his wife, I feel like there's a side of Lance that I don't know at all, and I wonder if anybody does."

Anderson said he and his family were headed back to Austin soon. As the Tour approached, Armstrong would be spending less time in Girona, and thus wouldn't require their help. They were sorry to be going, but as Anderson said, "Hey, that's life with Lance."

I remember leaving the café with two impressions: (1) Armstrong would be a hard guy to work for; and (2) if Anderson had ever basked in romantic notions about his job, those days looked to be over. I could easily picture Anderson—by any measure a proud, independent-minded person—knocking heads with his demanding boss.

As soon as that fall, the world would get a more precise indication of just how hard those heads could knock. To sum up: Armstrong would fire Anderson and then sue him, alleging that Anderson was attempting to extort half a million dollars from him. Anderson would then countersue for breach of contract, defamation, and infliction of severe mental distress.

But at the moment, while I sat there with Anderson in the afternoon sunlight at the café, Armstrong and Crow winging their way back from Tenerife, things seemed almost peaceful.

CHAPTER 10

HAMILTON'S SECRET

Tyler Hamilton's first race with his new Phonak team was the week-long Paris-Nice stage race in early March, and it didn't go badly. It went horribly.

He was sick, for starters. He'd caught the flu in the days before, and was forced to go on antibiotics. Cyclists prefer to avoid antibiotics, because they depress performance for a week or so, but Hamilton had no choice. He had fever, chills, the works. So he swallowed the pills, and had his Phonak team send a backup rider to Paris, in case he wasn't able to ride.

"Just in case," Hamilton said, trying to be cheerful. But beneath the cheer was frustration. What was sickness but crashing of a different sort? He'd done all the usual careful things—washed his hands frequently, kept antibacterial wipes handy, used his knuckles instead of his fingertips to press buttons on elevators and teller machines. But a bug had gotten him, snuck past the gates.

"It'll be tough to race when I'm feeling like this," he said. "But it's important for the team that I go."

Perhaps so, because even with Hamilton's presence, Phonak raced poorly. While CSC controlled the race by riding as an unbreakable unit, the green-and-yellow jerseys of Phonak were scattered like posies throughout the bunch, their strength wasted.

"We were terrible," Hamilton said afterward. "And I wasn't in good enough shape to help much."

It is not an easy thing to persuade a talented professional athlete to give every last ounce of his effort and pain for another's glory. *Domestiques* means "servants," and when it comes to cycling, the age-old complaint still applies—it's awfully hard to get good help these days. Setting aside humankind's nobler impulses for a moment, the *domestique*'s motivation springs largely from primal instincts: fear, greed, and love. (There's also insanity: In 1947, after French national champion Rene Vietto lost a toe to sepsis, he insisted his *domestique*, Apo Lazarides, cut off one of his own toes to match. Vietto's toe can be found preserved in formaldehyde in a Marseille bar, notably unaccompanied.)

Hamilton's team-building approach was to go slow and gentle, to extend the vibe he established at training camp. Where other leaders might have barked orders, Hamilton asked about families, he picked up tabs, he opened doors, he exposed them to the depths of his niceness. On the bus, he took them aside one by one and tried to earn their trust. He had seen other ways of leading, and those didn't suit him.

"A natural leader like Armstrong will simply tell everyone what he wants to happen," Phonak's codirector Jacques Michaud said. "Tyler approaches things from the other side. He leads by example, he brings people along."

In the weeks after the Paris-Nice debacle, Hamilton's results improved by small degrees. At Criterium International, he was twelfth; at Pais Vasco, he was fourteenth, at Liege-Bastogne-Liege, a classic which Hamilton had won in 2003, he was ninth. More important to Hamilton, however, his team was showing signs of coming together.

"It's something you feel as much as something you see," Hamilton said later. "It's when we get to the point that you don't have to look or wonder where a rider is in the pack, where he knows what his job is, and does it."

Late April brought one of the pressure points of the Swiss team's season: the Tour of Romandie, one of Switzerland's biggest races, and one which Hamilton had won the previous year. As if to emphasize the moment's importance, a new team bus was delivered just before the start. It was not a normal team bus. Its exterior was decorated with a giant photo of a maniacally grinning old man—Swiss Tour champ Ferdi Kubler, it turned out—proffering a Phonak hearing aid. In a parking lot filled with sheeny buses decorated with eagles, cats, and other stylized images of speed and power, Phonak's bus stood out for its resolute uncoolness. On the inside, however, the bus had everything: a six-hundred-horsepower motor (Postal's was only 350), two showers and bathrooms, kick-ass TV and stereo, and leather couches that faced each other so the team could huddle up before a race—a far nicer setup than Postal's old blue bus, though no one was so unkind as to point that out. Ferdi's Love Bus was the perfect Hamilton-mobile: humble on the outside, gleaming perfection on the inside.

The team rode well at Romandie, taking two of five stages. More important, however, they rode as a team, using their strength in the service of Hamilton and each other. In the third stage, Oscar Camenzind led the peloton to the base of a climb called Pas de Morgins, then teammate Alexandre Moos took over and won the stage, with three Phonaks finishing in the top four, including Hamilton. They followed the basic template of successful stage racing: getting someone into the lead early, then working as a group to chase down anyone who threatened.

Entering the final time trial, Hamilton had a narrow nineteen-second lead. His radio malfunctioned, so he had no idea how he was doing as he rode the twenty-kilometer course. The team was gathered at the finish, however, and their reaction told the story. They greeted their leader with a distinctly un-Swiss level of emotion, hugging, crying, dancing in triumph. Afterward, Hamilton reinforced his goals for the Tour, saying that he was aiming for a top-three finish. It was a statement he'd made often in recent months in response to the incessant questions, a statement that fit with his humble, baby-stepping ways. But this time, Hamilton added something new.

"I'm aiming for the podium," he said. "But I'm attentive to the fact that I'm also in a position to win."

When Hamilton returned to Girona, he was feeling good. He would now rest, return to the States for a few days, and prepare for May's training camps in the Alps and the last pre-Tour race in June.

Things were clicking. His bike sponsor, BMC, was working on a new time-trial bike with some top racing-car engineers. The Tyler Hamilton Foundation was growing steadily: they had cooked up an idea of showing a big stage of the Tour at movie theaters across the country. Hamilton had been on the covers of an embarrassing number of cycling magazines during the spring, each of them priming the world for the coming Hamilton-Armstrong showdown at the Tour. Best of all, Hamilton hadn't touched pavement, a feat which he attributed to his secret weapons: a vial of salt and a bottle of lucky water.

After his crash in last year's Tour, a friend gave him two good-luck charms: a vial of salt and a bottle of special water. Hamilton, who wasn't normally superstitious, had worked the voodoo into his race-day regimen, faithfully stowing the salt in his jersey pocket and taking a single sip from the water bottle, which he kept in his suitcase.

"I forgot the salt one day last year, in the Tour of Holland," he said with a smile. "I crashed, cut my hand, and cracked my femur. So since then, I haven't forgotten it. Knock wood."

"Nobody knows how hard it really is on him," Haven Hamilton said. "After the Tour last year he went through a real down period when he didn't touch his bike. This is a guy who rides every day, no matter what—our wedding day, Christmas—and he couldn't bring himself to ride. It was like post-traumatic stress, like a price he pays for being the way he is. So if this year feels different, that's a good thing. He's due for a little good luck, don't you think?"

To appreciate how due Hamilton is, one must go back to the 2003 Tour, to a sunny afternoon in the riverside village of Meaux, finish of stage 1. Hamilton carried high hopes for the Tour, all of which literally crumpled on a narrow curve near the finish, when the usual thing happened (one rider twitched, another put a foot down), sparking a hideous splintery pileup that flipped Hamilton neatly over his handlebars at 40 mph.

"That hurt a lot," Hamilton said.

Two doctors X-rayed him, shaking their heads. The right collarbone was fractured, a clean crack in the shape of a V. The Tour's official newspaper was notified, headlines were written: "Hamilton Out." Then a third doctor examined it, and noted that while the bone was broken, it was not displaced. In a Hamiltonian stroke of luck, the fracture had occurred near the spot where he'd broken his collarbone the previous year—a mass of fresh bone growth had helped prevent the fracture from spreading. *"C'est possible,"* the doctor said.

Hamilton, pale and bandaged, wobbled out for stage 2. Space was cleared in the team car; his suitcase was packed and brought to the first feed zone in anticipation of his dropping out. Haven, having driven overnight from Girona, pondered how she'd console him. But he finished the 205-kilometer stage in the lead group, and the Tour was never the same.

"On a pain scale of one to ten," Hamilton said, "that was ten."

"It is the finest example of courage that I've come across," decreed veteran Tour doctor Gerard Porte, adding that your average person would have taken three weeks off work. Historians rooted eagerly through the Tour's ample cupboard of noble wounded—Pascal Simon's broken shoulderblade in 1983, Honore Barthelemy's broken shoulder, dislocated wrist, and partial blindness in 1920; Eddy Merckx's 1975 finish with a broken jaw—and watched as Hamilton steadily surpassed them all. The squad of camera operators featuring Hamilton as centerpiece of a 2005 IMAX movie (tentatively called *Brain Power*) kept filming, scarcely believing that God could script so perfectly. Back in the States, his brother, Geoff, stayed up late to police the Web page, deleting some of the more heated offers left by teenage girls who make up a high percentage of Hamilton's fans. Inevitably, it went so far as to tip the other way: a rival team director accused Hamilton and CSC of faking the fracture, precipitating the rarely seen spectacle of a team parading X-rays to prove one of their riders is injured.

Barred by antidoping regulations from taking any actually useful painkillers, Hamilton turned to less conventional methods: physiotherapy and scads of Tylenol. His handlebars were swathed in padded tape and his tires deflated a notch to provide a small measure of cushion. Each night CSC's lanky Danish healer, Ole Kare Foli, worked while Hamilton tried to sleep, applying acupressure and "channeling energy."

It seemed to work. On the steeps of Alpe d'Huez a few days later, Hamilton not only rode in the lead group, but attacked four times. It was great, authentically heroic stuff, and soon everybody was going crazy, and the crazier they got the humbler and nicer Hamilton became (radiating that friendly glow, saying "thank you" a hundred times a day, asking other people how *they* were feeling), which, of course, only made everybody crazier.

Then things got suddenly worse. Favoring the injury, Hamilton compressed a nerve in his lower back, triggering a new pain that dwarfed the ache in his collarbone. The night after stage 10, Hamilton lay on his bed, his torso twisted in rictus, his breathing restricted. Foli tried to massage him, to loosen him up for the needed spinal adjustment, but the pain was too great.

"That really, really hurt a lot," Hamilton said. "At least what I remember of it."

Haven's recollections were clearer. "Ty was lying there in the dark, he couldn't move," she said. "Then he says, 'Just do it, do the adjustment now.' Ole went to straighten him out and Tyler's screaming and Ole is crying and I'm crying, wondering what could be worth all this."

Eight days later, Hamilton provided a succinct answer with his performance on stage 16, a day in which he was nearly dropped early on, ridden back to the pack by his teammates, then broke away and rode alone through the mists up one of the Tour's steepest climbs, his eyes reduced to slits, his cheeks, according to one breathless account, streaked with tears. ("I don't think I was actually crying," he said later. "But it did hurt a lot.") He outrode the superior power of the chasing pack for one hundred kilometers and won his first-ever Tour de France stage, giving television commentators plenty of time to let their voices dissolve with emotion as they declared it one of the longest and most courageous solo breakaways in Tour history. "That felt really good, because I did it not just for me but for everybody else," he said.

One of the people who mattered most to Hamilton was his trainer, Luigi Cecchini. Before the Romandie race, I had met Hamilton in a café, and we talked about his relationship with the Italian doctor.

"He's an amazing guy," Hamilton said. "I started working with him when I was on CSC. We talk every night, to go over the workout. Every few weeks I go visit him in Tuscany to work with him. I think of him like my European father."

He went on to describe Cecchini's beautiful home in Tuscany, the large communal gatherings every Friday, his art collection, even the low, reassuring sound of his voice. He described Cecco's famously precise workouts: specific wattages for certain times, everything calibrated, everything administered with exquisite sensitivity. Cecchini was an artist, Hamilton said, and he should know. When he was at Postal, Hamilton had been tested by Ferrari a few times with Armstrong.

"At Postal I was trained to be a diesel engine," he said. "I could go a million miles at the same speed, but I had no explosiveness, nothing to separate me from the pack. Cecco is rebuilding my engine. It's taken a long time, but it's starting to happen."

I asked Hamilton about his power numbers. He said he was pushing 400 watts at threshold, and should be 10 percent more by the Tour.

I did some napkin-math. By the Tour, then, it should be 440 watts.

How much do you weigh?

Sixty-two kilos.

More math, resulting in a magic number of seven watts per kilo. Well above Ferrari's Tour-winner threshold of 6.7. Also, as it happens, slightly above Armstrong's number.

Is that right?

Hamilton's eyes went serious for a moment, then he started to say how the numbers change a lot and how they don't mean much, and a race, as he so well knows, is so much more about other factors, about team and health and recovery and luck.

But even with that, the truth of his situation had a chance to sink in. Here was a guy who might well have the engine to beat Armstrong—if he didn't crash—and who knew it.

Then Tugboat's leash got tangled up again in the chair, and Hamilton was reminded of something that happened a while back in the Chicago airport.

They were flying back to the States with Tugs. Haven and Tyler went to the baggage department to visit Tugs during a long layover, with the intention of letting him have a walk. But when they opened his cage, the dog bolted, sending security personnel chasing after him in the airport, and nobody could catch him. It was a story that pleased Hamilton—the long confinement, the opportunity, the unexpected burst for freedom.

"Good old Tugs," Hamilton said, ruffling the dog's ears. "You sure surprised them, didn't you?"

CHAPTER 11

DR. EVIL'S CHEESE

The sport of cycling consists of two races. There are the races we see on the road; then there is the shadow race between the drug testers and the cheaters. In the early days of 2004, the shadow race kept slipping to the surface.

There was Phillippe Gaumont of the French Cofidis team, admitting blood-doping, describing how he would rub salt on his testicles until they bled, to get a medical allowance for banned cortisone. There was ex-Kelme rider Jesus Manzano providing authorities with a list of the twenty-nine illegal drugs he said he'd taken at his team's behest, including Oxiglobin, a product for anemic dogs, and describing how he went into seizure and nearly died when they accidentally gave him the wrong person's blood at the 2003 Tour de France. There were police surveillance audiotapes of Italian cyclists getting doping advice from a doctor they'd jauntily nicknamed "Chemical Ali," and newly released videotapes of top Italian riders injecting themselves at the 2001 Giro. There was the widening scandal on the Cofidis team, which suspended racing in April when several of its riders were implicated in an investigation.

By summer, three former world champions—Belgium's Johan Museeuw, Britain's David Millar, and Switzerland's Oscar Camenzind—would be caught, popped, nailed, busted. The sport began to resemble one of those Agatha Christie novels where the guests kept disappearing one by one. But while the scandal index seemed to be on the increase, the rider behavior that caused it was nothing new. Cycling's greatest beauty—the purity with which it tests body and mind, the freedom of the road—has long left it open for those seeking an edge. Which, if history is any guide, meant pretty much everybody.

Doping wasn't illegal in the early days, and cyclists experimented freely with strychnine, cocaine, ether, and, after World War II, with amphetamines, which had been mass-produced to keep soldiers and pilots awake (British troops alone used 72 million tablets). Riders would empty their jersey pockets in front of journalists, showing them the pills that kept them going. From the start, the focus was on stimulants; the point was to numb pain and fatigue. Interviewed on French television after he retired, Tour champion Fausto Coppi said all riders took drugs, and anyone who claimed differently knew nothing of the sport. The interviewer asked if Coppi had used them. "Yes, when it was necessary," he replied. And when was it necessary? "Almost always."*

Jacques Anquetil, who won the Tour five times, was frank on the subject. On a bet, Anquetil once rode the Grand Prix de Forli time trial without amphetamines, just to see what would happen. He won, but rode more slowly and suffered greatly. "Never again," Anquetil swore as he got off the bike. He later said, "Only an idiot thinks that a professional cyclist who rides 235 days a year can hold himself together without stimulants."

After British rider Tom Simpson's death on Mount Ventoux in 1967 (which was linked to amphetamines in his system), testing became more stringent. In the seventies, the emphasis moved away from stimulants and on to the harder stuff: steroids, human growth hormone, and, in the late eighties, erythropoeitin, or EPO, which stimulated the production of oxygen-carrying red blood cells, thereby boosting performance by an estimated 15 percent. EPO

---

*For a full and sometimes darkly funny treatment on the subject, see Les Woodland's *The Crooked Path to Victory: Drugs and Cheating in Professional Bicycle Racing* (San Francisco: Cycle Publishing, 2003).

came with one slight side effect, however: an increased likelihood of funerals. In the late eighties and early nineties, a dozen Belgian and Dutch riders died in their sleep when their slowed hearts were unable to pump the sludgy, EPO-thickened blood (a problem neatly solved by setting alarms for the middle of the night so users could speed their pulses with a few grave-dodging calisthenics).

In the thirteen months leading up to the 2004 season, seven riders had died of heart attacks: Dennis Zanette, 32, Fabrice Salonson, 23; Jose-Maria Jimenez, 32; Johan Sermon, 21; Michel Zanoli, 35; Mario Ceriani, 16; and Marco Rusconi, 24. Some were active pros, some recently retired, some promising amateurs. Together they were, depending on where you stand, either proof that cycling is stressful enough to ruthlessly expose any hidden genetic abnormalities, or evidence that things might not be quite right. Imagine the public reaction, for instance, if seven NCAA and NBA basketball players suffered heart attacks in a single year.

For most fans, the sport of cycling exists on the edge of a looking glass, and what you see depends largely on where you live. For Americans, doping is entwined with questions of character, with goodness and evil. For Europeans, doping is simply something cyclists are known to do. *C'est le métier,* the French say: It's the job. It's the classic prelapsarian divide; the same divergence that occurs when a politican is caught out with a mistress: Americans get outraged—*How could he?* while Europeans shrug—*But of course.*

Neither approach is accurate, of course, and the divide is widened by the maddening difficulty of policing a territory as endlessly complex as the human body. Accusations come cheap, reputations are forever tarnished by a single headline, and absolute proof is nearly impossible to achieve.

Which brings us to Michele Ferrari's cheese.

It was a beautiful hunk of Parmesan cheese. Fat, firm, transmitting its nutty fragrance even through a shield of plastic wrap, it sat like a slab of Italian marble amid the landscape of paper and pencils inside Dr. Ferrari's briefcase. He had hand-carried it from Ferrara, his hometown, as a gift to his favorite client.

"This is a special cheese," Ferrari said, hoisting it, his slender nostrils dilating to inhale its essence. "Lance will like it, I think."

It was Thursday, March 25, the day before Ferrari's fifty-first birthday. He stood in the sunshine of his golf-course lab with George Hincapie, Floyd Landis, and Mike Anderson. Ferrari had flown in this morning from his home in Italy for another round of testing. There was one question: Where was Armstrong?

"He could not have forgotten," Ferrari said, his lips pouching out in a rictus of concern. "We spoke only last night. Perhaps he is with Sheryl, do you think?"

"Who knows?" Landis said. "Who ever knows?"

In the two weeks since the narrow bike failed, Armstrong's schedule had received a shot of adrenaline. He had flown from Tenerife to Lake Como, Italy, to do some riding with old friend Jim Ochowicz, and visit the family of Fabio Casartelli, a former teammate who died in a crash in the 1995 Tour. He had flown to Madrid to receive an award from the Spanish newspaper *Marca*. On March 20 he had been scheduled to ride in Milan–San Remo, the season's first major one-day race, but had begged off at the last minute, saying he had a touch of bronchitis. And now, two days before the start of his next race, Armstrong was nowhere to be seen.

Anderson's phone rang.

"Uh-huh," he said, eyeing Ferrari. "Cool. Okay. Right. I'll tell them."

He hung up the phone and pointed north, toward the shadowy bulk of the Pyrenees. "He's out there," Anderson reported. "He'll meet you later back at his place."

Ferrari absorbed this information. He turned to his briefcase.

"When he is not feeling right, he sometimes needs to take a longer ride," he said to no one in particular. "To do a test is perhaps not as useful."

Ferrari began to arrange the graph paper and lancets on the BMW's trunk.

"Who knows?" Ferrari speculated. "Perhaps he did not sleep well last night."

I ask if something as simple as a night's sleep would make a difference.

"Ahhh, small things, they can be big things," Ferrari said, holding up a long index finger. "Sleep, it is important."

"Naps are illegal, right, Michele?" Landis asked teasingly.

Ferrari turned to Landis, his birdlike features alight.

"Of course!" he said, his tones rising to high sarcasm. "Napping is a competitive advantage."*

"That wouldn't be right," Anderson said drolly.

"Spaghetti too, of course," Ferrari said.

"Bread," Landis offered.

Ferrari drew himself to full height, as if he were delivering an address to Congress.

"According to Italian law," he recited, his index finger bobbing along, "it is illegal to use any substance or method which enhances athletic performance. So of course naps, they are not allowed."

"*Any substance or method*," Ferrari repeated slowly, to let the idiocy of the law sink in. His dark eyes roved, and landed on the briefcase.

"The cheese!" He raised his voice in a parody of triumph. "This has many carbohydrates and fats which aid in performance, and so it is highly illegal. It must be banned! It is a good thing that there are no police around, no?"

If Ferrari seemed well-practiced at this sort of routine, it was for good reason. He'd been on trial since 2001 for allegedly administering illegal, performance-enhancing substances to cyclists. Ferrari's next trial date was in three weeks, in fact, which had put a

---

*This is not completely a joke. Sleep increases the body's production of human growth hormone, which assists in recovery and overall rejuvenation. Napping, then, isn't just napping: it's a skill. Historically speaking, the king of snooze was Barry Hoban, a British rider of the sixties and seventies who completed a whopping eleven Tours in twelve tries, thanks in part to his near-narcoleptic talent for nodding off minutes after the completion of each stage. But Hoban may have a new rival.

"Floyd is very, very good at sleeping," Ferrari told me admiringly. "Lance is not bad, yes, but Floyd, he sleeps two hours each afternoon, sometimes three!"

crimp in what had been tentative plans to accompany Armstrong to the States.

"It is unfortunate timing," he said. "In many ways."

Dr. Ferrari's trial conformed to dramatic convention. First came the splashy SWAT-type raids on offices and team hotel rooms, the file boxes paraded before a titillated media, the damning signatures on suspicious prescriptions. Then the indignant denials by riders and the doctor, the volley of claims and counterclaims, all of it usually winding up in a dispiriting tangle. These are mud-spattered operas, and Ferrari's version thus far had followed the script to a T, with one unexpected twist being the testimony of a beakily intense Italian named Filippo Simeoni, an active professional rider who said yes, Ferrari had taught him how to use EPO and how to avoid getting caught.

"A damned liar," Ferrari called him. When Armstrong, who was not involved in the trial, echoed the same sentiment in an April 2003 interview in *Le Monde*, a furious Simeoni upped the ante by suing the American for libel.

"It is all crazy," Ferrari said by the car, waggling the point of the cheese wedge around his ear. "It makes no sense."

Many bales of media hay had been made questioning Armstrong's continuing relationship with Ferrari. Many observers, including three-time tour winner Greg LeMond, had condemned Armstrong for the association. They pointed darkly to Armstrong's apparent reluctance to reveal the relationship, which was brought to light in 2001. They archly wondered why Armstrong kept Ferrari on exclusive contract (Ferrari can work with other riders, provided they are not Tour contenders), and raised the question of whether Ferrari had a more vital impact than Carmichael on Armstrong's success.

From a distance, Carmichael is by far the more important member of Armstrong's coaching team. Armstrong and Carmichael have worked together since 1990; their close relationship is touted in Armstrong's books and innumerable articles, as well as in advertisements for Carmichael Training Systems, the personal-coaching company of which Armstrong is part owner. Armstrong is the poster boy for the CTS method, which involves the detailed analysis of training data sent over the Internet. Since Armstrong won his first Tour in 1999, CTS has grown from a bedroom company to one with three thousand clients and $5 million in revenues in 2003, and which has doubled in size each of the past few years. Along the way, Carmichael has become a celebrity in his own right: earning as much as $20,000 per speech, and working as an OLN commentator. He had also written several books, including a new one on sports nutrition, and planned to launch a signature line of frozen foods.

Ferrari, on the other hand, spent more hands-on time with Armstrong: one week a month during the season, Ferrari estimated, including the six to eight weeks before the Tour, excepting races. Ferrari had visited Armstrong in Austin, and accompanied him to training camps in Tenerife, the Alps, Arizona, Nice, and many other locations.* In addition, Armstrong called Ferrari most nights of the Tour to go over his performance and talk about the next day. During Marco Pantani's breakaway in the 2000 Tour, a concerned Armstrong had Bruyneel call Ferrari from the team car to get his opinion on whether Pantani could keep this pace going (he couldn't, Ferrari predicted, rightly). Perhaps noting the success of the CTS model, Ferrari recently started an online training business of his own, which he named 53X12.com (the numbers refer to the largest gear ratio used by most professionals).

When *USA Today* writer Sal Ruibal asked Carmichael in July 2004 to explain how he worked with Ferrari, Carmichael described a system by which Armstrong sent his daily training data to Ferrari, who analyzed the numbers and forwarded his observations to Carmichael, who then adjusted Armstrong's training accordingly. But when I had asked Ferrari to describe his working relationship with Carmichael in February, he shook his head.

---

*The closest Ferrari got to prime-time exposure was an uncredited moment during episode 3 of *The Lance Chronicles*, when his hands could be seen drawing a drop of blood from Armstrong's finger in Tenerife. Tenerife, by the way, was not identified, either, referred to only as Armstrong's "European training camp."

"I do not work with Chris Carmichael," Ferrari said, pronouncing the name with slow precision. "I work for Lance. Only Lance. When he calls, I come. We are not married, you see, but still, I am here when he needs me."

Whatever the balance,* it was clear that Armstrong was close to both men; both served his needs in their own way. What's more, Armstrong was untroubled by Ferrari's controversial reputation. The facts were clear: Ferrari had never been convicted of anything; neither had Armstrong ever tested positive. Retaining the most brilliant trainer was not that different from retaining the best bike engineers—Ferrari was the human version of the Shit That Will Kill Them, made more effective by his dark reputation. Even if Ferrari did little more than hand Armstrong water bottles, Armstrong's competitors would still have to deal with that seed of doubt, wondering if just maybe there was some magical dust swirling around inside that bottle.

Yet one might just as easily turn the question on its head. Why did Ferrari keep working with Armstrong? Ferrari might have had his fun with Parmesan cheese, but behind the joking lay the very real possibility of, at worst, a two-year prison sentence, and, at best, the constant attention of an aggressive Italian justice system that had already raided his house twice and tapped his colleagues' phones. Working for Armstrong probably paid well, but on the other hand, Ferrari didn't particularly need the money. He was a

---

*To explore this question, I took a poll. Here are the results:
- Postal director Bruyneel (diplomatically): "I would say both Ferrari and Carmichael are very important to Lance. Each in their own way."
- Armstrong agent Stapleton (emphatically): "Ferrari's the trainer, but Carmichael's the coach. He's got final say."
- Postal team chiropractor Spencer (carefully): "Ferrari's brilliant, and I think there's no doubt that Lance listens to him carefully. On the Tour, I can say that Carmichael is just not that involved. I think he's busy with TV stuff."
- Current Postal teammate Landis (incredulously): "Come on. You've met them both. Who would you listen to?"
- Former Postal teammate Vaughters (knowingly): "That is a very interesting question. There are a lot of people who would say that it is *the* question."

physician, his children were grown, he lived in a lovely home with Antonella, his wife of thirty years. There were almost certainly less risky ways to make a living.

The same question could be asked more pointedly of Luigi Cecchini, who owned a beautiful Tuscan estate, bought his art at Sotheby's, whose wife owned a Gucci emporium, and who gave off the air of a man who had no need to risk anything in life, certainly not his freedom. Why would these two undeniably smart men, with so many resources at their disposal, insert themselves with full knowingness into this dark circus of wiretaps and allegations?

What was so irresistible about being notorious?

In the exceedingly unlikely event that a Hollywood screenwriter is commissioned to write a script about two rival sports doctors, he might consider having the two start out as school chums, earnest science dweebs. Perhaps our screenwriter might be tempted to construct a dramatic arc where the dweeb friends would (1) participate in some groundbreaking discovery, (2) race and train together, using the power of their discovery to transform themselves into top athletes, and (3) inevitably split, becoming warring father-figures to their own sets of athletes, who in turn would compete against each other. Then the screenwriter would speedily realize how hopelessly contrived it all sounded, and chuck his outline into the trash. Yet such an outline would be a reasonably accurate description of the relationship between Michele Ferrari and Luigi Cecchini.

They are cast quite nicely: Cecchini is short, shy, and rich; the former race car–driving son of a shirt-manufacturing magnate. Cecchini tired of the luxe life in his thirties and surprised his family by entering medical school. Ferrari is the taller, more excitable one, the middle-class son of a ribbon-maker, a promising runner who'd severely injured his Achilles tendons following the misguided advice of a coach who ordered him to train by leaping up hills. Both were exceptionally bright; neither had any reverence for the stony dogma of sporting tradition. They were looking for new, bright truths.

Their father figure was Francesco Conconi, the sleepy-eyed doctor at the Ferrara Institute who in the late 1970s had begun investigating a simple question: how does one measure the highest sustainable level of athletic effort? Conventional wisdom had it that the answer lay in a number called VO2 Max, which referred to the body's peak ability to move oxygen, and which could be measured in a lab with a treadmill, electrodes, and a mask to ascertain the contents and volume of each breath.

Conconi, however, didn't like working in the lab. What good was a truth if you needed treadmills and electrodes to unearth it? He stayed outside, pursued his ideas, and in 1982 published a modest-looking article titled "Determination of the Anaerobic Threshold by a Noninvasive Field Test in Runners" in the *Journal of Applied Physiology*.

A fancy enough title for a simple study that consisted of watching athletes run a length of track faster and faster until they collapsed. Conconi measured their heart rates and found that heart rate and speed were related in an interesting way. As the runner went faster, the heart rate increased proportionally—up to a certain speed, where heart rate flattened out, increasing less for every additional unit of speed. Conconi graphed his results, and saw the same pattern again and again—a faultlessly straight line with a little cat's tail at the end, like this.

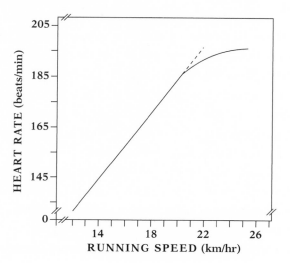

Conconi honed in on that cat's tail. He rightly saw it as a vital shift, a red warning line that marked the tipping point from the steady, repeatable equilibrium to an economy of loss. The anaerobic threshold, it was called, marking as it did the point at which the body stopped burning primarily oxygen and started burning other, less replenishable fuels and producing a crippling surplus of lactic acid.

It was devastatingly simple. In this point, Conconi found a straightforward way to express the peak efficiency of the human organism. Prior to Conconi, athletes spoke of endurance as an abstract concept, as if it were an extension of their character. After Conconi, they spoke of it in terms of a number they could easily find and track.

The consequences of this discovery, beyond igniting what would become a multimillion-dollar business in heart-rate monitors, were simple and far-reaching. The anaerobic threshold number was an answer, but also a more tantalizing question: if true sustainable strength lay at this threshold, to what heights might that number be lifted? And, more to the point, how?

Ferrari was Conconi's prize student, and wrote his thesis on anaerobic threshold; Cecchini studied at Ferrara for one year. They were also cyclists. On their bikes, the two set out to explore the territory of this threshold, to investigate factors like hematocrit, the percentage of oxygen-carrying red blood cells; or glycogen stores, or lung capacity— all of them potential levers to nudge that holy number upward.

This stage, of course, is where our Hollywood screenwriter might insert a turning point, where his characters become unable to resist the temptation to dabble in the dark arts. They would use their physician's access to pharmaceuticals to inject themselves with various substances so that their bodies might perform to their ultimate capacity. But to hear Ferrari tell it (Cecchini has not spoken to the press since 1996), it wasn't like that, not at all. They trained, they measured themselves by various criteria, they trained more. They were pioneers, a couple of doctor buddies out riding.

"It was Conconi, Cecchini, and me," Ferrari said. "It was crucial that we were athletes and that we tried it all ourselves. We were the first athletes we studied, and you have to taste, to really taste what it means to ride for five hours, to have the hunger bonk. Only if you've tried it and tasted it yourself can you understand."

And if the trio chose to taste more illicit substances—and Italian courts have produced strong evidence that Conconi did—there was a lot on the menu. Steroids and stimulants were old hat, but EPO was just becoming available. Blood transfusions were not illegal, and had, in fact, been quietly used by American cyclists in the 1984 Olympics. As our screenwriter might ask, what chance did ethics have in the face of science and art? Ferrari and Cecchini were the inheritors of a tradition that stretched to Michelangelo and da Vinci. Here was a chance to explore the old Italian idea of perfectability: building the ultimate endurance athlete.

Cecchini, the chubby scion who had come to cycling to lose weight, transformed himself, logging 50,000 kilometers in his peak years, the equivalent of riding a Tour de France each month. Ferrari, the former runner, wasn't too far behind, pushing 320 watts at threshold and weighing a mere 67 kilos. When he and Ferrari raced together, however, Cecchini usually won. "He was superstrong," said Ferrari, who does not use the term lightly. "Super, superstrong, eh?" Conconi was no slouch, either, defeating far younger cyclists in hill-climbing races until he was well into his sixties.

From the sport's earliest days, professional cyclists mostly trained according to the dictum expressed by Eddy Merckx: "Ride lots." It was a relatively unscientific approach that consisted mainly of long, steady training rides interspersed with the more violent efforts of racing, which were thought crucial to achieving winning form. But with Conconi's number, the door to a new approach was opened.

The first concrete proof had come in 1984, when Conconi's star client Francesco Moser won the Milan–San Remo spring classic without racing earlier that season. The cycling establishment was thrown for a loop. Moser's win marked the start of a new era: scientific training. The power in cycling, which had been held by coaches and *soigneurs*, began shifting into the hands of the doctors, the ones who knew how the machine really worked. Ferrari and Cecchini worked together as team doctors with the famed Italian Ariostea team from 1990 till 1992. Ferrari then moved to another Italian team, Gewiss, and helped Swiss rider Tony Rominger demolish the hour record, one of the sport's most hallowed marks (the distance a single rider can cover in sixty minutes). Along the way Ferrari picked up a nickname, "the Myth."

In 1994, just after three Gewiss riders finished an unheard-of 1–2–3 at Fleche Wallonne (a race in which Armstrong finished well back), Ferrari gave an interview to reporters from *La Repubblica* and *Corriere dello Sport*. He was quoted as saying "The limit is the antidoping rules; everything that is not prohibited is allowed" and "If I were a rider, I would use the products which elude doping controls if they helped to improve my performances and allowed me to compete with others." About EPO, he was quoted as saying "EPO is not dangerous, it's the abuse that is. Even orange juice can be harmful if you drink ten liters of it." Ferrari said he had been misquoted, but the damage was done: Gewiss fired him the following day. He was now officially notorious.

Ferrari struck out on his own, working privately with Gianni Bugno, Tony Rominger, Moreno Argentin, and Eugeni Berzin, among others. The following year, his athletes took four of the top five spots in the Giro d'Italia, along with top spots at the Tour of Romandie, the world championship road race, Paris-Tours, and the Tour of Lombardy. Meanwhile, Cecchini was making Tuscany a hotbed of top cyclists: Paolo Bettini, Mario Cipollini, Andrea Tafi, and Michele Bartoli all numbered among Cecchini's clients, as did the top three finishers at the 1996 Atlanta Olympics road race—Pascal Richard, Rolf Sorenson, and Max Sciandri.

It didn't all go smoothly, of course. Their mentor Conconi was investigated for doping, an endless trial that ultimately exceeded the statute of limitations. Judge Franca Oliva, however, wrote a forty-four-page report in which she expressed her conclusion that Conconi was guilty. "The accused did, for seven years and in a systematic manner, aid and encourage the athletes named in the court's indictment with their consumption of EPO," the judge wrote, "supporting them and encouraging them in their consumption by a reassuring series of health tests, with examinations, analyses, and tests intended to establish and maximize the impact of this consumption on athletic performance."

In the fall of 1995, Ferrari got a call from none other than Eddy Merckx asking if he might consider taking on a friend of his, a twenty-four-year-old American named Lance Armstrong. Ferrari knew of Armstrong—who didn't? Armstrong had won the world championship at the unusually tender age of twenty-two; he'd been the youngest-ever winner of a Tour de France stage; he also had the reputation of being difficult. But Ferrari had a full slate of clients, he was not looking for more. Mostly out of politeness, Ferrari had Armstrong come to his home in Ferrara for some testing.

"I did not want to take him," Ferrari said. "Then we did a test and I saw his numbers. Very quickly I changed my mind."

To imagine Ferrari testing Armstrong for the first time is like imagining what it's like for an orchid collector to lay his eyes on an elusive specimen after years of searching. In walked this big, confident kid. ("Very big," Ferrari remembers. "Very, very big.") His resting pulse was around thirty. He could generate over five hundred watts for long periods and produced very little lactic acid. His hematocrit level—his percentage of oxygen-carrying red blood cells—was in the range of 47 percent (low- to mid-forties being normal for most people; 50 percent having been established by the UCI as the legal limit). His leg muscles had an unusually high percentage of efficient, slow-twitch fibers.

"Champions, they are naturally selected," Ferrari said. "They begin at their own level, and Lance was at that level, for sure."

Before they could get very far, however, in October of 1996 Armstrong was diagnosed with cancer. When he returned to racing, the nature of the project had changed. Armstrong had lost fifteen pounds, mostly in his upper body. Ferrari, independently but parallel with Carmichael, started to look for methods that would help Armstrong adapt. One idea came from an unlikely source: Kenyan marathoners.

Ferrari had watched the East Africans come to dominate the long-distance running scene, and, as a former runner, he was fascinated by what seemed a glaring inefficiency in their form. Rather than the lovely antelope strides of other runners, the Kenyans ran with short, quick steps. They didn't run, they scooted. It was hardly pretty; moreover, it had been shown by many studies that the ideally efficient running stride was long, not short. All the same, these inefficient Kenyans seemed to win an awful lot. An idea began to form.

"I had started on high cadence a few years before, with Rominger," Ferrari said. "I understood something was changing. When I saw the way the Kenyan runners were running, with little steps, very fast, it got me thinking if perhaps this was not more efficient by some other measure."

It was a counterintuitive thought. The most efficient pedaling cadence, everyone knew, was on the order of 70 to 80 rpms; anything faster wasted energy. But as Ferrari realized, that number came from the lab, not from the field. In the field there were other factors, like the buildup of stress and lactic acid in the muscles in a long event like the Tour. In the field, the only efficiency that counted was getting over the line first.

It was a tradeoff: to lose efficiency in pedaling in exchange for gaining it in resiliency, and it was only possible if Armstrong's engine could make up the difference; in other words, if his threshold was pushed high enough. It was a bold idea, one that appealed to Ferrari because it represented a logical step in the evolution of the ultimate athlete; one who shifts the stress from powerful but unreliable muscles onto the more resilient cardiovascular system. They worked with Armstrong to raise his cadence from the conventional range to 100 rpms, a move that Ferrari regards as the key to all that has happened since.

"I believe that the high cadence is the secret, if there is a secret, to Lance's performance in the Tour de France," Ferrari said. "Cancer, cadence . . . life is strange, eh?"

When he made that comment, Ferrari and I were driving behind Armstrong, Landis, and Hincapie on a 180-kilometer training ride in the Pyrenees. Ferrari went on to explain the advantages of high cadence. When Armstrong attacked at 500 watts and 100 rpms, the maximum force on his muscles was about 54 kilos, or 118 pounds. If he were to attack at the same wattage at a more conventional cadence of 75 rpms, the peak force on his muscles would be 160 pounds, 35 percent more.

"Every time, unh, unh, unh," Ferrari mimicked, his face contorting. "It creates too much *streeeeeehhhhs*. The muscle tightens, the blood does not flow. For Lance's muscles, it would be not so good."

But Ullrich pedaled at conventional cadences—why didn't he speed up his cadence, too?

"Probably Jan has a different kind of fiber in his muscles, fast fibers that are able to work at higher tension and with higher lactic acid," Ferrari said. "So perhaps Ullrich is doing exactly what he should be doing. And besides, I hear Ullrich has a very good trainer."

Ferrari laughed. He had not spoken with Cecchini in a few years, but thought of him fondly. I asked if there was perhaps a friendly rivalry between the two.

"No, no, no," Ferrari said. "We do our work, that is all. We do not keep track."

A few moments later, Ferrari was ticking off his victories. "Nine Giros, six Vueltas, all of the spring classics, two Paris-Roubaix, five Liege-Bastogne-Liege, and of course six Tours de France."

Six? Armstrong had only won five, right?

"Ahh yes," Ferrari said, delighted. "Even Lance does not know about this one. We should all have secrets, no?"

If Dr. Ferrari harbored other, darker secrets, he was not going to tell them to me, and certainly not now. Ahead of us, Armstrong led his teammates up a steep climb. His legs were firing out. A human being moving up a mountain, set against an afternoon sky. It was a beautiful sight, and it was plain that Ferrari thought so, too. It was not hard to imagine Cecchini in Tuscany behind Hamilton and Ullrich, watching them, feeling the same.

"Foom, foom, foom," Ferrari said, in time with Armstrong's pedaling.

"He is strong today. Not as strong as later in the season, but he is strong."

I asked Ferrari if Armstrong represents some peak of human athletic performance.

"No," he said quickly. "I don't think so."

I did a double take. Really? Armstrong is not the peak?

"There are many more parameters to explore," he explained, but turned cryptic when I asked what they were.

"I'm looking into the area of breathing," he said. "Like with scuba divers or yogis. I think this is an area that might have potential, to achieve greater oxygenation of the blood. Naturally, of course."

We were nearly on top of the mountain; France to our right, Spain to our left. Below, the whole of the Old World spread out before us in the mist.

I was still stuck on the idea that it would be possible for a cyclist to be far better than Armstrong.

"Yes, yes, for sure," Ferrari repeated. "We are nowhere near the ceiling."

Ferrari looked out at the view. He watched Armstrong's legs fire into the pedals.

"Foom, foom foom," he said.

CHAPTER 12

HOA-NOA

Armstrong is a man that needs stress to work optimally. He isn't functioning at 100 percent when things become too relaxed, and he won't hesitate to stir things up a bit, if that tension isn't already there.

—JOHAN BRUYNEEL, *GAZET VAN ANTWERPEN*,
JUNE 8, 2004

"Hoa-noa," Johan Bruyneel kept saying. If he said it once, he said it half a dozen times, painstakingly forming each syllable in his slow, Schwarzeneggerian voice. "Watch *hoa-noa*. Keep an eye on *hoa-noa*. Do not let *hoa-noa* get away."

To the ears of the U.S. Postal team, eight riders gathered in the cramped confines of a Bluebird RV in western Georgia, it sounded like their reserved, rational Belgian coach had blown a gasket and had resorted to incanting a voodoo spell.

Hoa-noa, hoa-noa, hoa-noa.

So what if it was voodoo? After all, they could use some magic. Their bus, donated by a wealthy fan, was fetched up in an anonymous parking lot in Carrollton, Georgia, thousands of miles from cycling's natural European habitat. While Hamilton and Ullrich and the rest of Armstrong's rivals duked it out amid the cathedral spires and cobbles—this week held no fewer than three classic one-day races: Flèche Wallonne, Amstel Gold, and Liege-Bastogne-Liege, all of which Armstrong had raced in the past—the Posties were marooned in the land of hot asphalt and fried batter, about to start a race whose very name sounded like the punchline to a joke involving a hillbilly and a beret: The Tour de Georgia.

The bus was nice enough, but the generator kept crapping out, an event that would have been less nerve-wracking if the vehicle hadn't been constantly surrounded by an alert mass of fans. Outside the windows, the crowd murmured and stirred, having sorted themselves into the customary strata: first came the infirm, the aged, and the newly sick, supported by crutches and wheelchairs and family members. Then, just behind, held aloft by their parents, floated the children. Then, behind them, stood the mix of elbowy den mothers and politely yearning grandparents, overalled farmers and golf-shirted NASCAR fans, their hands clutching books and Bibles and homemade collages, their eyes glinting and squinting with Armstrongian determination. What they wanted was Lance. Not a picture (though they'll take thousands); not to speak to him (though they'd shout his name until they were hoarse). No, they wanted him, the actual thing. They wanted to touch him, to grasp him, to pluck threads from his jersey and hair from his head, to bring home some blessed sliver of the magic stuff. It was a variation of the scene Armstrong creates anywhere in America, but here, in the red-clay Baptist stronghold of the Deep South, where God and the Devil do their daily battle amid the kudzu vines, it resonated more strongly. On a scratchy car radio outside the bus, "Break These Chains" was playing on WTGIF (Thank God I'm Forgiven).

"This is not a normal race for us," Bruyneel said later. "Very little here is normal."

The team had chosen abnormality for three reasons, and their names were Luke, Isabelle, and Grace, the children of Armstrong and his ex-wife, Kristin. Armstrong's children. Luke was four, the twins were two and a half. Armstrong had not seen them in the last two months; visits had been sporadic since the couple's initial separation in January of 2003. The legal aspect of the divorce had proceeded smoothly, perhaps helped by the fact that Kristin had hired mediation specialist Bill Zabel of Schulte, Roth & Zabel, who also guided George Soros, Howard Stern, and Michael Crichton through their settlements. The last details of the divorce settlement, reported to be $15 million, had recently been finalized, which was good timing. Armstrong had built his season around a five-week April return to the States. "I would rather lose the Tour and see my kids," he said in January, "than win the Tour and not see them."

Seeing the kids also had meant finding a race hard enough to imitate, if not replicate, Armstrong's normal April racing program. And if the American calendar had lacked such a race, then it was necessary to create one. Over the winter, Armstrong had zeroed in on the Tour de Georgia, a one-year-old six-day stage race that was on the verge of cancellation, and that, after some overtures and a conference call between race organizers and Armstrong, Bruyneel, and Carmichael, had been summarily brought back from the grave.

With Team Armstrong's guidance, race organizers had upped the course's difficulty, and added a specially tailored time trial, a hilly twenty-one-kilometer track that would serve as a miniature version of the tour's penultimate Besançon time trial. Sponsors had flocked on board and so had two European teams, Bjarne Riis's Team CSC and Domina Vacanze, headlined by flamboyant Italian sprinter Mario Cipollini. It had been an impressive show of influence. In a matter of weeks, the race went from nonexistence to becoming perhaps the most prominent stage race ever held in America, one that would later be estimated to have drawn 750,000 spectators and $70 million to the region.

On other levels, things hadn't worked out quite so smoothly. Despite his plans, Armstrong hadn't spent much time in Austin with his children. Nobody knew why—and everyone knew better than to ask, as the answer would inevitably have two sides, both of which could be filed under the general heading of "Divorce Is No Fun." But the bottom line is that he'd been in the States three weeks now and had spent four days in Austin before decamping to Sheryl Crow's Craftsman house in the Hollywood Hills.

"It didn't work out like he thought it would," said Dave Bolch, the team *soigneur* who accompanied Armstrong on his stateside leg. "All I know is that we were there, and then we left."

Over the next weeks, Armstrong was exceptionally busy, even for him. The BlackBerry was vibrating and clicking. He did endless rounds of media, commercials, photo shoots; he would soon be on the covers of no less than six national magazines. He scouted out training rides in the hills above Los Angeles. He would go out for four hours, and then stay out for five, six, accompanied only by a follow car.

"If he is upset, he wouldn't be the kind to talk about it anyway," Korioth said. "It all comes out on the bike."

Divorce seemed to be the month's theme. As Armstrong arrived in Georgia, the warm air buzzed with rumors that the team was about to lose its title sponsor. The U.S. Postal Service, which had bankrolled the team since 1996, had come into criticism from several watchdog groups, which questioned the wisdom of continuing the $9 million sponsorship in light of the agency's budget shortfalls and rising mailing costs. Team supporters countered by adding up the publicity value of a Tour victory ($55 million a year, according to a 1999 study), and increased European market share attributable to the team's high profile. Regardless of the debate, the Postal Service's contract was up at the end of 2004, and they showed few signs of wanting to renew.

Armstrong's interest in that development was more than figurative. Capital Sports & Entertainment, the agency of which Armstrong was part owner, had recently merged with Tailwind Sports, the company which had been managing the team—and of which Armstrong was also a part owner. (As with any sponsor, the Postal Service's duties start and end with check-writing; the daily business of the team, including contracts and budgeting, is handled by a for-profit management organization.) The merger, which had been finalized over the winter, formalized the dynamic that had been in play for some time: it was Armstrong's team. But with the Postal Service likely backing out, the question became, would there be a team to own? Bill Stapleton and Bart Knaggs of CS&E had been quietly sending overtures to potential sponsors, seeking a company that might pony up the required $12–14 million a year. They'd received a few desultory nibbles, but all discussion had stopped at the same unanswerable question: Was Armstrong going to ride the Tour next year? Which, in essence, was the same as asking the question: could he win *this* year?

How all this related to a large Belgian man mouthing tribal words at the front of a bus is difficult to say, but suffice it to say that Johan Bruyneel was well accustomed to the challenge of standing on the borderland between Armstrong and a world that didn't always conform to his wishes. So Bruyneel solved the problem by gathering all the distractions and distilling them into another, more compelling distraction, one he named *hoa-noa*.

"Lance, keep your eye on *hoa-noa*," he reminded.

Bruyneel, the son of an Izegem jeweler, stood six feet tall but seemed taller. His brown eyes were large and watchful, with thick, hobbitty brows. He wore drapey coats and held his arms straight at his sides with palms back, as stage actors are taught to do. His fingers were long, like a guitarist's, and they plucked gently at the edge of his cell phone, as if to some tune only he could hear. His life hinged on a chance conversation in a hotel lobby in 1998 with Armstrong, who was looking for a new director. Before that encounter, Bruyneel was an injured, ex-journeyman cyclist, hoping for a job in public relations. After it, he was on his way to becoming the most successful director in cycling history.

It was easy to imagine that first conversation, because in a sense they were still engaged in it. Armstrong leaned in while Bruyneel remained watchfully upright, offering information here and there in the calibrated doses of a man steering a powerful sports car. For Bruyneel, Armstrong provided the physical talent he lacked as a rider. For Armstrong, Bruyneel provided a level of discipline and know-how that had been lacking in his precancer career. Bruyneel, like many of the key people in Armstrong's life, related to him less as a father figure than as a big brother—the nice, deferential sort, who knew lots of nifty stuff—Frank Hardy to Armstrong's impetuous Joe. Bruyneel spoke five languages; he had ridden for French, Spanish, and Belgian teams; he knew the riders, the methods, the other directors. He combined tough-guy Belgian granite with an open, rational sensibility that he learned by riding under the progressive leadership of Manolo Saiz at the ONCE team. After Bruyneel agreed to take the job, he sent an e-mail to Armstrong, a message most significant for what it did not contain: no directions, no plan, no paternal advice, but rather a simple vision. "See you on the Champs Élysées next year, wearing the [world champion] rainbow jersey and the maillot *jaune*."

"It's not best to tell Lance what to do," Bruyneel said. "Better to make suggestions. To give little impulses."

Bruyneel specialized in impulses. Whenever he came across an article questioning whether Armstrong could win in 2004, or praising his rivals, he would cut and paste it into the text of an e-mail, complete with highlights of pertinent phrases. *Washed up. Showed weakness. Older and vulnerable.* Whenever Mayo or Hamilton spoke openly of their ambitions to win, Bruyneel would find their words and beam them on. He did not do the same for Ullrich's pre-Tour comments. "Ullrich's words, they, how do you say? An evergreen," Bruyneel said.

In his everpresent briefcase, Bruyneel carried another tool: a list of one thousand names in tiny computer script. They were the names of the Division I riders. At the beginning of each season he had circled sixty names—the hot sixty, by his view, the riders to watch out for, and thus the ones to sign once the season was over. Bruyneel updated the list during the season, with feedback from Armstrong, fellow coaches, and other riders.

Back in December, when star climber Roberto Heras unexpectedly left Postal and signed with Bruyneel's old boss Manolo Saiz at the new Liberty Seguros team, it took Bruyneel thirty minutes to track down a name he'd been watching: a quiet thirty-year-old climber named José Azevedo, who was riding for a small team in his native Portugal. Azevedo, who had ridden for Saiz in 2003, came cheap, signing for less than half of the $1.5 million Heras earned. Better still, Heras's contract called for a $1.4 million buyout clause, which effectively meant that they had enough money left over to sign another good rider.

While other coaches like to pinch their riders to see how fit they are, Bruyneel applies pressure with the large, dark lenses of his eyes. If Armstrong has The Look, Bruyneel has The Gaze. He employs it mostly from a distance, from dim doorways and car windows. He gazes at asses and legs and arms, but particularly at faces. Riders sometimes catch Bruyneel staring at them from across the room at breakfast. It is a touch unnerving, this X-ray vision, particularly when the rider doesn't know it's happening (and Bruyneel, discreet as ever, doesn't go out of his way to tell them). Riders find it doubly unnerving when those brown eyes pick up some hidden sign that even they have yet to notice. For example, Bruyneel's favorite way to measure a rider's condition is to watch him as he rides back to the peloton after taking what polite television commentators like to refer to as the "natural break." (Sometimes riders stop to pee; sometimes they let fly from the bike. Either way, they frequently have to catch up afterward.)

"There is something in the way they pedal after they piss," Bruyneel said, shrugging. "I don't know why, but it is definitely there."

"If he's looking at you closely, it's probably not such a good sign," says Postal rider Tony Cruz.

"A rider with a good face might have a bad day," Bruyneel pronounced. "But a bad face means a bad day almost always. Except Ekimov. Ekimov always looks like shit."

Today, however, Bruyneel's eyes were fixed on a different goal. With the Georgia air cluttered with unfamiliarity and distraction, Armstrong and the team needed a focus. They'd already sung the prerace, strictly-here-for-training refrain. Bruyneel had also made two late moves to amp up the quality of the team, replacing two inexperienced riders with Tour veterans Pavel Padrnos and Viatcheslav Ekimov. Like other directors, Bruyneel selected race lineups from Postal's roster of twenty-five riders. Bruyneel's additions meant that the Georgia team had no fewer than four members of what would likely be the Tour team. Now, a few minutes before the stage, he found something else.

Hoa-noa, hoa-noa, hoa-noa.

Horner. As in Chris Horner, the defending champion, who rode for a domestic team called Webcor Builders. As in the radiantly confident, freckle-faced, thirty-two-year-old American racer whose personality reminded some of Armstrong himself. Chris Horner was currently in twenty-fifth place, one ahead of Armstrong, but he'd caught Bruyneel's attention for a different reason.

"I thought Horner would motivate him most," Bruyneel said later. "This is a guy who dares to say that he's going to win and going to beat everybody, so let's pick him."

Bruyneel's strategy with Horner was subtle but simple. Today was a rare two-stage day: a relatively short 126-kilometer stage in the morning, followed by an afternoon time trial. The morning's stage finished with three laps of a steep course on the streets of Rome, Georgia. Horner, an aggressive rider, was sure to make a move, to try to gain time on Armstrong and the rest.

If Armstrong marked Horner, the thinking went, Armstrong would likely finish in the top handful of racers and thus get more rest before his time trial began (competitors start in reverse order of standings, two minutes apart—thus the twenty-fifth place finisher would depart fifty minutes before the leader). Starting later in a time trial is always an advantage, not just for the extra rest but also because Armstrong would have the chaser's advantage of knowing his competitors' split times, which would put him in his preferred position of hunter.

The larger questions—whether Horner was a true threat, whether the extra few minutes of rest mattered, whether Armstrong would ride better if he chased—were wildly debatable. Horner was good, sure, but then again so was CSC's Jens Voigt, who stood four seconds ahead of Armstrong in the Georgia standings. So, for that matter, was Bobby Julich, Voigt's teammate and former third-place winner in the Tour, who was currently tied with Armstrong. But Bruyneel hadn't chosen Voigt or Julich; he'd chosen Horner, the cocky American, the mirror of Armstrong. All of the distractions and problems were distilled into a single name, a pointed suggestion.

"He listens to me," Bruyneel said. "I sometimes have to say things many times before he does, but eventually he will hear. He does not always agree, but he hears."

At some point, Armstrong heard. He didn't say anything, he just shot Bruyneel The Look, the meaning of which his friend John Korioth later translated.

"The tenth time Johan said it, you could see Lance get pissed. He was like, 'You want me to watch Horner? How about he watches me fucking win the race, OK?' Johan saw it, and then he shut up. Finally."

Before the race could begin, however, Armstrong faced another task: escaping the bus. Which was difficult enough in the Tour de France, where he had the muscular assistance of two bodyguards, several gendarmes, and steel barricades. Here in Georgia, there was only a puny roll of fabric tape, one that had long ago given way to the force of the fans' love, a force which now pressed and surged and yelled his name so that it echoed around the parking lot: *Lance, Lance, Lance!*

Armstrong stood on the top step and looked through the tinted window, figuring things out.

Finishes were easier. You could strategize a finish. Armstrong could cross the line and head to the prearranged pickup spot, and be on the bus or in the team car before anybody was the wiser. The Belgies loved it; they even timed how long it took between the first racer crossing the line and the bus roaring off, the record being under five minutes.

The key for Armstrong was being on the bike. In a crowd, being on his bike was like being invisible. Once he got rolling, his hands firmly on the bars, he could weave in and out of all but the densest throng at five miles per hour, doling out an occasional tap or a hello, then watching their faces as they realized who it was—too late! It was beautiful, the kind of gotcha joke that Armstrong loved. Instead of the crowd invading his space, he was invading theirs! Sometimes he would get to the finish and hide out in some race official's car, then Armstrong would borrow a cell phone to ring up Bruyneel, and when his coach asked where in the hell he was, Armstrong got to say, "I'm twenty feet behind you, in the car." Dave Bolch, a Postal *soigneur,* called it "the Batman move."

There was no Batman move possible now, however; not even a second entrance on the bus (which the Postal team bus had). No, Armstrong was definitely trapped, sealed in by the intense love of what looked to be several hundred people. And he needed a way through.

Armstrong pulled on his team cap, which had the advantage of hiding his distinctive hair and making all the Posties look alike. He let a few teammates provide interference, then he stepped down. The crowd surged forward; his teammates scattered like lemmings. Armstrong grabbed his bike, which had been placed as usual by the door, handlebars forward. Someone shouted his name, and they began to close in.

But Armstrong was already ahead of them. He shielded himself with the bike and searched the front row for his goal: a white-haired woman named Iris, who had an artificial leg and the foresight to pass a note onto the bus. Other people had passed notes, too, but for whatever reason (prayer, Iris later vouched) their notes were not chosen, their faces were not noted and memorized from behind the glass.

Armstrong saw Iris, reached for her. The crowd backed off instinctively, sensing that something was up.

"You ready?" he asked.

"Yep," Iris said, smiling hugely and showing her yellow disposable camera.

Armstrong's eyes lowered to the clunky, toylike camera, and he squinted, eyeing it closely. The crowd leaned in—this was what they wanted. Seeing him ride his bike was fine and good, but seeing him *render judgment*—well, that was better, because you didn't just see it, you felt it. Then you felt something even better, because Armstrong took the camera in his hands. Held it up so everybody could see it.

"You *sure* this thing is gonna work?" he asked.

A ripple of pleasure flashed through the crowd. He was challenging this one-legged grandma, testing her! It was like a parlor trick, a quick unveiling of the will, executed with such an easy, locker-room style, the exact same way he addressed huge crowds, pushing them, teasing them, wanting them to rise up. Iris rose.

"I'm sure, dang it," she said loudly, and everybody laughed at her boldness, including Armstrong.

The photo was snapped. Armstrong got on his bike, and said well, he was sorry but he'd better get to work. People tried to surround him but he started paddling with his leg, getting moving. *Soigneurs* swept people back. The crowd parted reluctantly, and he glided off, Batmanning through the crowd toward the start line.

People milled about the bus, thrill giving way to disappointment. He had been there—right there—and now he was gone. A middle-aged man approached John Korioth, having deduced that Korioth was Armstrong's good friend, College. The man told his story. His name was David, and he had leukemia. David had come from California to see Lance. This was his third straight day outside the bus; each time Armstrong had stopped for ten seconds, talked to one person, and bolted. Now David was more than upset; he was pissed. He wanted thirty seconds, no more. What more could he do? Was there a way, any way?

Korioth fixed David with a long, steady look.

"I sure hope you didn't drive all that way for this," Korioth said. "Because in front of you there's a guy whose wife and kids both have cancer, and in front of that guy are ten more people who've got something worse."

Korioth watched David's face go slack as the information sank in.

"I'm sure it sounded harsh," Korioth said later. "People come to him with expectations; they have this connection to him that goes very deep, and it's endless. If he stops for five seconds, it could be five hours, and Lance understands that the only way to have any kind of life of your own is to sometimes be perceived as somewhat of an asshole."

How else can you explain the depth of it, except through harshness? The line outside the bus starts with Iris. Behind her stands the widow of the pastor in Michigan who died after being hit by a car, could Lance write a letter to be read at the funeral? Behind her stand the parents of a twelve-year-old Pennsylvania boy wondering if Armstrong might have a minute to make a phone call. Behind them stand others, more and more every day, every minute, like the parents in France who wrapped up their sick child in a white blanket and met Armstrong in a field. Could Lance just touch him on the forehead, just once? Please?

How do you satisfy that much need?

You can't.

More interestingly, what kind of person *tries anyway*?

For most people, that answer comes easily: a saint. One who lives a simple, powerful message of hope. And for the many who consider Armstrong a kind of citizen saint, the evidence is plentiful: his Augustinian journey from impetuous youth to seeming maturity and wisdom; the Old Testament savagery of his affliction; his eloquent relishment of suffering; his triumphal arrival at a far-off mountaintop—it's all right there.

But as Armstrong has said a thousand times, he doesn't qualify. He does not believe in God, the afterlife, or anything but the here and now. "I think too many people look to religion as an excuse, or a crutch, or a bailout," he wrote in his second book, *Every Second Counts*. "I think that what you've got is what you've got, here and now." Armstrong wears his unreflectiveness like a badge of honor. Sheryl Crow got him a book on meditation; he couldn't get through it.

Yet it is difficult to imagine anyone more capable of inspiring people to religious heights. At his speeches (for which he charges $150,000, and with which charitable organizations can raise multiples of that figure), he sometimes plays a homemade video that a friend took while Armstrong was sick, a video that shows a skinny bald guy on a stationary trainer, weakly grinding away. "I couldn't beat anybody's grandma," he'll say. Then he'll tell how the doctors carved his head up like a pumpkin, to find tumors like so many snowflakes—a blizzard of tumors, in fact. His story is dark and unflinching and revelatory. It is replete with angels (his mother, Linda, his nurse, LaTrice Haney) and devils (Cofidis, the French team that refused to honor his contract), and visitations. Armstrong continually sneaks in time to help out someone with cancer, take them on a bike ride, pick them out of the mob just like he picked out beaming Iris.

"The obligation of the cured" Armstrong calls it—and there was no doubt that he'd fulfilled that commitment a hundred times over. The barest list of his services to the cancer community would fill several pages; stories of his inspiration would fill volumes (and do). But that isn't enough.

Care packages, yes. Fund-raising clubs, yes. Resource centers, yes. Fund-raising rides, yes. Survivorship centers, yes. Lobbying in Washington, yes. Bugging President Bush (getting in his face!), yes. A couple years ago, the American Cancer Society wanted to cohost an event, and the answer was no thanks, we'll do it ourselves. Screw the American Cancer Society—LAF is going to be bigger, better, smarter, newer.

The newest idea was a bright yellow bracelet that Armstrong wore for the first time in Georgia. Donated by Nike, the bracelets were sold for $1 and emblazoned with the LAF's LiveStrong logo; the money goes to LAF's survivorship education program. Armstrong unveiled them at the press conference ("I'll wear it the rest of my life," he said). In the audience, his agent, Bill Stapleton, fiddled self-consciously with his own bracelet and tried to sound optimistic.

"It's one of those 'change the world' ideas," he said. "If things go right, who knows, it might catch on."

Catch on it would. By year's end, no fewer than 30 million Americans would be wearing bracelets, including many prominent athletes, celebrities, politicians, and others whose lives have been touched by cancer.

And yet, even as his influence grows, even as these bracelets multiply and fly out into the world, the question lingers. By what depth of desire or need does Armstrong—this irreligious saint, this selfless man with a big ego—embrace his role so completely?

There are the obvious reasons, of course. He does it because he believes he was given a second chance, and because his instincts call for him to maximize that chance. He also does it because he's good at it, whether giving a speech to a thousand people or teasing Iris. In those situations, we see Armstrong at his provocative best, pushing people toward a new belief: Cancer patients are not sick. They are fighting death.

Those people, in turn, form a deeply loyal fan base, which helps Armstrong in several ways. Not just by elevating his reputation (and, it must be pointed out, giving him public-relations Teflon with which to deflect criticism), but by providing him with thousands of people who, at some level, want him to succeed. It's a feedback loop: a distant, loyal makeshift family whom he loves and inspires, and who in turn love and inspire him, a spiral of belief that finds its expression in the Tour.

Sainthood has its downsides, of course. He inevitably disappoints people, like poor David from California. The line stretches forever, and it gets longer every second. He can't possibly fulfill all the demands, he can't overcome that endless field of reaching hands, that pulling, clutching frenzy, that appetite.

And yet Armstrong seems uniquely suited to handling the downside. When they come at him, Armstrong does not, as some would, shrug and smile and endure while letting some secret seed of resentment take root. No, he plays a game of hide-and-seek with them, a game that works because he has understood from the start that in order to get close to someone you have to be willing to push them away; in order to love you have to be ready to fight.

David from California stood by the bus for a long time, still pissed off. He watched Armstrong ride away, then he walked to his car.

There wasn't much time. He had to get on the highway, if he was going to get to the finish line in time to try to see Armstrong again.

CHAPTER 13

THE RIGHT BREAK

At ten a.m., after the Carrollton barbershop quartet warbled the national anthem, the Tour de Georgia peloton started north, toward Rome. They rolled through the dappled hills, past the Carrollton High School Trojan marching band, past the Camaros and the McMansions and the fields still dewy in the morning light. Small children lined the road, waving flags, smiling their toothpaste grins and sending their birdlike calls into the pines: Lance! Lance! Lance!

This was a strange sight. I'd just come from seeing Paris-Roubaix, a race known as the Hell of the North, and had seen almost no children. In fact, I'd asked a local about maybe bringing my kids, and they laughed out loud. Bring children? To a *bike* race? It didn't take long to figure out why. European one-day races are about drinking, smoking, eating terrible sausages, and placing your kneecaps inches from a rampaging river of cars and bikes.* This was a celebration of a manly, unhealthy, savage world, a festival of Old World barbarism, all crashes and pain and a roaring, oceanlike sound of men shouting. There was

---

*The Tour is more kid-friendly, but it doesn't change the fact that attending a bike race is a combination of excruciating boredom and unbelievable excitement that stems from the math: You wait hours to see something that lasts twenty seconds, and afterward you usually have no idea what the hell happened—who's winning, who's losing. So you solve it by making your own good time: hence the wine, bread, and festive atmosphere of anything-goes fun. Kids catch on fast. At one race, in Portugal, we looked down to see our three-year-old daughter mooning the peloton as it passed.

drama, sure, but it was of a darkly fated variety, the sort felt at an Aztec altar just before the priests cut out the beating heart of some unlucky, beautiful youth and held it up to the gods. The closest I came to seeing children at Paris-Roubaix was when the race passed a lonely bar, and a half dozen aging drunks tottered out to stare with yearning, bleary eyes at the idea of the young men they used to be.

In Georgia, however, there were children, thousands of them, along with balloons and flags and sunflower yellow jerseys. The finish area featured a health fair, with screenings for several types of cancer, blood pressure–testing centers, tanned legions of pro bono personal trainers ready to wield their life-changing advice. The strongest beverage I saw was Fanta, and I got the distinct impression that anyone lighting a cigarette would have been gang-tackled. Cycling, through Armstrong, had somehow been married to wholesomeness and health, a notion that provided marketers with much grist, but which any European might have noted with a gimlet eye.

No matter the atmosphere, today's pace was healthily fast, and rider after rider tried to escape, motivated by Armstrong's presence at the front of the peloton. For the vast majority of Tour de Georgia riders, American pros who would likely only see the Champs Élysées as tourists, this was the Tour de France. Riders started competing for the honor of being chased down. Eleven times, riders took off, and eleven times they were brought back, mostly by Postal. This was in strict accordance with the sport's standard pattern seen on most flat stages.

Part I—a lot of dramatic attacks, as a series of racers try to get away from the peloton.

Part II—one racer or group succeeds in establishing a gap, and the race settles down for its middle portion. Somewhere in that middle, the tables turn, and the peloton begins to chase down the breakaway. The rule of thumb is that a hard-chasing peloton can make up ten seconds per kilometer on most breakaways.

Part III—the escapees are caught (eight times out of ten) precipitating the demolition-derby madness of a sprint finish; or, alternatively, the escapees actually escape (two times out of ten) and duel it out to the finish line.

Mountain stages, of course, were an entirely different animal, since gravity tends to sort riders more dramatically. Today was a fairly flat stage, complicated by a few factors not normally found in European races. First, the field was filled with American riders, who have a tendency to be more aggressive than their European counterparts. Second, the finish was a series of four laps on narrow city streets, including one nasty turn of 110 degrees. Armstrong had already experienced the charms of this racing, in the first few Georgia stages.

"I looked over at Lance, and he was totally gripped," Tony Cruz said. "He's not used to this, I don't think."

"Here [in America] it's a whole different art," Armstrong said. "You can tell the guys here are used to racing differently. You have no friends, you have no allies. . . . There's a different hierarchy in the European peloton."

As each break went, Bruyneel speedily judged its potential from the team car; it was as if names from his list lifted off the page and set off down the road. If those names were deemed threatening in any way, Bruyneel ordered Postal to chase, and the break would be immediately reeled in. Finally, after thirty-five minutes, an acceptable situation presented itself. Jackson Stewart of the Ofoto team successfully broke away and the race settled down. The gap was established at two minutes, and Bruyneel began talking.

In regular existence, Bruyneel is not a particularly chatty person, but put him in the team car, connected to his team by their earbud radios, and he turned into a one-man news channel, providing constant updates on weather, wind, and upcoming terrain. Most of the bulletins came as directives, the most common being, Stay in the front. "Stay in the front" is a short way of saying a lot of things: Keep working hard, protect Armstrong, and, above all, don't get caught up in crashes. Not crashing was perhaps Armstrong's highest priority in this race, so Bruyneel made sure that there were riders around Armstrong at all times.

"Stay in the front. Stay in the front. The front, the front, the front."

Bruyneel, of course, couldn't actually see the front, relying instead on the crackly pronouncements of race radio, and a map (in Europe, he has a dashboard-mounted television). Bruyneel didn't pay attention to any one of these things; rather he seemed to look in between them, paying attention to all three. He had an acrobat's calm, eyes in the middle distance, watching over some inner balance.

What Bruyneel wanted was for nothing to happen; for the race to proceed, in his words, normally. If the race was normal, free of any insane attacks or unlucky crashes, then the strongest riders would do well, and he usually had the strongest riders.

"There are not so many tactics in our races," he said. "Even in the Tour, except for last year, my job is relatively easy."

When he did choose to get tactical, however, Bruyneel was no slouch. It was his idea to have Armstrong pretend he was hurting during the famous stage 10 of the 2001 Tour, creating the moment that has become known as The Look. The situation was this: Postal was weak; several riders were having a bad day. An earlier breakaway had put Armstrong, along with other contenders, a more than hefty thirty-five minutes in arrears to François Simon, a middling French rider.

Bruyneel had an idea. He told Armstrong to flail along the back of the peloton, to persuade the others that he was hurting and could be dropped. When motorbike-riding radio reporters came alongside the team car to ask what was wrong with Armstrong, Bruyneel feigned ignorance. "I don't know," he said.

Ullrich and his Telekom team took the bait, riding hard for eighty kilometers and putting pressure on Simon as Armstrong and Postal played possum in their wake. When they reached the base of Alpe d'Huez, the final climb, Armstrong came to life in what might be one of the larger "gotcha" moments in Tour history, staring down Ullrich as he passed and going on to put what would be an insurmountable 1:40 on the German.

Here in Georgia, Ullrich had been on Bruyneel and Armstrong's minds, which is to say on their BlackBerries, quite a bit. The day before, Ullrich had competed in the Flèche Wallonne, a one-day classic in Belgium. For Ullrich, this ranked as an important day.

After his mediocre performances at the Murcia and Setmana Cata-lana races, Ullrich had spoken with great optimism about Flèche Wallonne as well as Liege-Bastogne-Liege, which he would ride this Saturday. He'd been doing a lot of training, and looked forward to hitting a new level. This was a new start, Ullrich had said.

Halfway through the race to Rome, Bruyneel's voice came on Postal's team radio with a bit of news. The Fleche results were in.

"Rebellin won the race, with Di Luca second and Kessler third." Fine, everybody wondered. But where was Ullrich?

Bruyneel let it drop casually. "Oh. Ullrich didn't finish."

He didn't finish! Not due to the relative nobility of a crash or injury—no, as it turned out, Ullrich had simply quit! He'd run out of gas and bailed on the Mur de Huy, a steep 1.3-kilometer climb. Word was he'd pulled over, handed his bike to a mechanic, and headed back to the team bus. Nobody was saying why. Maybe that old knee injury was bothering him, maybe he was still too big.

Not only that, but Ullrich had announced he was dropping out of Saturday's Liege-Bastogne-Liege race. "The level of competition was too strong for his current condition," his team said. His next race would be in a month or so. It didn't have to be spelled out. A monthlong break? There were seventy-two days until the Tour. Take away the month and he would come back with forty days left.

Now, on the road in Georgia, with that piece of information buzzing pleasantly in their brains, Armstrong and Bruyneel were feeling good. Bruyneel read Flèche Wallonne's top ten.

"Scarponi, Vino, Kloden . . ." Bruyneel's voice droned. The rest of the Postal guys only half-listened. But Armstrong listened to every name, thinking about Ullrich, in part because he knew that Ullrich would be thinking about him. Ullrich liked to pretend he didn't pay attention to results, but such willful ignorance was beyond the bounds of Armstrong's belief.

"I wonder what Jan thought when he heard I won [the time trial] in Portugal, that I'm winning in February, when I'm nowhere near my peak," Armstrong had said a month before. "And I was thinking what I would do if I heard Ullrich had won a time trial in February? I think

I'd get straight down and do fifty sit-ups just to say to myself I was doing something. . . . I think a lot about my opponents. I'm no good at bullshitting. I think about Ullrich all the time."

From Armstrong's perspective, it set up nicely. Ullrich would wake the following morning with a question on his mind, the same question that all his rivals would share, because what they wanted—what they hoped for—in their moment of weakness was to be given a touch of slack, for Armstrong (who was in Georgia strictly for training, after all) to have an off day, or crash, or at least finish in the pack.

And what would Ullrich see?

Bruyneel kept reading the names in his stoic, slow voice. "Vandenbrouke, Serrano, Zberg."

What would he see?

As they neared the outskirts of Rome, the pace picked up. The pack caught Stewart with sixteen kilometers to go, left him behind, and swung onto the streets for the three finishing circuits of four kilometers each. Mario Cipollini's team moved to the front, followed by Horner and his team.

Bruyneel incanted. "Stay in the front, stay in the front. Watch *hoa-noa*. The finish is tricky."

In the town of Rome, spectators began to hear sirens, the roar of engines, and behind them, an unfamiliar sound. A sound few of the Americans had ever heard; a deep, whirring churn, like the inhalation of a monstrous breath, and as the pack drew closer—going far faster than they'd imagined—the sound grew louder and louder until they appeared, a flashing, sinuous rush of raw power, a storybook dragon. A five-year-old girl covered her ears and cried.*

Everyone in the crowd looked for Armstrong. Twice, the peloton buzzed the grandstand, and each time its passing was followed by a brief, churchlike silence. Then voices would pop up.

---

*It's tough to communicate the speed and power of the pro peloton without resorting to numbers, but here's the bottom line: no other animal or machine—not a racehorse, not a rainbow trout, not an F-105 fighter jet—can move through space as energy-efficiently as a human being on a bicycle.

"Did you see him?"

"I think I saw him, on the left."

"Did anybody see him?"

"I saw him! I did!"

Bell lap. One last climb of Second Street Hill before a downhill run to the line. Armstrong was near the front, behind George Hincapie, watching Horner and Julich and a Cuban named Ivan Dominguez. They went up together, past an American flag. Then down over the last kilometer, through two left turns.

Hoa-noa, Bruyneel said. He didn't yell, he simply talked louder.

Hincapie followed, as did Dominguez. Armstrong was behind them, head up, catlike.

Go go go go go.

They fanned out across the road. Dominguez took off left, American sprinter Ben Brooks to the right. Armstrong followed, then cut to the middle. The primal scene: Three guys racing like hell to the line, moving too fast to see anything but the shape of three bodies with their arms stretched out, their heads bowed as if in reverence.

The guy in the middle won. He was wearing blue.

The announcer couldn't figure it out for a second. The crowd leaned in, waiting. Then the announcer shouted the name everyone wanted to hear.

Explosion. The little girl hugged her mother. Another woman was crying. Men pumped their fists and Armstrong raised his, the yellow bracelet catching the light.

The announcer did his throaty best to explain just how impossible this was, how Armstrong never wins a sprint, how it was like an Olympian miler suddenly winning the hundred-yard dash—and yet the crowd didn't buy it for even a second, because on some level this was exactly the story they had expected all along. Lance won? Of *course* he won!

All the elements were visible as Armstrong prepared to climb the podium: There was his coach, Carmichael, the one who believed in him! There was Sheryl Crow, handing him a water bottle— sneaking a kiss! There, at the foot of the podium, in a dream-pink dress and silver crown, stood the stunningly lovely Miss Georgia, her hair cascading, her creamy toes curling in expectation of giving Armstrong a bouquet.

And yet, when the podium moment arrived, Armstrong wasn't greeted by Miss Georgia, but by a chunky, blond-haired woman in a white T-shirt and jeans. The crowd puzzled for a moment, then there was an audible sigh of pleasure as they got it (gotcha!). She was a cancer survivor—a fighter! A death-defeater! Armstrong and the woman embraced. A salty tear traced the curve of Miss Georgia's perfect cheek, and she was not the only one crying.

Later that night, at the press conference held in a church, Armstrong sat beneath a banner that read PEOPLE CONNECTING IN CHRIST. He had won the time trial, too, of course, a double stage-win that put him in the yellow leader's jersey. "Show of Force," the headlines woud read. When reporters asked him about his big day, Armstrong scratched his head and smiled and acted faintly surprised. He didn't plan on winning, he said, hadn't sprinted like that in years. It had nothing to do with Ullrich's failure or anything else. It had just happened. He shrugged.

"Some could even say [Ullrich's] preparation is going better than mine," he said.

As it turned out, the early reports from Flèche Wallonne were wrong. Ullrich had indeed quit, but he did not return to the team bus. He rode his bike straight to the hotel. He booked a six a.m. flight out of Brussels with his physiotherapist, Krohme. They drove to the airport in the darkness.

He didn't say much. He sat on the plane and looked out the window.

He had screwed up, and he knew it. There were reasons—he'd been sick in January, again in March—but still, he'd fucked up.

He had had such hopes for the year; he had felt so strong. The other times, yes, he had been too heavy—but this time, he had added muscle. The knee was not bothering him, in fact it *had* felt better. He was a few pounds over, sure, but he hadn't expected to have to abandon.

He had already spoken with Cecchini on the phone, he had heard that low, comforting voice. Cecchini did not sound worried. He said he would send a new training program. They would throw everything else away. They would start over, he knew how to do it. There was still time.

The plane arrived in Zurich, Switzerland, around seven a.m., and Ullrich drove to his home near Lake Bodensee. Though he had been up most of the night, Ullrich did not take a nap. He ate a bowl of muesli, then he found his bike and went out in the silver morning light, looking for a steep climb.

Fat boy was finally pissed.

CHAPTER 14

THE THIN BLUE LINE

If you had checked the Union Cycliste Internationale elite road-race rankings two months before the Tour de France, when Armstrong returned to Europe from the States, you would have seen this:

6th	Lance Armstrong	1,753.00 pts
8th	Alexandre Vinokourov	1381.50
10th	Iban Mayo	1186.00
13th	Jan Ullrich	1162.00
18th	Ivan Basso	1062.00
22nd	Roberto Heras	1028.25
26th	Tyler Hamilton	944.00

The numbers, of course, were a rough gauge at best (particularly since they went back to last year). What mattered to Armstrong was both more immediate and more subjective: How did his rivals look?

From the bottom:

- Hamilton looked quietly good. He'd gritted his way through the ice storms of Paris-Nice in March, and had done a little better at each successive race. The word around Girona was that Hamilton was putting up big numbers on training rides, though of course Hamilton would never have admitted to that.

- Heras looked decent. The 5' 7", 130-pounder had talked in the press about his weight-lifting regimen (which was priceless in itself, just for the image of the hummingbird-like Heras pumping iron) and about riding an impressive 1,000 kilometers a week. He'd had no notable victories, and had finished most races in the pack, which probably meant he was keeping his powder dry, aiming to peak at the Tour.

- Basso looked solid; he was a vital cog of CSC's machine-like run of early season success. He was skinnier than in years past (the influence of Cecchini, no doubt) and was showing his Tour ambitions by addressing his main weakness: time trialing. With director Bjarne Riis and a teammate, Basso had visited a wind tunnel at MIT in Boston to improve his position and refine equipment.

- Ullrich? Well, Ullrich had disappeared. Rumors had him spotted riding in Tuscany and Switzerland and every place in between; he had put forth word he would not emerge until the end of May at a race in Germany. What he was doing was clear enough: He had likely embarked on long, steady rides designed to burn off weight and build base-condition. This was comforting, being the kind of training most riders would do in February and March, not May.

- Mayo, the twenty-six-year-old Basque, looked good, if unproven. He'd improved the form he showed back in Murcia and was looking skinny and fast. This month, however, would bring Mayo's first real test, a two-week series of Spanish races he'd entered with his Euskaltel-Euskadi team.

- Vino—well, Vino was Vino: strong, aggressive, fearless. He finished well in big races (third in Liege-Bastogne-Liege, fifth in Fleche Wallonne), he showed a nose for finding the right break. Then again, Vino had recently made some noise about his own chances at the Tour, lightly questioning the presumption that Ullrich would be T-Mobile's team leader. Could there be a rift? Armstrong hoped so. It was the kind of thing that would make for tactical opportunities. It was also the kind of thing that would never, ever happen on his team.

But in truth, more of Armstrong's attention was focused closer to home. Early May was the time of year when Armstrong and Bruyneel started narrowing down Postal's Tour team, the eight support riders. To most knowledgeable observers, there were eleven candidates, roughly arranged like this:

SURE THINGS: José Azevedo
Triki Beltran
Viatcheslav Ekimov
George Hincapie
Floyd Landis
Chechu Rubiera

ON THE BUBBLE: Michael Barry
Benjamin Noval
Benoit Joachim
Pavel Padrnos
Victor Hugo Peña

In one of bike racing's most reliable ironies, these fairly anonymous names would have a large say in whether or not Armstrong would win the Tour. The eight would ride in front of Armstrong, blocking the wind, increasing or slowing the pace as he and Bruyneel dictated. The team would function as a literal and figurative extension of Armstrong's strength, the lever by which he would lessen his own pain and, he hoped, bring pain to his rivals.

Building the Postal team was roughly similar to creating an eight-headed, sixteen-legged version of Armstrong, a kind of multi-limbed deity: the Hindu god of megawatts. As with creating any god, construction was the simple part. The real trick was keeping the sucker in line; ensuring it behaved properly through regular and timely application of Armstrong's hot Look and Bruyneel's cool Gaze. To understand that process, it's helpful to take a look into the beating heart of the team, the dinner table.

At any race hotel you can see them, several islands of tables in big dining rooms, each team creating its microhabitat, sending up its distinct set of sounds. In fact, it would be possible to close your eyes and identify the nationality of each team solely by the sounds: the Italian teams hold passionate debates, the French teams complain artfully, the Spanish chatter and nurse endless coffees.

And what of the residents of the Postal Nation, those seven or eight men who were presently being tested to see if they possessed the physical and emotional qualities to become the Shit That Will Kill Them? Well, they were harder to hear, because they were usually off in a private room, walled off behind the impermeable glass of Belgie team procedure, but at every race during the spring you could hear them nevertheless—a curious, bubbling, keening noise that drew you closer, until you recognized the sound and the strange reality that lay behind it. Because these guys who were being subjected day and night to The Look and The Gaze, who were being ruthlessly molded into the Hindu god of megawatts, were laughing.

Not just laughing but giggling, chortling, wheezing, cackling—several cultures worth of laughter that echoed from appetizer to dessert. It built slowly through each meal. The *soigneurs* and mechanics ate first, serving as a kind of collective Ed McMahon to set the tone for the later arrivals of the coaches and riders, working running jokes and starting new ones, greeting each rider as they entered in their delicate senior-citizen's walk, the laughter building and building, climbing toward its hilarious peak.

Ha hooo hooo hah hah haheeeeeeah hah hooooooo!

There was big George Hincapie, gently folding himself into a chair with his shy, murmuring laugh. Hincapie was an archetype of Postal riders, peerlessly strong and peerlessly nice. He was 6' 3", 170 pounds, and, in the phrase of cycling journalist Jamie Nichols, possessed "the killer instinct of a timid woodland animal." His essential niceness, in fact, was widely believed to be the reason he didn't win more races (three in the last five years), though on the upside it was also the reason that he was dating Melanie, an incredibly luscious Tour de France podium girl.

There, chattering pleasantly away between bites, was Manuel "Triki" Beltran, the smallest and most talkative of the trio of Spanish climbers. Beltran fairly vibrated with energy, stories, superstitions, and a high cackle of a laugh. He did not seem to inhale. He talked so often during steep climbs that it occasionally drove his teammates mad, though he compensated with an accompanying absentmindedness that made for good comedy. Cleaning up after a race last year, Beltran accidentally doused himself with massage oil, mistaking it for soap solution they used to towel off road grime, and was so caught up in his story that he simply never noticed.

Then, usually sitting together, were Padrnos and Ekimov, the Eastern Bloc goombahs. It took some getting used to, seeing such hard faces take on soft expressions of laughter. Padrnos, a giant of a man, nicknamed Jaws because of his uncanny resemblance to the Bond villain, smiled gently and checked if anybody wanted more water. Eki was quieter but no less considerate, and when he laughed, the skin on his face stretched unnaturally, a grimace of hilarity.

And there was Chechu Rubiera, the son of a milk deliveryman, a rosy-cheeked picture of Spanish civility. A college-trained engineer who was married to a lawyer, Rubiera emanated an openness and sweetness that seemed almost otherworldly. At night, he sometimes wore pajamas with teddy bears on them.

And Victor Hugo Peña, a big, broad-shouldered Colombian who had a shark tattoo on his shoulder and who carried himself in a gliding manner, easing around the room with an alert double-decker smile. There, quietly tucking in, was José Azevedo, the new guy, from Portugal. New guys on Postal were usually quiet, and he was no exception, though he showed a quick alertness, just as he did on the bike, to the mood and movement of conversation, passing the salt, scooting over, deferring. He was an apt replacement for Heras, who had been so shy that he hardly ever spoke.

This season's newest face was also the youngest. Spain's Benjamin Noval was twenty-five years old, a spring colt of a man with large, wet eyes and delicately curled lashes. On the bike, he rode with liquid power. Off it, he walked with a quiet, careful step, looking furtively around corners. Postal's coaches were most pleased.

"He looks good," Dirk Demol said in April. "He is a quiet, nice person, a hard worker, and he has the correct attitude."

The correct attitude could be summed up in two attributes: Tough as hell, and a little shy. In fact, so prevalent was the Postal personality that other racers joked that Armstrong should run an ad: WANTED *strong, docile cyclists; housebroken a plus*. Even their edgier behavior—mooning their coach from a bus window, snapping naked photos of themselves with other people's cameras—had the token rebelliousness of tenth-grade boys on a school field trip. They might go to a strip club in training camp, but they giggled about it. It was funny! In fact, just about everything on the Postal team was funny—the Belgies were funny, the mechanics were funny. There was just one thing that wasn't funny: not doing your job.

"When you don't come through, even in a small race, you get this vibe. It's cold, business-like. You feel like a salesman who didn't reach his quota," said Tony Cruz.

"Things are much better if you do your job," Rubiera said. "For sure it is better that way."

"Lance is a difficult person," Ekimov said. "When he says jump, you jump, no matter what."

"I think everybody's afraid of Lance," Landis said. "If you're not, then you haven't been paying attention."

There were three parables that new Postal riders learned early. The first was the Parable of the Two New Guys, and it went like this: Two new guys were signed by Postal, and just after training camp they went to train with Armstrong for two weeks. Wanting to impress their new leader, they rode with him up mountain after mountain. They did everything he did, just as hard as he did it, and at the end of two weeks the two new guys had suffered major knee injuries from which they have never recovered (in the proper Belgian telling of the story, the last two words were ominously extended, so that the alarmed listener believed for a half-second that the two new guys had actually *died*).

The second was the Parable of Kevin Livingston. Livingston had been Armstrong's top *domestique* and best friend (they'd moved to Austin together, and later trained with Ferrari together). After the immense success of the first two Tour wins, Livingston had asked for a raise. Armstrong had said no—he wanted to use the money to sign more riders. Livingston had gone elsewhere, and after his new team went bankrupt, he ended up riding for Telekom, Ullrich's German team. In parable form, it came down to a simple message: Armstrong chose improving the team over keeping his best friend. Then there were the other versions of the Livingston parable, the other riders and coaches and *soigneurs* who'd crossed swords with Armstrong or who had underperformed and who were now gone: Cedric Vasseur, Johnny Weltz, Chann McRae, Frankie Andreu, and Christian Vande Velde. Armstrong and John Korioth, the best man at Armstrong's wedding, had gone two years without speaking after a dispute over the direction of the Lance Armstrong Foundation, of which Korioth was executive director.

"There's a pattern," said Jonathan Vaughters, Armstrong's former teammate. "People get close, and then something inevitably goes haywire."

The cause of the rift seemed to vary in each instance. Sometimes it was a simple argument ("Two stubborn guys being stubborn," is how Korioth described their split, which has since healed), sometimes it was disputes over money, as with Livingston. But the core argument was often the same: failing to live up to Armstrong's standards.

"We all look in other people for what we want to see in ourselves, and that's why he's so hard on people," Bart Knaggs of CS&E said. "He says if somebody doesn't work as hard as me, I don't respect him."

"Even now, we only get by because we're not in his field, in his wheelhouse," Knaggs continued. "He'll bang on us about getting stuff done and we can never, ever say, did you do your workout? It's a tough limb to be held under."

The third parable—which, providentially enough, mapped out the path to avoiding the dangers described by the first two parables—was the Story of Eki. Thirty-seven-year-old Russian Viatcheslav Ekimov was the only rider on Postal—indeed, perhaps the only person in Armstrong's world—whose work ethic was beyond question. This status was underlined frequently, most of all by Armstrong's assertion that Eki was "nails." Which raised the question: what does it take to be "nails"?

This is what it took. When Eki was fourteen and living at a sports club in St. Petersburg, he rode 38,000 kilometers in one year, an average of 450 miles a week. In 1996, as a professional, he nearly doubled it ("That's not possible for a human," Landis said incredulously). But it was true—Eki had twenty-five notebooks full of training logs to prove it. Eki had ridden thirteen tours and finished every one. Eki never missed a training day. Eki was never late or unprepared. Eki coached himself. Eki was Eki. Armstrong liked saying the name; he said it with a clicking relish. And when Eki strolled into the dining room wearing that face—that old-man's face under the great goombah flourish of hair, those deep circles under his eyes, like an Eskimo spirit mask, the delicate rosettes of old scars lacing his knees, not to mention that ass, that eternally tiny turbo-powered ass—the younger riders looked, knowing *that is what Lance wants me to become.*

For these nice, shy, strong men sitting around the dinner table, riding for Postal was like inhabiting a Disneyland built on a lava dome, a landscape of wonder and opportunity, studded by impressive monuments (rock star Sheryl! Mount Eki!) and scary crevasses, and made all the more fantastic by the hot knowledge that if you screwed up, you would vanish in a heartbeat.

So the Postal riders did what most people would do in that situation: they made an instinctive calculation of all the pluses and minuses, the salary (pretty good) and the individual glory (smallish, but lasting) and the risk and unpredictability, and all those were absorbed into their minds and their guts. Life as a Postie was hard and bizarre and inspiring and scary, and, for those willing to stay, it became, well, kind of funny. In fact, it was freaking *hilarious*! So they laughed.

They laughed at breakfast and at dinner; they laughed when Armstrong walked in and after he left (though they tended to fall silent and watchful as he walked toward the table). They laughed after dinner, when the Spanish guys played chinos, a counting game where the loser had to buy coffee. They got serious when they had to—and there were plenty of times of silence or even desperate quiet, when Armstrong was in one of his moods, or things were bad, or Bruyneel was laying out the game plan. But the rest of the time, they laughed—Hincapie with his soft murmur; Beltran with his dolphinlike whinny; even the giant Padrnos laughed, the basso profundo fizzing of an undersea volcano.

All except one.

CHAPTER 15

THE BOOK OF FLOYD

The Ordnung: A structure of yieldedness, suffering,
servanthood, humility, defenselessness, and an expression
of faithful community life. By living defenselessly, one
learns to love one's enemies and trust in God's power for
protection.

—ADAPTED FROM THE *MENNONITE ENCYCLOPEDIA*

In a homogenous barrel of Postal *domestiques*, twenty-eight-year-
old Floyd Landis stood out. He had bristly red hair and muscular
arms, the latter a souvenir from his previous career as a professional mountain biker. His face was small and sharp, with a long
nose and an upturned chin, the face of Dickens's wiliest orphan. Its
repertoire of expressions was narrow, but it excelled at one, which
was outrage. When Landis was outraged, which was frequently, the
large eyes would bulge cartoonishly, dangerous red flowers would
bloom high on his cheeks, and the nostrils would flex in quick
bursts, as if his nose were trying to wriggle away from an oncoming
explosion. He would add to all this a small and incredulous smile,
which overlaid the outrage and softened it into an expression of
towering amazement.

"Can you believe that?" the face said.

Landis was well practiced in this amazed smile, perhaps because
he had seen so many directed at him over the last few years. During
his brief career—first as a mountain biker, then as a road racer—

Landis had demonstrated a knack for doing things that no one had ever imagined before. One night, after several mechanical difficulties, he raced his mountain bike down a steep hillside with no tires—passing racers on a downhill, sparks spraying off the bare rims. He rode wheelies for miles—uphill. Another time he was tired after a race and, rather than walk the quarter mile to the hotel, he simply curled up in a banner and lay down on the pavement. When a dumbfounded teammate asked why Landis he hadn't walked to the hotel, Landis fixed him with an amazed look. "I was tired," he said. "So I slept."

It was usually portrayed as run-of-the-mill eccentricity—that wacky Floyd, crazy like all those mountain bikers. But, in fact, there was nothing the least bit eccentric about it. This was a purposeful, rational process. It was as if, his former teammate Will Geoghagen once said, Landis had just been defrosted from some distant past, and needed to figure out everything anew. His life was nothing so much as an experiment, one that might have been titled "Reactions That Occur When an Unfrozen Mennonite Is Mixed With America."

Landis had been raised as a Mennonite in a small town in Lancaster County, Pennsylvania. He left home for good at age twenty, and proceeded to become one of the strongest mountain bikers in the world. When he changed to road cycling in 1999, he quickly rose through the ranks, and soon became one of a half-dozen riders to whom was affixed the damning tag of "maybe the next Lance Armstrong."

Landis arrived as the complete package. He was 5' 10" and weighed 150 pounds; his threshold was in the range of 440 watts, his magic number within shouting distance of Ferrari's magic 6.7. He could climb and he could time-trial. Most of all, he was tough, in a borderline-insane way, an attribute he had displayed most recently when he broke his hip in early 2003.

"Broken hip" doesn't do it justice, actually. It was a complete oblique fracture of the right femoral neck, which meant that he'd broken the top off his femur. It had been fixed by drilling three four-inch-long titanium pins into the bone. The pins were poorly placed, however, and muscles and ligaments kept snagging on the bolt-

heads as he trained. In early May, Landis went in for another surgery to have them replaced; the next day he caught a flight to the
team's pre-Tour training camp. He was still limping when he arrived
at the start in Paris.

He rode the Tour, got stronger as it went on, and finished the
race as one of Armstrong's strongest teammates. As his wife, Amber,
summed up, "Floyd is one tough bitch."

There was something about Floyd, in the sheer animal guts of
that comeback, that reminded people of Armstrong. It showed a
force inside him, something in the way he looked at the world. His
similarity to Armstrong was a source of strength and, some feared,
a potential problem.

Here was the problem: Landis and Armstrong had become
friends.

It had begun right from the start. Armstrong was drawn to Landis, his freshness, his offbeat sense of humor. In 2002 and 2003,
Landis spent five weeks before the Tour with Armstrong and Ferrari
in St. Moritz, just the two of them riding, day after day. They did a
few things in the off season, too. When Armstrong started dating
Sheryl Crow in 2003, he invited Landis to join them at the Country
Music Awards after-parties.

Sure, Landis occasionally did some weird stuff—like the time
after Armstrong announced his divorce when Landis left "Freebird"
by Lynyrd Skynyrd on Armstrong's answering machine. But as Armstrong told friends at the time, it was little-brother stuff—okay,
because after all, it was Floyd. Armstrong, for his part, tried to play
the big brother. When Floyd and a buddy spent a rainy training day
trying to see how many cappuccinos they could drink, Armstrong
found out and gave him a talking-to.

Afterward, a bummed-out Landis phoned Geoghagen.

"I really pissed off Lance," he said. "I drank fourteen coffees and
he yelled at me and now I've got this killer headache and I think he
hates me."

A second later, Landis said, "I knew I could do it, though."

Geoghagen laughed, but he also winced inwardly. *That was just the kind of thing Armstrong would have said*. Lance and Floyd, Floyd and Lance, the two were peas in the take-no-shit-from-anybody pod, no question. But the position of being Armstrong's friend was a tricky one for anybody, especially for Landis, for whom docility came with difficulty. When something bothered him, or struck him as unfair, he spoke up. He asked questions, he tested limits—it was as if something were compelling him.

When the Postal team won the team time-trial in the 2003 Tour de France, Landis asked if he would get the $20,000 bonus that his contract called for when he won a stage—the team time trial was a stage, right? (No, it was later determined.) Early in the 2004 season, when Bruyneel handed him a bottle of water that had been salted to prevent dehydration, the others drank obediently while Landis spat it out and demanded regular water. When they were driving back from a race and it was 110 degrees and nobody would turn on the air conditioning or open a window for fear of catching cold, Landis spoke up—did any of them really believe that? He openly asked teammates about their salaries, a verboten subject on Postal. But to Landis it made sense. Shouldn't they know? Why should the team have such a huge advantage in negotiations?

This year, the rumors had started to circulate that there was tension between Armstrong and Landis. They were so weak as to hardly qualify as rumors—they seemed based on silly, insubstantial things: a look, a word, a bad joke. Then there was the fact that Landis hadn't attended the first recon trip to the Alps (which was explicable—he'd just returned from the States). Then, in late May, Landis was left off the team for the weeklong Tour of Languedoc-Rousillon, a stage race that, by the looks of Postal's lineup, was a dress rehearsal for the Tour.

Other riders heard the rumors and felt unease descend. Didn't Landis know the score? Didn't he know the Livingston Parable? Didn't he know that there could be hell to pay?

Mennonites believe that God's message shines most brightly through an unadorned surface. When Floyd Landis was sixteen years old, his parents' message to him shone as clear as if it had been painted in bright white letters on the clean brick wall of the family house: If you continue competitive cycling, your soul will burn for eternity.

It was written down, as it happened. In Romans 12:2 and 1 Peter 3:3–4 and several other texts—if not in particular then in a vivid generality. Floyd knew these texts well, having attended church three times a week, on Wednesday, Saturday, and twice on Sunday with his parents, brother, and four sisters.

Sitting on the hard wooden pews as a boy, Landis had felt rather lucky. He was a Landis, of a plain, decent family, not well off in money but rich in spirit. He lived in Farmersville, near the towns of Landis and Landisville. His distant ancestor, Hans Landis, had martyred himself for the cause back in Switzerland in 1614. His more recent ancestors had come to Lancaster County in order to build lives of hard work, humility, and, above all, separateness from the world. To live, as the Mennonite saying went, *in* the world but not *of* the world. For the Landises, that meant no television. No dancing. No revealing clothing. No uncovered heads for the women. No swimming in public pools, no coveting of worldly goods of fame and sex and ego, no mingling with the unrighteous, and no back-sliding. Other things, however, were permitted: radios, cars, zippers. And, when Floyd was fifteen, a bicycle.

It was a secondhand beater made of heavy steel and painted fluorescent orange. He used it to go fishing and ride to his job at the Dairy grocery store. His friend Eric Gebhard got one, too, and they rode together. One afternoon, without telling their parents, the two boys went to a race in a nearby town. It happened to be a Sunday, which Mennonites regarded as a day of rest. Vigorous exercise was expressly prohibited.

Floyd thought about this. It wasn't the first time he'd wondered about this sort of thing. At his public high school, Floyd had obediently worn long sweats during gym class while the others ran about in shorts, a difference that gradually struck him as odd. He had never been a rebellious kid, but he'd always been a logical one. Did

God really care if you wore shorts or not? Would God really send you to hell for riding in a bike race on a Sunday? Landis decided that He probably wouldn't. Landis and Gehbard entered the race, and Landis won.

He won a few more local races. He found cycling magazines and read up, and started to do some training. Something about the sport—the training, the riding, the suffering, made sense to Landis, if not to his increasingly concerned parents. He tried to placate them with small measures: after all, he didn't wear those revealing cycling shorts, but rode in cotton sweats, which tended to become waterlogged and weighed ten pounds by the finish. But it didn't help; his parents still worried that their son was headed for the wrong end of that big sorting bin spoken of in the Mennonite Confession of Faith: "The righteous will rise to eternal life with God, and the unrighteous to hell and separation from God."

That moment wasn't that far away, either. A lurid kingdom of temptations lay outside Farmersville, in Philadelphia and New York and everywhere else where the unrighteous had carried the day. To leave the safety of the people to pursue a worldly life among them—in sports, no less! So the Landises talked with their son. It would be Floyd's decision; it would mean nothing if it wasn't. But they wanted him to know—they had to let him know, that his soul was at stake.

"I had a choice," Floyd said. "You can bike and burn in hell forever, or not bike—hey, it's up to you."

He kept riding. He rode after school and he rode after his job at the Dairy. When Floyd was seventeen, his father hit on a scheme to keep Landis from riding, loading him up with an endless list of chores: paint a building, clean the garage, help patch the car's radiator, a rural Pennsylvanian version of Hercules' labors, the end of which would find Floyd exhausted and the sun long since set.

So Landis rode at night. He found a headlamp, and put on layers of clothing against the chill—five layers in winter, topped by an orange hunting cap. He devised a system to keep his feet dry: socks, plastic baggies, socks, his $5 tennis shoes, and a final sheath of plastic bags. Somewhere he had read that top cyclists ride five hundred miles a week, and so he decided to do that, a program that kept him riding until two or three in the morning, sometimes in ten-below weather.

"I basically said screw it, I'll show you fuckers," Landis said. "I love my parents—they're good people. But I was also determined to get out, and I knew my bike was the only way."

Sometimes his father followed him in their car, unable to believe that his son was training in the ice until two in the morning, every morning. They assumed he must be doing something else, drinking beer or seeing a girl on the sly. Floyd saw the headlights shafting through the trees, but he did not turn around, nor did he mention it when he got home. He kept riding. His speed increased, his muscles grew stronger, his heart grew bigger, but the pain was always there—heart hammering in throat, back throbbing, legs glowing hot.

Landis won the junior national mountain biking championship at eighteen and moved to California at twenty, in 1996, because it was "as far away as I could get from Pennsylvania and still be on the planet." When he arrived, he had never tasted Mountain Dew or coffee or sex. He had seen one movie, *Jaws*, which had frightened him so badly his mother had to come take him home. With the help of biking friends, Landis set out to educate himself about this strange world. Though in typical fashion, he ended up educating his friends.

"We would make lists of movies for him to see, music he had to hear," recalled Geoghagen. "He loved *Apocalypse Now*, but he hated *Platoon*, and he would get so pissed about the stuff he didn't like—he'd say, 'Why did you have me watch that?'

"Things are very cut and dried with Floyd," he continued. "Right or wrong, no in-between. He won't admit it, but a lot of his suppressed religious beliefs inform how he sees the world."

"*Sixteen Candles*!" Landis would shout. "Why would you tell me to see that movie? That is a waste of energy, a waste of a movie, a waste of time, a waste of waste!" Or when someone would toss out a pop-culture catchphrase, like "Scooby snack," it would provide Floyd another opportunity to hold forth. "Why do you have that stuff junking up your brain?" Being around him was like being around a raging Old Testament prophet, trashing the landscape in search of some true thing.

His racing was similarly biblical. At his first twenty-four-hour relay race Landis was so excited that his teammates had to lock his bike in a closet to keep him from riding it too much the night before. He crashed on his first lap, tacoing his wheel, and so he adopted the slightly unconventional tactic of riding a wheelie down the mountain. He found a San Diego–based coach, Arnie Baker, who was pleasingly eccentric: Baker had Landis ride all day in a tiny gear, then the next day in a huge gear, or ride one-legged. When tested in a lab, Landis scored a VO2 Max of ninety, one point higher than that of Miguel Induráin.

When the mountain-bike scene faded in the late nineties, Landis made the jump to road racing, a move that posed as many cultural questions as athletic ones. To generalize: roadies thought mountain bikers were Neanderthals and hippies; mountain bikers thought roadies were effete Euro-poseurs. Landis did not enjoy being perceived as a hippie, much less an unskilled one. It was unfair—in fact, it was wrong. So Landis set out to correct things.

He showed up for his first road race wearing a garish jersey, a visored helmet, and a pair of brilliantly colored Argyle socks, pulled high. He made his way slowly to the front row, a slight smile sharpening his face. He wheeled a bike with a monstrously big fifty-six-tooth front chain ring, so large that it resembled a pie plate. A slow crater of disgusted amazement widened around Landis. He paused, allowing their eyes to take in the full glory of his appearance. Then, in a loud voice that rang with Mennonite clarity, Landis said what he'd planned to say, a reading from the First Book of Floyd:

"If there's anyone here who can stay with me, I will buy you dinner."

Laughter. Landis remained quiet, then replied.

"You shouldn't laugh, because that gets me angry. And if you make me angry, then I'm going to blow you all up."

More laughter.

The race began, and Floyd rode up to the leaders. Then past them. He pressed the pace, slowly at first and then faster and faster, pushing that pie plate until it hummed, until the others felt like they were trying to follow a motorcycle.

"You like my socks?" he asked. "How do you like them now?"

They gasped for air.

"I'll take that for a yes," Landis continued. "How about if I go a little farther up the road, and you can tell me how they look from there?"

Landis won his first race by fifteen minutes, including a stop to repair his punctured tire. He won his second race by forty-five minutes.

"Get Floyd emotionally involved and there's no way he'll back down," Geoghagen said. "He will go until his heart literally explodes."

Landis fairly burst onto the road-racing scene, finishing third in the Tour de L'Avenir as an unknown in 1999. He rode domestically for two years, then was signed by Postal after the 2001 season, and promptly finished a stunning second to Armstrong in the Dauphiné Libéré. He married Amber Basile, who had a daughter, Ryan, and bought a home in Temecula, near San Diego. He was making around $200,000 a year.

He liked riding for Postal; he wasn't bothered by the relative anonymity. Sure, there were some ironic moments in the States where passers-by would mistake him for Armstrong or ask the standard question—"You mean he has a *team*?" After the Tour, Armstrong would be invited on Leno and Letterman, while Landis would go talk to the Conestoga Valley Middle School, sharing the bill with the local unicycle troupe, but he didn't mind. Landis didn't want Leno or Letterman; he wanted to ride his bike, earn money, and win races.

Besides, anonymity suited him, because it made his life simpler. Landis may have left Farmersville, but there was surely a little Farmersville left in him. He was resolutely skeptical of flash-bang technology, wind tunnels, and the like. "You want to go faster?" he would say. "Pedal harder." His Girona apartment was practically a furniture-free zone. When he wanted to lose weight, he simply stopped eating for two or three days. ("I get pretty grouchy, but it works.")

More stunning to his fellow cyclists, Landis even walked, routinely making the mile-plus stroll into Girona's old town from his apartment near the university. "I don't know why these guys complain," he said. "It only hurts because they never do it. Of *course* it hurts, but then you get past it."

But still, this was his third year, going on his third Tour, and Landis couldn't figure out quite where he stood on the team, and with Armstrong in particular. Landis's season so far had been solid, if unspectacular. He'd raced a fair amount, won the Tour of Algarve in Portugal, and come within a hair of winning a stage in Paris-Nice.

But in late May, with most of the rest of the Tour team having just completed the Languedoc-Roussillon race, Landis sat at a café in Girona, his mind full of questions. There were plenty of perfectly good reasons Bruyneel and Armstrong hadn't picked Landis: he'd had an unusually heavy spring racing schedule, the team needed to try out new riders like Noval. But those reasons didn't ease the questions that kept bubbling in Landis's mind, one of which was, why did Armstrong and Bruyneel wait so long before announcing the Tour team?

"They do this every year, waiting until the last minute," he said. "In my opinion, they treat us like kids. It's not like we're going to quit riding and start drinking beer if we find out we're not on the team."

Landis shifted restlessly. He kicked off his shoes and set his socked feet on top of them. He had ridden six hours that day. He weighed 152 pounds and, according to Ferrari, his threshold was 456 watts. His watts-per-kilo was at 6.6, a hair shy of the magic 6.7 level. Mathematically, he was closer to Armstrong than ever before. But only mathematically.

"I don't know what Lance wants," he said suddenly. "Sometimes he can be a normal guy and be your friend, after the Tour. But now, it seems like he's somewhere else . . ." he trailed off.

"I'd really like to know him better. I'd like to know what that guy wants. I would love to know what's going on inside his head, but he doesn't want to let anybody in, for whatever reason. He has a hard time being close friends. He reminds me of somebody who wants to be president—it doesn't make sense, really, to want it, but he still wants more and more and more."

I asked if maybe it had something to do with Armstrong getting motivated for the Tour. It required so much of him, perhaps there was not much left for friendship.

"Maybe," he says. "Lance is really good at forgetting. Once he clicks past something, he doesn't think about it again. But all this that people say about his needing to pick fights to get motivated, I don't know. To me, lasting motivation doesn't come from a set of circumstances. If nothing happened at all—if there were no fights, he'd still be motivated. Whatever it is that's driving him, it doesn't have anything to do with daily stuff. It's deep, and it's always there.

"Lance is a complicated guy. His nature wants things to be perfect, so whenever anything goes wrong he feels like he can fix that reason and be perfect. But you know what? Sometimes stuff happens for no reason. Sometimes shit happens, and you crash, and that's it."

Landis rearranged his knife and fork, reset his water glass on its coaster. He gave a wry smile. "I guess I'm like everybody else. I'd like to figure him out better."

The idea of Armstrong as a secretly lonely person, perpetually isolating himself in the tower of his unreachable standards, had some traction among some of those who knew him. It fit what they saw as a familiar pattern, the elements of which Landis knew by heart: Armstrong's closeness with his mother, Linda; the absence of his father; the easily triggered feelings of betrayal. *You're not my dad*—that's what Armstrong used to shout at coaches when he was a teenager, wasn't it? What were these on-off friendships except an echo of that original rebellion, the aggression of a wounded, approval-seeking kid—*you're not my dad, not you, not you, not you*, either.

Yes, Landis might have understood it. But in the end, the kid from Farmersville didn't go for fancy psychological explanations.

"Lance doesn't want a hug," Landis said. "He just wants to kick everyone's ass."

CHAPTER 16

ATTACKERS

Gora ta gora Euskadi   Up and up Basque Country
Aintza ta aintza   Glory and glory
Bere goiko Jaun Onari   To its Good Lord from above

—Anthem of the Basque homeland,
lyrics by Sabino Arana

If, one warm evening in late May, Lance Armstrong had walked out of his apartment and climbed the narrow path atop Girona's ancient city wall, he would have seen the crest of the Pyrenees rising to the northwest. If he had looked toward the setting sun, his eyes would have tracked toward the mountainous region of Spain marked on the map as Basque Country. There, in the orange-tinted light, resided a slender figure named Iban Mayo, better known to Armstrong as the single reason that he nearly lost the 2003 Tour, and a likely reason he might lose this year.

It wasn't that Mayo was winning; it was the dominating, effortless style in which victory came. Sixty days remained before this year's Tour, and Mayo was simply riding away from the peloton. He'd just finished a ten-day blitz in which he won no fewer than five times. At the Alcobendas Classic, a two-day, three-stage race held northwest of Madrid, he won a mountaintop finish, a sprint finish, and finished second in a time trial. At the Tour of Asturias, Mayo entered the last day trailing by forty-nine seconds. The stage didn't suit him; it was rolling hills, nothing too steep where a climber might make up such a large margin. But with fifty kilometers to go, Mayo attacked on a cobbled rise near a fishing village. When the peloton reached the top, they looked around, expecting to see him. But Mayo was simply—incredibly—gone.

Armstrong was familiar with the feeling. He'd been introduced to it vividly at the 2003 Dauphiné Libéré. Mayo had attacked Armstrong repeatedly on the climbs, an act which, while mildly significant at the time, had since become regarded as the Shot Heard Round the World. "Mayo took Lance catabolic," was how Chris Carmichael put it. "Lance went so hard that he broke down, and entered the Tour flat instead of improved."

Mayo was a sharp-edged mix of beauty and arrogance. He stood 5'-9" and weighed 130 pounds, with swept-back hair and a long white scar on his right arm, which turned pink when he rode hard. He had returned to his home in Durango after his five wins in order to prepare for June's rematch with Armstrong at the Dauphiné, and also because he was Basque.

"Because he was Basque" was the answer to most questions regarding Iban Mayo. It explained his mix of spirituality and aggression. It explained his adherence to throwback training techniques. It explained why he was able to come back after a nearly fatal car accident seven years ago. It also explained why he, of all the contenders, was the one Armstrong understood least. Like his countrymen, Mayo was a specialist in the tactics of rebellion and ambush.

It wasn't far off to say that it was in his blood. Basque Country is a mountainous kingdom the size of New Hampshire, which is home to Europe's only indigenous people, population two million. The Basques have been rebelling since A.D. 218, and have fought off or outlasted, in rough order, the Romans, the Visigoths, the Muslims, the Franks, the Vikings, the Normans, and Napoleon, and Franco. Honed by this Darwinistic whetstone, the Basques have produced a line of extraordinarily hardy, determined, large-eared young men who have been drawn to extremes: they built Columbus's ships, they founded the Jesuit order (Ignatius Loyola and

Francis Xavier were both Basque),* and, like the Irish, perfected the kind of fierce, bonfire-lit patriotism that is possible only when a rural, spiritual people rises to war against brutal oppressors (during the Franco era, the mere speaking of the Basque language could get you arrested). In more recent years, some of those young men have expressed their rebelliousness through the terrorist acts of ETA, the Basque separatist organization. Others by racing bikes.

Basques and bike racing. It is an overstatement to say that cycling is the primal act of national identity, but not all that much of an overstatement. Large races are treated as national holidays. Basque highways are under restricted speed limits to enable training and racing on weekends; Basque radio crackles with live play-by-play of junior-high races. The de facto national team, the neon orange–clad Euskaltel-Euskadi, is supported partly by the sponsoring phone company and partly by its fans, whose subscriptions cover nearly half of the team's measly $4.5 million budget (Postal, by comparison, would spend nearly three times that amount in 2004). The Basque cooperative, Orbea, manufactures bicycles in numbers similar to the pistols they once forged. Seventy Basques ride in the four-hundred-strong pro peloton, which made Basque Country, per capita, the most fertile cycling ground on earth. "An emanation of our people," is how Euskaltel rider Haimar Zubeldia described it, and no rider emanates more essential Basque spirit than Mayo.

Mayo lived in a nondescript apartment in the city of Durango; he'd just moved out of his parents' home a few months before. He trained with monklike simplicity, meeting his teammates at ten-thirty each day in the square, and rode without follow cars or power meters. He carried himself quietly, which led many to believe he was bashful. But when Mayo did speak, his face changed. His eyes flashed quick and prideful. Words came in unstoppable torrents, as if some inner dam had cracked.

Mayo grew up a welder's son in the village of Igurre. He played

---

*Not to mention five-time Tour winner Miguel Induráin, known to the world as Spanish, but known to the Basques as one of their own.

soccer and basketball, and showed talent in school races. In 1997, when he was nineteen, he became a Red Cross ambulance driver. His driving career ended when his ambulance crashed head-on into a stone wall. Mayo's legs were broken; he sustained deep wounds to his right arm. He came home and spent the next two months in a wheechair. After evaluating his options, he decided to study to be an electrician. Everyone agreed that this was a wise decision. He could make a decent living, and stay close to the village, and it wouldn't place too many demands on his ruined legs.

In a year Mayo was back on his bike, working on a toes-down pedaling style that demanded less from his damaged joints. He turned professional with Euskaltel in 2000, and won a few shorter races the following year, including the Midi Libre and the Classique des Alpes. But he didn't seem like a Tour-quality rider. No less an authority than his countryman Joseba Beloki classified Mayo as "a simple shooting star who will never hold up in a three-week tour," a label that seemed accurate when Mayo finished a gasping eighty-eighth in his first Tour de France in 2002.

At the 2003 Dauphiné, however, Mayo showed up a changed man: faster, skinnier, more aggressive. He surprised Armstrong by winning the 5.1-kilometer prologue time trial; then, after Armstrong crashed on stage 5, Mayo began his attacks. These were not the one-off, death-or-glory attacks of Vinokourov; Mayo engaged Armstrong in a more subtle game. He yo-yoed his speed, putting on surges, and, when Armstrong caught him, off he'd surge again, daring Armstrong to match him. It was not an efficient tactic, if Mayo were trying to win the race. But if the goal was to upset the champion, it worked.

"We know [Mayo is] being ordered to vary the tempo," Armstrong said frustratedly.

On the twenty-five-mile-long Col de Galibier, Mayo surged his way to a gap, which grew to thirty seconds. On the way down the mountain, Armstrong caught Mayo and drew alongside, giving him a long look. Mayo didn't seem to notice and kept attacking, out-sprinting Armstrong to the line. Armstrong won the overall by 1:12, but the damage was done.

"Lance should have let Mayo win that race," Ferrari said later. "He dug too deep after his crash. He let his pride take over, and he paid the cost at the Tour."

A month later, Mayo put on a similarly electrifying performance in front of half a million fans on Alpe d'Huez, riding away from Armstrong and putting 2:12 on the champion in a bare nine kilometers. Mayo went on to finish sixth in the Tour, but his Alpe d'Huez ride bode well for his 2004 chances, especially since there would be an uphill time trial at Alpe d'Huez. The plotlines were clear: 2004 would be a climbers' Tour, and Mayo, if he was on form, looked to be the best climber.

The key to this notion lies inside that seemingly offhand qualifier—"if he was on form." Form is one of the more mysterious elements of bike racing, possessing an otherness that is revealed in its preposition. One does not get *in* form; rather, one tries to get *on* it, as one might walk across an ice-covered ridge, a visit made trickier by the fact that even the rider is never quite sure where the edge begins.

The word was originally used to describe racehorses in the eighteenth century, and its meaning remains unchanged, referring to the elusive moment when all systems are working at optimum efficiency. It is made possible by supercompensation, that physiological tendency of bodies under stress to protect themselves by getting stronger . . . up to a point. After that point—the edge of the icy ridge, so to speak—the body protects itself by shutting down. For Tour riders, the trick was to get as close as you can to the edge without slipping over.

"A privileged equilibrium between quality of muscles, acuity of intelligence and force of character," the French philosopher and writer Roland Barthes called it. Stepping out on the razor, the riders call it, a journey into the realm of physiological irony. On the bike, they feel invincible; the pedals seem to float. Off it, they move slowly, delicately. Body fat plummets to malnutritive levels,* they are hollow-cheeked

---

*Tour riders are very skinny, far skinnier in person than they look on television or in photos. Their upper arms are so slender that you could almost wrap your thumb and index finger around them. The wife of one American rider says that she can tell the Tour is drawing near when she can start to see her husband's internal organs—his liver, his kidneys—beneath his skin.

and paper-skinned; they might get out of breath climbing a short flight of stairs. White blood cell counts drop by 30 percent; their bodies become vulnerable to all manner of colds and disease. They push elevator buttons with their elbows to avoid germs. They sniffle. They live on the boundary between pathetic sickness and intoxicating power. They push, like Icarus, to see how high they can fly.

"You feel invincible, so you want to go, go, go. It feels so good," veteran American sprinter Fred Rodriguez said. "Then you wake up one day and it's over."

For most riders, stepping out on the razor is part science, part magic, the most magical part being that you get better at it as you get older. Having experienced and managed many peaks (Armstrong's lasts roughly forty days, Ullrich's is the same), they are less prone to play Icarus. They memorize their razor.

In this, Armstrong is assisted by an immune system that matches his extraordinary cardiovascular system. Last year's Tour excepted, he rarely gets sick. In fact, he is so reliably healthy that others in the cycling community were moved to heights of disgust.

"It's unbelievable," Haven Hamilton said. "Ty is real careful, but Lance, he does everything and hardly ever gets sick. I've even seen him"—she winced in horror at the idea—"*bite his fingernails.*"

"Besides not crashing in five Tours, the most amazing thing is that Lance doesn't get sick," said former Postal rider Vaughters. "Everybody else will be sick, coughing, dying. And he's fine."

Younger cyclists, however, hold a trump card of their own. Their bodies are capable of abrupt ascents to new levels of performance, a hard-to-predict moment that Ferrari called the *salto de qualità*—the leap of quality. Armstrong made his in 1999 training when he broke Tony Rominger's record ascending the Madone. Ullrich made his in his blowout time-trial win at the end of the 1996 Tour. This leap is so dramatic and essentially mysterious that the cycling world has another word for it: revelation.

It so happened that a twenty-two-year-old named Damiano Cunego was providing an intimidatingly clinical example of revelation at this very moment, in the three-week Giro d'Italia. In the space of a few days, Cunego had transformed himself from a promising but callow rider into a lord, winning climbs, sprints, and dominating a grand tour in a way none had predicted. From Armstrong's point of view, Cunego was not a threat—not right away, anyway. He would not ride this year's Tour de France (given the timing of the peaks involved, few could hope to do well at both). But Cunego's performance (not to mention his numbers: 420 threshold, weight of sixty kilos, a magic number of 7.0) made him one for Armstrong to watch.

Mayo, on the other hand, posed a more immediate riddle. During his glittering string of five wins in ten days, he had seemed unbeatable. But to Armstrong, the question was this: Was Mayo making a *salto de qualità*? Or was he peaking too early? Evidence was mixed. On the one hand, Mayo looked ungodly strong. On the other hand, he also looked ungodly skinny, to the point that he already had smile folds. The smile fold was a telltale event that happened when a rider's cheek lacked the fat to form a dimple. When they smiled, their skin pleated over on itself, forming a tight crease that served as a signal flag: body fat was dropping, the rider was inching out on that razor. For Armstrong, Mayo's smile folds were a comforting sight, beacons of a young rider tempting fate. Mid-May was too early to be on the razor. He couldn't possibly keep it up.

Could he?

"I've been asked a hundred times and I'll say the same thing—no," Mayo said. "The preparation has gone wonderfully, but I am at ease because I still have room to improve."

"His pedal strokes look powerful," Ferrari said admiringly. "He perhaps will be at a new level. But of course there is no way to know."

Despite his words, Mayo seemed to sense the danger. After his win at Asturias he announced that he was returning home to Durango. He would do no more racing until the Dauphiné.

Meanwhile, high on the other side of the continent, more activity was stirring. On May 25, Jan Ullrich emerged from seclusion showing a new face: grizzled, slender, and sunburned. He had no smile folds—no danger of that with Ulle—but his face and body looked lean and muscular. More to the point, that body was located in the Alps, as Ullrich had taken the rare step of reconning the Tour's mountain stages with four teammates, including Vino. For the German's many fans, it was a thrilling sight: the two teammates riding Alpe d'Huez for two days, then ascending the famed Glandon and the Madeleine passes, riding above snowline until a team car got stuck. Spirits were high: Ullrich said it reminded him of Rostock. Vino countered that it was more like Siberia.

"I did not melt," Ullrich summed up with a smile.

He was smiling a lot now. The Tour was barely a month away. He'd just spent five weeks away from racing, putting 3,000 kilometers into his legs. Though rumors had put him in Tuscany, in fact he'd mostly stayed near home, riding out of his door, either alone or with one or two teammates, following Cecchini's training program.

"He did everything perfectly," said Krohme, his physiotherapist. "Every day, to the letter. Now we see."

In his first race back, a one-day contest in Erfurt, Germany, Ullrich rode easily in the peloton as it chased a small breakaway. Then, near the finish, he attacked on a steep one-kilometer climb, a 14 percent rise similar to the climb that had broken him in the Flèche Wallonne race to Armstrong's golf-course test. For three minutes he dug hard, an all-out burst that separated him from the peloton and pulled him into fifth. Not a great result, but decent enough.

Two days later, Ullrich embarked on another test, a 23.7-kilometer time trial in Karlsruhe at the Tour of Germany. It was an unpromising day; blustery and sunshot. He rode to the start after following his usual routine and set off into a forest of cowbells. The fans were out in force, their faces stiff with Teutonic excitement: would he have it?

He shifted to the biggest gear. The Superman legs pressed down.

"I went hard, and all of a sudden, I began to feel it," Ullrich said. "I was surprised."

The crowd leaned in, viscerally aware that something was happening. Der Jan was waking up! The crowd took up the chant, and Rudy Pevenage began to smile a tough-guy Belgian smile. All the doomsayers had been wrong. Jan had done it again!

Ullrich crossed the line second, averaged nearly 32 miles per hour. Teammate Vino wasn't far behind. Both Pevenage and Ullrich did their best to play down their relief.

"I'm very satisfied," Pevenage said.

"His legs, they are different now," Krohme said. "They are structural again."

"The bad weight is gone, the good weight has remained," Ullrich said. "I don't know why everyone was so worried."

From rainy St. Moritz, Armstrong monitored Ullrich's rebirth. Armstrong had brought a small crew: Ferrari, masseur Ryszard Kielpinski, mechanic Juan Lujan, and Sheryl Crow. The weather was drizzly and cold, but Armstrong's numbers remained solid: his weight was down to 166 pounds, his threshold was 486 watts, giving him a magic number of 6.43. They were training two days hard, one day easy, with an emphasis on long, steady climbs.

"Good rides," Ferrari said. "The focus is on endurance."

While Armstrong performed another one-kilometer test, he and Ferrari chose not to undertake the longer threshold test they customarily started doing this time of year. In years past, the two tests have worked as a pair, the short rev and the long rev, a twin probe of Armstrong's stamina. This year, however, was different.

"We did not talk about it," Ferrari said. "If he doesn't wish to do it, then we do not."

There were other things to think about. Now, from the heights of St. Moritz, the map was starting to firm up. Mayo to the southwest, inching out on the razor. Ullrich to the north, waking up. Hamilton in the Alps, recently returned from Colorado, doing his methodical recon with his nice-guy Phonak team—a team that had looked surprisingly tough lately.

There was also one other person in the landscape, across the English Channel, in a thatched-roof town near Cambridge. A fifty-one-year-old man with sad, downturned eyes and one of those lovely Irish voices that made it sound as if he was singing.

His name was David Walsh, and he was in the final stages of his own measured, sincere effort to bring Armstrong down.

CHAPTER 17
THE CRUSADER

David Walsh met Lance Armstrong for the first time at the 1993 Tour. Walsh, an ambitious and outgoing writer for Dublin's *Sunday Independent,* was writing a book about the Tour de France. He was looking for a rookie to profile. Walsh and Armstrong spoke for three hours.

"I liked the guy," Walsh said, "I really liked the guy. I liked his freshness, his openness. He didn't mind telling you, I have to win. I have to be successful here, because I'm not going to accept being an ordinary guy. We clicked quite well."

In his 1994 book, *Inside the Tour de France,* Walsh captured all the ingredients: the bleak Texas background, the devoted single mother, Linda. We see the series of unreliable father figures, the white-hot competitive drive, the scale of his ambition. We see Armstrong win his first stage with a swashbuckling display of force. Most of all, however, we see Armstrong's unbreakable competitive spirit. Walsh recounted Armstrong's words at perhaps his lowest moment, after getting trounced in a time trial by champion Miguel Induráin:

> "The time trial, it's the biggest thing on my mind. I know I gotta learn how to do it. At the same time I know I can do it. I lost six minutes. I mean, it's plain as day, I know exactly where I am. I went all out, Induráin went all out. I'm six minutes down. But he's the greatest time-triallist there's ever been. Hinault never

killed people, never killed the competition like he does. So maybe it's not rational to compare yourself to him."

But Lance does just that.

"If I can get a minute a year, a minute a year isn't that much. I'm 21, he's 29. When you're 30 you're not gonna be nine minutes faster than you are at 21, but maybe in three years I will be three minutes faster. Then you are dealing with something manageable."

And suddenly Lance is flowing again. Looking to the next Tour and visualizing good times. Considering Induráin and seeing him as beatable. You want to say hold on, son, it isn't this simple, but you know that against his enthusiasm, your reason counts for nothing.

If Walsh viewed Armstrong with a fatherly eye, it was perhaps excusable, as he had children of his own: Kate, John, Simon, Daniel, Emily, and Conor, who, with his wife, Mary, filled up a small house in Kinnegad, County Westmeath, west of Dublin. From that house Walsh watched two months later as his young Texan friend became the youngest rider in sixty-three years to win the world road championships. Armstrong's win pleased Walsh immensely, proving as it did the accuracy of his instincts, not to mention increasing the likelihood that their paths would cross again. After all, Walsh had already written a book with Sean Kelly, the Irish champion. He'd always written about cycling as a thrilling contest of will and strength. But that would soon change.

In the summer of 1995, Walsh traveled to Australia to cover the Rugby World Cup for the *Independent*. While he was on the road, Walsh made a habit of speaking to his eldest son, John, every day. John was in sixth grade, a strong athlete and good student. He was videotaping all the matches to have them ready for his father when he got home.

"People say you love all your children equally, but I don't think that's true," Walsh said. "You love them all, but differently. And this kid I loved more than any person I've ever known."

John Walsh had brown hair and eyes that turned down at the corners in a way that made him look happy and sad at the same time. He also had a well-developed sense of justice. His teachers told of the day John's best friend, Andrew, scrawled something illicit on the chalkboard while the headmaster was out. The headmaster walked into the room, noted the writing, and inquired who wrote it. The customary stony silence ensued. The headmaster, hewing to form, announced that no one would leave until the culprit stood up. The headmaster waited.

"The silence went on and on," Walsh said. "Then John stands up, turns to his best friend, and says, 'Look, Andrew, just tell the master you did it and we'll get this dealt with."

Walsh paused and smiled sadly.

"John said that. So Andrew stood up, and said, 'Yes sir, I did it.' The teacher was bowled over, completely overwhelmed by John's maturity, leadership, his ability to stand up. John was ten. Ten years old!"

On June 25, 1995, twelve-year-old John Walsh was cycling on the road from Dublin to Athlone, and was struck by a car and killed. When I asked how his son's death affected him, Walsh folded his hands and took a deep breath.

"It was hugely catastrophic in our lives. We had five other kids at the time, and we felt we had to be there for them. We knew it would dominate our lives for all our lives, as it has. Nothing in life was ever going to fill me with a sense of awe, like before. It does that to you. But has it informed my work? It's impossible to say. This is so much more profound than any of that.

"My son's legacy to me was to have the courage to stand up to things," he continued. "John was a brave kid, he wanted to face the difficult questions. And if I carry a little of that with me, then I'm pleased about it."

The following summer, Walsh got his chance to face a difficult question, one involving Irish swimmer Michelle Smith. At the relatively advanced age of twenty-six, Smith had risen from sporting anonymity to win three gold medals at the Atlanta Olympics, exceeding Ireland's total for the previous sixty-four years. It was a marvelous moment, and Ireland embraced it as only the Irish can, which is to say with patriotic abandon. At two a.m., the night she won her third gold, fully half of the nation's televisions were tuned in.

But behind Smith's performance, some coaches and athletes had raised questions. She'd shaved an astounding seventeen seconds off two personal bests in three years. Her husband, Dutch discus thrower Erik de Bruin, was under a four-year doping suspension. Walsh had a decision to make: on one hand, a heartwarming comeback story, supported by the fact that Smith had passed all her drug tests. On the other, questions.

Walsh's story was headlined "Poison in the Golden Pool."

"What I wrote was, we must not believe this woman," he said. "What she has done simply does not make sense. It does not seem real, and so it must be proven real, not the other way around."

In the midst of national celebration, Walsh's words were seen as heresy. His children were harassed at school; he was vilified on talk shows and in letters to the editor. Walsh was also, it turned out, very likely right. Smith kept her medals, but two years later received a four-year suspension for doping. Walsh's story was seen in a new light—not of the suspicious crank, but of the astute moralist.

Emboldened, Walsh began to collect stories of clean athletes cheated by dirty ones, to assemble a secret history of sport. The task required discernment, but Walsh was not the kind to shy away. The stakes were too high. The payoff, which happened all too infrequently, was when one of the cheaters confessed, an event Walsh referred to as a "conversion to morality." His writing took on the feel of an extended sermon, preaching in the wilderness. He sorted athletes into the sheep and the goats. They were either good, clean, and perfect ("A lovely, marvelous lad," he would say, "one of life's good guys"), or they were tainted, fallen.

In 1998, two years after he wrote the Smith story, Walsh's relationship with cycling changed. At five thirty a.m. on July 8, three days before the Tour began, a white Fiat of the French Festina team was stopped at a French border crossing near Lille. Its driver was a balding fifty-three-year-old Belgian *soigneur* named Willy Voet. A search revealed 234 doses of EPO, 160 capsules of testosterone, 80 bottles of human growth hormone, 60 blood-thinning tablets, anti-hepatitis vaccine, syringes, and ten boxes of plastic medical drips. The ensuing scandal, which broadened to several other teams, became known as "the Festina Affair," and it nearly scuttled the Tour: riders were suspended; teams quit; Voet and the team doctor were arrested. Voet's ensuing book, *Breaking the Chain*, provided readers with a grisly picture of modern cycling, including stories of rampant pill-popping, in-race injections, and a unique method of providing clean urine to dope controllers, known by the simple if vivid name of "pipe up the ass."

"Everywhere the police looked, they found drugs. The idea that Festina were somehow a bad apple is complete bullshit, as anyone who knows the sport knows," Walsh said. "Nineteen ninety-eight was like two fingers that opened up our closed eyes, and said, look, see the reality? There. And once your eyes get opened like that, if you're in any way honest, you can't close them again. What was I doing? [The riders] have been robbing their clean colleagues of what should be the legitimate prize, and we, the journalists, have been idiots for the way we've been reporting it. I became an activist then, after 1998."

The Tour announced that 1999 would be a race of renewal. Walsh came to the race to see if it was true. He wanted to see if the average speed slowed, if the climbers had to gasp for oxygen as they once did, if the Tour would return to what he called a "more human race."

He saw the fastest race in history, dominated by the impassive figure of Lance Armstrong, who had recovered from testicular cancer three years before. Walsh also saw Armstrong become involved in a public dispute with Christophe Bassons, a rider who had been outspoken in his opinion that doping had not ceased. During the race, Armstrong sought out Bassons and told him that if Bassons felt that way, he ought to quit the sport. Walsh listened, and made up his mind.

"I believe that you can tell how someone feels about antidoping by the way they speak about it," Walsh said. "If you look, really look at their words, it cannot help but reflect their attitudes. Watching Lance and listening to him, I did not get a sense that he was our new icon, that this was the guy who can lead us into the promised land of drug-free competition. I got the sense that any people who wanted to really get into this doping question were the enemies. And I was going to be the enemy."

He took to the role with enthusiasm. Two years later, from his post as chief sportswriter of the highly regarded London *Sunday Times*, Walsh wrote an investigative piece that for the first time widely publicized Armstrong's relationship with Dr. Ferrari. Though some in the press had known that Armstrong was working with Ferrari (it had been mentioned in a 1997 *VeloNews* piece), there were many in cycling—including Vaughters, who was Armstrong's teammate at the time—for whom this was news. During the 2001 Tour, at a press conference in the Pyrenean city of Pau, Walsh raised his hand.

DAVID WALSH: The question here is one of perception— Michele Ferrari is going to answer the most serious doping charges, lots of people in cycling, because of the charges, regard him with grave suspicion. You present yourself as the cleanest of clean riders . . .

LANCE ARMSTRONG: . . . and I have the proof, which you refuse to believe . . .

WALSH: . . . let me finish the question—you present yourself as the cleanest of clean riders and yet you associate with somebody whose reputation is incredibly tarnished. That person is going to go to trial in two months' time. Would you not think it would be in the interests of cycling for you to suspend your relationship with Michele Ferrari until he has answered the charges of which he is accused?

ARMSTRONG: You have a point. It's my choice, I view him as innocent, he's a clean man in my opinion,

> let there be a trial. Let there be a trial, let the man prove himself innocent. Let there be a U.S. Postal affair in France, let us prove ourselves innocent. Let's let that play out and then we'll decide.

Walsh left frustrated. He had proven the Ferrari connection, but he needed more. Something bigger, something irrefutable. In the summer of 2002, he contacted former *L'Equipe* journalist Pierre Ballester, who had ghost-written Voet's book. After the 2002 Tour, Walsh and Ballester began to make calls. Walsh's approach was at once direct and vague: "I'd tell them, 'I'd love to do an interview about your time on the U.S. Postal team. It might be for a newspaper story, or a magazine, or a book,'" Walsh said. "Then, if they agreed, I would go to them and say, 'Look, if you want to tell the truth, I'm interested.'"

People responded; some old sources, some new. They spoke with former Postal doctor Prentice Steffen, former Postal rider Steven Swart, with former Postal *soigneuse* Emma O'Reilly. Walsh's and Ballester's notebooks began to fill. Given the likelihood of a lawsuit, Walsh and Ballester worked out a protocol: they would use only named sources. They would give important sources opportunities to review transcripts of their interviews and to read finished chapters. It was tedious work, and Walsh loved it.

"It was tremendous," Walsh said. "I've never felt more like a journalist than when I was doing this book. If you say to me, Why do journalists exist? I think we exist for this kind of work. I can't watch *All the President's Men* and not feel inspired by it."

Walsh and Ballester sought to keep their project as quiet as possible. "In 2001, Armstrong found out what we were writing [the *Sunday Times* article] about himself and Ferrari, and so he tried to diminish our story by leaking it to a newspaper," Walsh claimed. "We weren't going to let that happen again."

"David is an idealist," Vaughters said. "He would do this book if it cost him $100,000. He would do this book if it only sold one copy.

He's a stubborn person who pursues exactly what he thinks is correct, and he won't back down. In some ways, he reminds me a lot of
Lance."*

Walsh, who would go on to earn about $50,000 on the book,
worked on it nights and weekends. He kept writing his weekly stories for the *Sunday Times,* often about doping, and won Britain's
Sportswriter of the Year award three times. He wrote in clear moral
terms: his subjects were either unimpeachably heroic or the pits of
villainy. His authorial eye often seemed drawn to children in a
crowd, gazing at their sporting heroes. In one story, written in 2004,
a father lifts his child so the boy's fingers graze an unknowing
cyclist's back. Walsh invites the reader to consider what matters
more, the question of which athlete wins the Tour de France or the
deeper questions embodied by "the outstretched arm of the child."

It is a vast understatement to say that doping allegations were nothing new to Armstrong. As the world's premier cyclist, he was treated
with unparalleled levels of suspicion. Armstrong was tested thirty,
forty times a year, both in competition and out, and came up clean
each time. In 2001–02 the Postal team had been the subject of a
twenty-one-month French judicial inquiry that was eventually
dropped for lack of evidence. He cooperated with the sport's random controls, in which he was required to keep USADA testers
updated on his whereabouts so they could procure urine and blood
at a moment's notice. Armstrong went further, donating money to
testing programs. His agent wrote clauses into his contracts stating

---

*Pursuing this notion of some innate similarity between Walsh and Armstrong,
I asked Walsh if anyone had ever caught him cheating. He answered immediately, No, never. Then, a few seconds later, he remembered something. When he
was at University College, Dublin, Walsh captained his house soccer team. In a
big match, wanting desperately to win, Walsh told his two weakest starters not
to show up and instead brought in two talented townies—bangers, he called
them. Helped by the bangers, Walsh's team won, 4–1—but midway through the
game one of the starters he'd told not to come—a seminarian, it turned out—
showed up and dressed Walsh down in front of the team. "What I did was
totally immoral and unethical," Walsh said, faintly entertained by the memory.
"Armstrongesque, you might say."

that if he ever tested positive, the contract would be voided. What more could he do? Yet with each passing Tour, the questioning increased.

"You guys are like the weather," Armstrong said of the doubters. "Sometimes it's sunny, sometimes it's rainy. When it's sunny, you put on sunscreen, when it's raining, you put on a raincoat and you live with it."

Characteristically, Armstrong did what he could to influence the weather. His method of dealing with the media precisely mimicked the dope-testing system under whose shadow he lived. Basically, Armstrong tested journalists. He read everything written about him, sifting it for mentions of doping and other negatives. Writers of Web articles were unsurprised to get rebutting e-mails from him, sometimes moments after their articles had been posted. To anger Armstrong was to risk losing access—a potentially career-scuttling loss for underpaid cycling writers for whom access to the Postal team was crucial. To stay in bounds was to be a friend, a friendship that sometimes involved reporting to Postal on the activities of their less-circumspect colleagues.

"We have friends in the press room," Bruyneel told me, tilting his head mysteriously. "We know what goes on, and who is with who."

"You've got to be careful what you say," *VeloNews* writer Andrew Hood said. "The walls have ears."

Postal was the only team to snap digital photographs of journalists' faces. ("For the black list," spokesman Jogi Muller joked, lamely but accurately.) Behind the tinted windows of the Postal bus, Bruyneel, Muller, and Armstrong did their homework, monitoring the behavior of journalists milling outside.

"They cannot see us, but we can always see them," Bruyneel said. "You can tell a lot by who is talking to who, and how they are speaking."

Truth was, many in the Tour press room viewed Walsh with mixed feelings. While a minority supported him wholeheartedly, other mainline journalists saw his work as nakedly partisan ("Walsh is simply not there for the same reasons we are there," said one

American journalist who did not wish to be identified). Even so, Postal did its best to isolate its interrogator, chiefly by finding out who was so bold as to be friendly with the Irishman.

During stage 8 of the 2003 Tour, Postal press representative Muller was dispatched on a mission to find out whose car Walsh was riding in (writers, to save costs and energy, share vehicles). On a road near the Col de Galibier, Muller drove a team car alongside a suspected vehicle, which was driven by veteran Australian author and journalist Rupert Guinness, and which contained *VeloNews* writer Andrew Hood as well as someone else in the back hidden by tinted windows. After peering unsuccessfully for several moments, Muller hit on another gambit. He pantomimed, asking Guinness if he wanted to stop for coffee. Guinness somewhat wonderingly pulled over at the next café. When Muller saw Walsh step out of the rear seat, Guinness's name was added to the black list. ("Muller let me pay for the coffee, too," Guinness added ruefully.)

Through the spring of 2004, Armstrong and Bruyneel monitored Walsh closely. "On a scale of one to ten, it was a seven or an eight," Korioth said. "Lance kept saying, 'This fucking Walsh, he just won't leave it alone.'"

"We were concerned, of course," Bruyneel said. "There are many people who want to bring Lance down. We didn't know what was in [the book]. But then you have to realize that anyone who gets to a certain fame has people who want to write books like this. How many books have been written about George Bush? Are they true?"

"David Walsh is convinced Ferrari has some magic mystery potion," Bill Stapleton said. "He tries to connect these dots and prove something. He thinks we're ahead of the curve.

"But think about it for a sec," Stapleton continued. "We're building long-lasting, trusting relationships with people who are spending a lot of money—Coke, Nike, Subaru. If we're fucking lying, we can kiss it all good-bye. And if we were lying we'd do some stupid stuff to try to cover it up, wouldn't we? Does anybody think for a second that a secret that big wouldn't come out?"

In early May, Walsh contacted Stapleton and requested an interview with Armstrong. A back-and-forth ensued, after which Walsh agreed to send his questions in writing. On May 17, while Armstrong was returning to Girona from training camp in the Alps, Stapleton received a list of a dozen questions.

"They were ridiculous," Stapleton said. "It was all accusations, asking if he'd borrowed makeup to cover up syringe marks. I asked what it was for, and when Walsh was unwilling to tell me more about what he was writing, I tuned it out. There's no value in answering questions that lead to something negative."

In the second week of June, Walsh went to Paris for four days to meet with Ballester and lawyers for the publisher Le Martiniere. On the lawyers' advice, Walsh and Ballester cut several sections and pared down others. The final draft of the book, titled *L.A. Confidentiel: Les Secrets de Lance Armstrong*, contained interviews with fifty-two people. It had 385 pages and 103 footnotes, and an epigraph from Saint Jerome. On the morning of June 11, at an undisclosed location in southwestern France, the printing presses began to run.

CHAPTER 18

ONE MINUTE, FIFTY-EIGHT SECONDS

Le Mont Ventoux ne tolère pas le surregime.
(Mount Ventoux takes orders from no one.)

—MARCEL BIDOT, FRENCH NATIONAL TEAM MANAGER,
1952–1969

An hour before the Mount Ventoux time trial began on June 10, the Nantesse arrived. Her lipstick shone radium-bright; the fishnet stockings were strung taut; her blue high heels flashed like propane jets as she strode along the narrow cobbled sidewalks of Bedoin, the picturesque village at the foot of Mount Ventoux. She paused for a moment before she entered the teeming town square, straightening her fishnets and plucking her skirt hem. Satisfied, she stepped into the sunlight, but not before fixing her eyebrows in a supreme arch, as if she was surprised—shocked!—to see all the fuss.

The Nantesse (so named for being from the French town of Nantes) had come to Mount Ventoux because she is a cycling groupie, part of an elite sorority that includes the Basque Sisters, the Red Mouth, and one silent figure known only as the Stalker. It is not a pastime for the faint-hearted, requiring the resourcefulness to sneak past watchful *soigneurs*, the hardiness to withstand unceasing travel, and the courage to remain undeterred in the face of the medical link between cycling and erectile dysfunction. In the seventies, future five-time Tour winner Bernard Hinault answered a knock on the door of his Brittany home to find a Dutch woman who demanded he make love to her immediately (Hinault chivalrously declined, a decision that his onlooking wife approved).*

The Nantesse's presence at Mount Ventoux was the surest omen that today was the biggest day of the season thus far: stage 4 of the Dauphiné Libéré, the time trial up Mount Ventoux, featuring three of the big four—Armstrong, Hamilton, and Mayo. As with all things French, a large part of the day's importance lay in determinedly proving that it wasn't.

Throughout Bedoin's flag-draped streets, everyone was on top of their game. There was the avuncular former Tour winner Bernard Thevenet standing at the buffet, pondering which cheese would best accompany his red wine. There were the podium girls, distractingly gorgeous, slipping behind the sponsor's tent to sneak the day's first cigarette. There, warming up on their stationary rollers, were the riders, hollow-cheeked and sunburned, having inched their carcasses out onto the razor, singing ever louder, ever more unconvincing choruses of the strictly-here-for-training song. And here, all around Bedoin, floated the sweet taste of June in Provence, the springy curls of new grapevines snaking into the sweet air, the truffle-mad forests secretly abloom, and the old, Beckett-faced farmers with dirty leather boots and spotlessly clean tweed caps who just happened to come to town today to find—who knew?—a bike race about to begin.

---

*The cyclist with the most Casanova-esque reputation is a six-foot-four, blue-eyed, ivory-toothed hunk of Tuscan manhood named Mario Cipollini. The Lion King, as he calls himself, has owned a pet cheetah, wears a different pair of shoes each day, and when asked why actress Pamela Anderson's image was airbrushed on his handlebars instead of his wife's, replied, "Because I know what my wife looks like."

The thirty-seven-year-old sprinter is the subject of any number of fantastic rumors involving podium girls, rocking team buses, and, in one story, a sex act that took place during a race (behind a suitably modest hedge, one presumes). The reality, however, is that Cipollini, winner of forty-two stages in the Giro d'Italia and a dozen in the Tour de France, is secretly one of the peloton's most organized, methodical riders—Cecchini is his trainer, after all—and that his Valentino maneuvers are regarded within the peloton as some of the more spectacular diversionary tactics ever devised.

Most spectacularly ignored, however, was Ventoux itself, the single most death-enchanted rock in a nation specializing in death-enchanted rocks. Neither an Alp nor a Pyrene, Ventoux is a lonely freak mountain, a magnet for mad poets and misguided saints. The selfsame mountain on whose bone-white slopes British cyclist Tom Simpson had died while climbing in the 1967 Tour. It also happened to be one on which Armstrong had never won.

Sex and death and scandal—they were all there, vibrating the shiny elm leaves, along with the knowledge that this particular race had a history of foreshadowing Tour results. In 2002 and 2003, Armstrong had won the Dauphiné and gone on to win the Tour; in 2001, Armstrong had bestowed victory on then-teammate Hamilton. In 1975, when Thevenet thwarted Eddy Merckx's bid for his elusive sixth Tour win, he'd first beaten Merckx at the Dauphiné. Just in case anybody forgot, Thevenet reminded them.

"I think there is a sense of change in the air," he said.

Thus far Mayo had contributed to that sense of change by winning Sunday's 5.4-kilometer prologue, with Hamilton second and Armstrong third. Perhaps more impressive was the Phonak team's performance: Hamilton's shiny-faced boys finished fourth, sixth, seventh, and eighth in the prologue (the top four Postals, on the other hand, finished a mediocre 12th, 25th, 35th, and 60th). The first three stages had seen no change in the order, which meant that the big three would be the last riders up Ventoux today, separated by the customary two minutes: first Armstrong, then Hamilton, then Mayo. A perfect metaphor (though none would be so indiscreet as to call it that): Armstrong trying to escape, the others hot on the chase.

The real race, as the Nantesse and Thevenet and everyone else knew, had already begun in the tented shelters of the team encampments, where the three contenders were going through their warm-up routines. Time-trialing, unlike conventional racing, depends on a rider's willingness to push himself to threshold and remain there, suspended. Judging by the atmosphere of the three encampments, the three contenders looked to have three distinct approaches.

In the Euskaltel team's orange tent, set up near the town center, two mechanics were busy cutting holes in Mayo's cap. Twelve holes, to be precise, excised in careful ovals so that his hat resembled a kindergarten art project—a flower hat. They held up the hat and passed it between them, satisfied. Then they checked his bike, a tiny wedge of orange loveliness. Like the others, Mayo was testing a new bike: an orange Orbea with brake levers dotted with dozens of other, tinier holes, having been drilled out to save weight. To save more weight, the bike had been built with a compact frame, which essentially meant the core triangle formed by the top tube, down tube, and seat tube was reduced to the smallest possible dimension. In the *soigneurs'* beefy hands, the bike looked like a toy.

Mayo emerged from the bus, slightly hunched, moving in mincing steps. His skin was papery; his cheek delicate and hollow. His body looked as if it, like the hat and bike, had been systematically pared of every extraneous gram.

As he moved toward his bike, no one spoke to him; in fact, the unspoken agreement among the *soigneurs* and mechanics was to pretend that he wasn't there. Mayo swung his leg stiffly over the bike, an arthritic old man clambering aboard a child's toy. It was, for a moment, almost funny. *Him*? On *that*? The very idea that this skinny boy could win the world's hardest race seemed ludicrous.

Then Mayo started to ride. He accelerated through the gears, his toes downward. The rollers began to sing, and suddenly all that birdlike awkwardness turned into grace. His skinny legs whirled with elliptical perfection, his back straightened and lengthened proudly, his toothpick arms grew forests of veins. The tiny bike's rear wheel spun faster and faster, lofting a caressingly cinematic breeze into his curls. The body and the bike merged into a single organism of lightness and speed. The *soigneurs* stood back, as though Druids afraid of breaking whatever spell was being cast.

As if drawn by the sound, a crew of halter-topped teenage girls gathered around. They were French girls in summer, taut and tan, with lovely upsprung bodies they piloted through the village with perfect Gallic hauteur, a pose belied by the speed with which they materialized around the orange tent. First a few came, and then a few more, until there were a dozen miniature Isabelle Hupperts, a mob of lovely disdainfulness crowding around to look at this slender, lethal-looking figure. They abandoned all pretense of cool; they stared unabashedly at his gazelle-like legs, the loomed muscles of his calves, the delicate bones of his wrists, that long, telling scar on his arm. Some knew his story—*car accident, wheelchair, might win the Tour*. The girls stared and they memorized him and they whispered to each other but also to him. Mayo responded by ignoring them in the best Basque style, which is to say, magnificently. The Nantesse, playing the knowing veteran to these greenhorns, sashayed through to offer her best wishes, which Mayo accepted with a grave nod, then returned to the elegant privacy of his invisible bubble.

Meanwhile, forty feet away, team Phonak's camp emanated a different sort of love, overseen by the giant grinning image of leathery old Ferdi Kubler offering that hearing aid. Need water? A gel? Some ice? New wheel? The air buzzed with Boy Scout alertness, the ground scuttled with efficient Swiss *soigneurs*. Even the watching crowd was politely serviced (would anyone like a souvenir team postcard? a key chain? a magnet?). Instead of seventeen-year-old Eurohotties, the Phonak camp drew their mothers and grandmothers, a crowd that could appreciate this efficient, busy little kitchen, and especially the polite, boyish chef who oversaw it.

Hamilton wore a green cycling cap and a white crewneck undershirt. He was spinning aboard a black carbon bike with gold fittings and no logo, whose sleek flash seemed vaguely incongruous beneath him. From the bike, Hamilton's green gaze scoured the small team area, which was still crowded with teammates, since so many Phonaks were near the top of the overall standings. He was raising his eyebrows to get his teammates' attention and telling them how to ride the first five kilometers.

"*Tranquilo, tranquilo, premiero kilometro,*" Hamilton said, pressing down with his palms to show them. They mirrored the gesture back.

"*Tranquilo,*" they repeated obediently. "*Muy tranquilo.*"

Hamilton looked approvingly around the tent. Satisfied, he put on his sunglasses and retreated within his warm-up. He revved the bike, and the sweat dripped off his nose, splashing on the black frame.

Meanwhile, one kilometer north of town, next to a graveyard, the Postal team had set up its camp. If Mayo was all id and Hamilton was superego, the Postal camp was practical-minded ego. There might be things happening beneath the surface, but any emotion had been sternly funneled into the job at hand, a funneling which started and ended with Armstrong, who was warming up on his rollers, head down. He wasn't giving advice or checking on teammates, most of whom were long gone. He was concentrating.

There were reasons for seriousness. Bruyneel had just gotten word that *De Telegraaf,* a Dutch paper, had run an article the previous morning, which referred to the Walsh-Ballester book: "Armstrong is again in front of the firing squad," it said. Other newspapers were picking the story up. Armstrong's lawyers were drafting a letter to the *Sunday Times,* informing them that if they ran any story that alleged Armstrong had used performance-enhancing drugs— i.e., the book excerpt Stapleton expected—they would be promptly sued. Even the shiny presence of some new Shit That Will Kill Them—a new, light bike, freshly cooked, delivered by Trek day before yesterday—wasn't enough to lift the mood. Armstrong spun the bike on the rollers and stared down. Around him, the Belgies stood, watchful and tense.

Other rumors swirled around the bus, whispered by journos and industry types. The mid-May buzz about Floyd Landis had gathered force. Many were now convinced he was going to be left off the Tour team, that he'd fallen out with Armstrong over something. The scenario was made plausible by the highly caffeinated presence of Landis's agent, Mike Rutherford, who'd sprung five grand on a last-minute ticket from Colorado to France in order to speak with Bruyneel about Landis's future.

The buzz around the bus grew: Landis was on the bubble! Other evidence was produced: eight riders had been interviewed for OLN's *Lance Chronicles,* but Landis hadn't been among them. This was precisely the sort of red-meat rumor on which Tour-watchers love to feast. Richard Fries, a correspondent for OLN, excitedly sketched it out for a huddle of journalists. He likened the Tour scenario to Gettysburg, with Armstrong as Robert E. Lee, Hamilton as Ulysses S. Grant, and Landis as Jeb Stuart.

"This changes things," Fries said. "Tyler could just hang behind Armstrong, let his army exhaust themselves, then sweep in there like the Union Army. And with no Jeb Stuart to help him, what is Lee going to do?"

When start time finally came, Armstrong was first of the three to go. He rolled up to the start ramp. His face was tight, his jaw clenched.

"Put me on my mark," he told the starter.

The starter counted down. Twenty seconds.

Like a hitter in a batter's box, Armstrong went through his routine. He squeezed the brakes. He touched his earpiece, his glasses, his helmet. He took three deep breaths.

Cinq, quatre, trois, deux . . .

Armstrong lunged, a wolfish burst of power uncoiling, and disappeared up the road.

Hamilton was next. The crowd applauded warmly at his name, and he smiled shyly in return, causing a soft *awwwww* to ripple through the square. He looked loose, confident. When someone called for his *chapeau*, he removed it with a flourish and spun it into the crowd.

With thirty seconds left, he took his place on his black bike. He breathed deeply, and his eyes hardened. They locked onto the road ahead.

Cinq, quatre, trois, deux . . .

Hamilton made a silken acceleration, his head up, as if he were looking to see where Armstrong had gone.

Finally, Mayo. He walked slowly up the ramp, and sat down, hands folded. His *soigneur* solemnly rubbed his wheels with a white cloth. The Eurohotties cheered, but Mayo did not seem to hear them. He seemed to inhabit a waking dream, floating slightly above the world.

With ten seconds left, Mayo closed his eyes and crossed himself.

When the starter dropped his hand, he opened his eyes and flowed down the ramp, and those slender legs started to whir.

Three on the road.

Ventoux consists of three distinct climbs. The first six kilometers are a less-steep approach, an appetizer. The next section winds through ten kilometers of cruelly steep oak and pine forests. The final six kilometers, which are almost as steep, trace across Ventoux's upper reaches, a white, treeless moonscape.

Armstrong finished the lower slopes at 10:13, the day's fastest time thus far. That was good, but also expected; Armstrong's superior power gave him an advantage on the flatter sections over his lighter rivals. Hamilton came through seven seconds behind Armstrong. Then Mayo came through. The announcer reading out the split-times on race radio hesitated, as if unsure it could be correct: 10:04, nine seconds faster than Armstrong.

Bruyneel relayed the news to Armstrong in measured tones; there was a long way to climb. No need to overreact. Perhaps Mayo was burning matches. At the same time, Bruyneel knew all too well what was going on inside Armstrong's mind. Nine seconds! On the part of the course where he should have gained time? Too much. Way too much.

Mayo himself was surprised. He hadn't been trying that hard. In fact, he'd consciously gone easy. He didn't feel faster, but there it was, the kind of magical equilibrium a cyclist lives for, when the laws of the universe get turned upside down, and less energy somehow creates more motion. Though Mayo did not speak of it, some of that propulsion had been provided by Armstrong, in a quote he'd issued six months previous.

"No, I don't think Mayo can win the Tour," Armstrong had said. "I think you've seen the best of Iban Mayo."

While Mayo never spoke of Armstrong's slight, his coach, Julian Gorospe, made several references to the American's words, making it plain that, in his humble opinion, Armstrong was playing a dangerous game. One should not underestimate a welder's son from Igurre.

Mayo entered the steeper, wooded part of the course. His gazelle legs moved faster, the chain hummed, the tiny bike rocked back and forth. Up ahead, Armstrong churned his high cadence, trying to get away. The crowd leaned in. This was what they wanted, a rematch of last year, these two men on the mountain. People kept saying their names: Mayo, Armstrong, Mayo, Armstrong.

In between them, almost unnoticed, rode Hamilton, looking calm and composed.

"I felt good," Hamilton said later. "I went hard. I felt the way I wanted to feel."

His plan was working. After his rocky early spring, Hamilton's form was coming around right on schedule. He'd visited Cecchini several times in Tuscany, performing the power-building drills in which his trainer specialized, many of which involved being paced behind Cecchini's motorcycle. The two spoke each night, constantly revising training schedules and plans. While in previous years Hamilton had built around several peaks, 2004 was constructed with the Tour foremost in mind. Now, a month before the Tour, he was generating more power than ever. While not as far out on the razor as Mayo, he was getting lean, down to around 134 pounds or so. His and Cecchini's plan was to begin the Tour at 90 percent, then peak for the Tour's big third week.

"He's going awfully fast, awfully easy," said American rider Christian Vande Velde, who occasionally trained with Hamilton.

"We've been motorpacing a lot," said Hamilton's wife, Haven. "I think I've memorized every pebble on that road."

Best of all, the season had thus far been perfectly—to some minds, spookily—crashless. "Touch wood," Hamilton said whenever it was brought up. Then he quickly—almost uncharacteristically— changed the subject, saying there had been enough talk about crashes.

In fact, friends and journalists had noticed Hamilton had been increasingly outspoken about a number of things. In March, he had said his ambition was the podium; now he made no bones about it: he was coming to win. Before, he had played down any rivalry with Armstrong; now he seemed, in his own way, to be playing one up. He even talked about his "mean side."

"People think there's only one American racing bikes in Europe," he said. "There are others."

As if to prove it, Hamilton had been doing his recon, particularly of the Tour's middle stages in the Central Massif. "Those climbs are steeper than they look, especially on the stage to St. Flour," Hamilton said. "Anybody who doesn't go check them first is going to be very surprised."

Surprise—there it was again, Hamilton's favorite theme. Except that he wasn't so quiet about it anymore. He wasn't just ready to surprise his rivals; he was telling them. He was, in his Boy Scout way, talking trash.

Why not? He'd had his run of bad luck. He'd endured his crashes. He'd built one hell of a good team. He treated people with respect. And though Hamilton never said as much, it was impossible to listen to his words without hearing the voice of a man who feels his time is coming.

When Hamilton had first studied the Tour route, way back in October, one day had jumped out. Stage 13 to Plateau de Beille, lucky 13. A six-climb monster of a stage, the second day in the mountains. During recon, Hamilton had noted the last climb was a stairstep—steeper, then less steep, then steeper again. A hard acceleration on those steep sections would yield distance, not in great gulps, but a little at a time. Plateau de Beille: that was the one. Baby steps.

Now on Mount Ventoux, Hamilton watched Armstrong's figure grow larger and larger in front of him, now three bends ahead, now two. For a surreal moment, Hamilton thought he might catch and pass his former teammate. *Hello, neighbor*. How would that be for surprise?

Halfway up the mountain, the feeling hit Lance Armstrong for the first time. It was nothing physical, nothing to do with the pain moving through his legs or his mind. The feeling arrived softly. A flicker of awareness, a faintly ticking clock.

They're beating me.

One hundred thousand spectators leaned into the road, eyes

straining to see. The race was not televised; information traveled by voice and radio. The mountain vibrated with hidden knowledge. The people shouted; they showed their teeth. They'd been waiting for this moment, now they were tasting it.

They saw Armstrong emerge from the forest onto the white moonscape, now six kilometers from the finish. His face was tight, his lower jaw slightly jutted. Stopwatches clicked: how close were Hamilton and Mayo?

First came Hamilton, then Mayo. The picture clarified. Striving for calm, the race announcer enunciated the results of the second time-check: Armstrong had lost forty seconds to Hamilton. He'd lost a full minute to Mayo—the equivalent of a quarter mile.

On the mountain, disbelief gave way to pandemonium. The French crowd howled with surprise and delight. The mostly European press corps began to release half a decade of pent-up energy—the king is dead, long live the kings! Later, one of them would be seen dancing down in the press center, but on the mountain, the shimmying had already started.

In the support car, Johan Bruyneel, Armstrong's director, did something he'd never done before. He decided not to tell Armstrong how much time Hamilton had gained. Bruyneel had often used this gambit on young riders, who could be demoralized by an opponent's success. In fact, Armstrong would be furious when he found out what Bruyneel had done. But right now it seemed the director's best option. Better he ride blind.

"I had to decide," Bruyneel said later. "If I tell him, Lance might completely lose motivation. He might say, fuck it."

Armstrong's head tipped forward, his teeth bared. Later, some of his rivals would see the time gaps and say that he had been bluffing. They would be wrong. Armstrong was ascending Ventoux faster than he'd ever done, and it was making no difference.

Armstrong crossed the line red-faced, grabbed a towel from a *soigneur*, and rode off to rendezvous with Bruyneel and the team car.

"That," he said, climbing into the passenger's seat, "was not good."

Armstrong sat down, burning with questions. Why the fuck hadn't Bruyneel told him Hamilton's splits? How the fuck was Mayo so fast? What the fuck was going on?

Bruyneel waited, then applied the soothing Belgian cure of fact.

"Five weeks," he said slowly, holding out his fingers for emphasis. "We have five weeks before the Tour climbs."

Armstrong sat, staring out the window.

"Mayo is not superman," Bruyneel continued. "He has not lost his last five races." To reinforce his point, Bruyneel named each race: Asturias, Navacarado, Alcobendas—names, soothing names. "He cannot stay at this level for five more weeks. It is not possible.

"What percent are you now?" Bruyneel asked. He didn't wait for an answer. "85? 90? What will happen when you get to 100?"

Bruyneel gave a whoof-shrug. Armstrong didn't say anything.

The car wove westward down Ventoux's flank, toward the setting sun. Back at their rooms in St. Paul Trois Chateaux, Bruyneel got out pencil and paper. He calculated the percentage of time Armstrong had lost to Mayo on the steep part of the climb, which figured to be 1.5 percent.

Just before dinner, Bruyneel took the paper to Armstrong's room, showed it to him. Two minutes might sound big, but 1.5 percent? Everyone knew the formula: 1.25 percent for each kilo (2.2 pounds). And how many kilos was Armstrong going to shed before the Tour? One kilo, right?

There it was, then. One kilo, 1.25 percent. Now the gap with Mayo wasn't two minutes, it was twenty seconds. Twenty seconds! Twenty seconds was nothing. Armstrong kept the paper.

Meanwhile, the media along with everyone else was still fixated on the contenders.

"I have reached a new level," the Spaniard announced.

In his comments, Hamilton focused not on his success, but on that of his team. No fewer than five Phonak riders had finished in the top thirteen, a show of Postal-like dominance. By contrast, Armstrong's next-best teammate—Landis, as it happened—finished 14th, with the rest of the top five trickling in 15th, 20th, and 32nd.

Most observers took the result as proof that Armstrong now had a two-front war on his hands: Mayo and Hamilton surging away in the mountains, with Jan Ullrich crawling up his back in the time trials. Armstrong would have to play both ends against the middle.

"The truth is, we didn't expect that," Bruyneel said a day later. "It's evident that we have to improve. If they improve, too, then we have a problem."

The day after Mount Ventoux, the Dauphiné peloton gathered under threatening skies at the start in Bollene. Up front, under an arch of flags, Hamilton was chatting with the rest, surrounded by the usual morning routines of stretching, ass-checking, and good-naturedly comparing ailments. Mayo stood, remote as ever, wearing the leader's yellow jersey.

As departure time drew near, riders and press started looking around—where was Armstrong? Had he pulled out of the race? His bike stood by the door of the bus, waiting.

The announcer counted down to the start. Bells were rung; horns were honked. Some beaming small-town despot scissored a ribbon; the great processional of departure began—riders and motorcycles and cars. Still no Armstrong.

Instinctively, the press began to sidle toward the Postal bus, headlines forming in their brains. "Armstrong quits."

It wasn't until the last riders had crossed the starting line that the door to the Postal bus breathed open. Seizing his bike by the handlebars, Armstrong pointed it in the direction of the departing cars and hopped aboard on the run, weaving through the team cars in order to catch up.

From now on he would be racing from behind.

Infochemically speaking, the following Sunday, June 13 was a big day.

It began with the news that Ullrich had won the opening stage of the Tour of Switzerland. Ullrich, who was racing with teammate Vinokourov, had outsprinted four other riders to take a narrow win and don the leader's jersey. Observers took note, remarking that they could not remember the last time Ullrich won a sprint.

The *Sunday Times*, while persuaded by the letter from Armstrong's lawyers not to excerpt the book, instead ran a story written by one of the paper's editors, Alan English, which included some of the book's allegations. The French magazine *L'Express,* shielded by France's more lenient libel laws, ran a long excerpt that was soon being translated on the Internet. The book would be in stores on Tuesday.

Armstrong's agent, Bill Stapleton, phoned Billy Campbell, president of the Discovery Network. Three days before, Discovery had signed a three-year, $30 million deal with Tailwind Sports to replace the Postal Service as the team's title sponsor. Stapleton had previously warned Campbell that this book was on the way, but had guessed the release would come closer to the Tour.

"Here it comes," Stapleton told Campbell.

After attempting to ascertain the book's contents, Discovery's top executives called a meeting, which turned into a debate. On the one hand, the book would do damage; cause an unseemly string of lawsuits, rumors, bad press. On the other, the book didn't seem to have any absolute proof. In the end, despite the awful timing, Discovery decided to stick by Armstrong.

For Bruyneel, however, the timing was perfect. "It worked out well," he said. "Here you have a guy who wants to see the biggest rider lose, and destroy his career. If that's what he wants, if it's what Walsh works three or four years for—and then just on the day the book comes out, boom, that rider gets a three-year contract with a new team? I don't think Walsh feels very well when he sees that."

CHAPTER 19

TO THE EDGE

Bruyneel located a copy of *L'Express* magazine in the Lyon airport, and translated the twelve-page excerpt for Armstrong and Crow as they flew across the Atlantic to the June 15 sponsor announcement press conference at Discovery Channel's Maryland headquarters.

Armstrong listened as Bruyneel read the account of Emma O'Reilly, who had worked as team *soigneuse* and Armstrong's personal masseuse from 1998 to 2000. He listened to O'Reilly's allegations of lending Armstrong makeup to cover needle bruises on his arm before the 1999 Tour. He listened to O'Reilly's account of how Armstrong had asked her to dispose of syringes, how she had shuttled mysterious pills across borders, how she had kept a diary that included mention of Armstrong complaining that his red blood cell count was 41 percent, far below the UCI's 50 percent ceiling.

The O'Reilly diary portion of the excerpt read: "Without thinking, I replied: 'Forty-one? That's terrible. What are you going to do? Everyone in cycling knows that you can't win with a red cell count of forty-one.' He looked at me, and said, 'Emma, you know what I'm going to do. I'm going to do what the others do.'"

Armstrong listened as Bruyneel read the words of former teammate Stephen Swart, who alleged that Armstrong "participated fully" in a Motorola team decision to start using EPO in 1995. He listened to the account of former Postal team doctor, Prentice Steffen, who said he was fired when he refused to cave in to riders' requests for performance-enhancing drugs, requests that Steffen attributed to Tyler Hamilton, among others (allegations that Hamilton subsequently denied).

In full form, the book was exhaustive—and exhausting. It had a rummager's sensibility, moving back and forth in time and space to construct a dark alternate universe to belie the usual apple-pie Armstrong story. Walsh and Ballester pointed out that cancer had been linked to the use of performance-enhancing drugs, some of which can cause the mutations in fast-growing cells, such as are found in the testicles. In a chapter entitled "The Unique Metamorphosis of a Cancer Victim," Walsh and Ballester spent dozens of pages analyzing Armstrong's illness and recovery, speaking with several doctors who found his subsequent performance too amazing to be rationally explicable. They recounted the shadow-filled histories of Michele Ferrari and Francesco Conconi, and described the testimony of the Italian rider Filippo Simeoni, who claimed Ferrari had provided him with EPO and instructions on how to use it without being detected.

In addition, the book offered grimly alternative accounts of widely accepted landmarks in Armstrong's story, such as that of Cofidis, the French team that Armstrong said betrayed him when he got cancer. (The book quoted Cofidis officials wearily pointing out that they paid Armstrong $676,630, nearly two-thirds of his 1997 salary.) Or that of Armstrong's 1993 sweep of a three-event, million-dollar American racing series. (Walsh located cyclists on a rival team who alleged that Armstrong paid them $50,000 to not race hard against him.) Or that of Armstrong's well-publicized brush with the doping controls in the 1999 Tour, when he had a false positive for illegal corticoids based on what was officially determined as his preapproved use of a saddle-sore cream. (Walsh attempted to prove that the positive test was genuine; he quoted O'Reilly as saying Armstrong had told her he'd taken an illegal corticoid the previous month. O'Reilly went on to describe a scene of Armstrong and team officials huddled in panic as they tried to cook up an explanation for the positive test and to locate a team doctor to write a post-dated prescription for the saddle-sore cream. "When we leave this room," O'Reilly recalled team officials saying, "we all have to have the same story.")*

"Informative and serious," wrote George Vecsey of the *New York Times,* one of the few Americans to read the book in French. "Particularly on the depressing state of cycling."

Within hours of the book's appearance, Armstrong's lawyers filed suit in England against the *Sunday Times,* David Walsh, and Emma O'Reilly ("We won't discriminate," Armstrong said), and in France against *L'Express* and publisher Le Martiniere, seeking an injunction in order that Armstrong might submit a statement of denial into all copies of the book (the request was denied, and Armstrong was fined a symbolic euro for wasting the court's time and ordered to pay $1,800 in court costs).

"My impression of Walsh all along was that he's a writer with a conclusion, who builds premises to get where he wants to get," Stapleton later said. "He finds disgruntled ex-employees and relies on them, and at the end of the day, you can't build a house around someone with no credibility.

"The level of detail is remarkable," Stapleton continued. "But let's look at the ten worst pieces of so-called evidence, and assume they are true. It still doesn't prove anything."

Armstrong's own reaction to Walsh was more primal.

"Walsh is a fucking scumbag. He's a liar," Armstrong would later tell me. "His angle is that he hates me, and I hate him. He connects dots, and if you look at what the dots are, they're pretty shady.

"If I could go back and kiss David Walsh's ass, maybe I should have," he continued. "But I think they're bad, unethical people, and I'm not going to play that game, and if I have to suffer through it

---

*Interestingly, Walsh and Ballester's book contains numerous anecdotes and testimonials flattering to Armstrong. These include accounts of his thoughtfulness toward Postal team personnel (gifts of Rolex watches), as well as stories that illustrate his skill as a detail-oriented leader, such as the time he spotted sugar cereal on the training table and demanded that it be substituted by a healthier alternative. Seen through the dark lens of the book's central allegation, however, even the sunniest anecdotes can't help but take on a sinister tinge. In Walsh and Ballester's telling, granola stops seeming like just granola.

and get books and articles written and investigations launched by scumbags, then so be it. They will never get it, because there's nothing to get."

As the clock ticked down toward the Tour, people in the cycling world started to feel a familiar vibration. One of them was Patrick Lefevére, the highly regarded director of the Quick Step–Davitamon team.

"A lot has been made of his new girlfriend and the fact that he's seemed more relaxed off the bike," Lefevére noted, "but I think that will be offset by another factor: the book. I think that Lance is very angry, and it will be his rivals at the Tour who feel the full brunt of that anger."

Vino didn't see it coming. He was positioned midway in a snaking line of seven riders, flashing at 35 mph down a tidy street in the Tour of Switzerland's second stage. On a turn, he edged out of line a few inches, trying to get a view.

The steel pole caught Vino flush in the face and shoulder. He bounced over a traffic island, across the road, and hit a tree. That's where he was when Ullrich wheeled past, seeing his friend wiping away the blood, dazedly trying to get up.

Spectators held him back. Vino had a concussion, severe bruising, and torn ligaments in his shoulder that would require surgery. His Tour de France was over.

T-Mobile manager Walter Godefroot said, "Our team's strategy at the Tour is destroyed."

"There are worse things," Vino said from the hospital, with Kazakh knowingness. He would get on his bike again the day after surgery, secretly trying for a comeback. But it would be no use.

Those around Ullrich could see his mind shift. He was alone now, his hunting partner gone. In the next few days, Birgit Krohme sensed an acceptance. Perhaps this was how it was meant to be: Ullrich against Armstrong, strength against strength. For the next few days, through 1,200 kilometers of the Tour of Switzerland's demanding mountain stages, he rode with the leaders, feeling his form come.

"He is just gliding through the other riders," British rider Bradley Wiggins marveled. "It is awesome to watch."

A few days later, on June 20, Ullrich performed his own dress rehearsal for the Tour. It happened at the Tour of Switzerland's final stage, a 25.6 kilometer time trial, which began with Ullrich trailing the leader, Fabian Jeker, by forty-one seconds. The scenario was what Ullrich had trained for: a dramatic, last-day comeback; a test of pure German power.

"I go today to my borders," Ullrich said before the race.

The day didn't start particularly well. In the first fifteen kilometers, he'd only made up sixteen seconds. But as he entered the last ten kilometers, Ullrich found something. Tight in his aero position, churning the big gear of his trusty Walser narrow bike, he powered through the streets of Lugano.

In the last ten kilometers, Ullrich made up twenty-six seconds on the leader, including eleven seconds in the last kilometer alone. Jeker faded; Ullrich flew toward the line; and when the race clock stopped, he had won by one second.

He stood on the podium, soaking up his first stage-race overall win in five years, loving the feel of the moment. Just after he stepped down, he took off his shirt and let everybody see just how fat the fat boy was now.

In London, bookies tightened the odds. Armstrong was now 1.9:1; Ullrich was 2:1.

Meanwhile, Tyler Hamilton was back in Girona, looking for more wood to knock on, because the lucky salt had failed him two days after his performance on Ventoux, on stage 6 of the Dauphiné. He'd crashed descending the ominously named Col de la Morte. He'd been rounding a hard left turn when the rider next to him started to slide out. Hamilton went down hard on his left side, missing a retaining wall by inches. His left forearm was caked in blood, his hip burned and cut. On the bright side, he hadn't broken anything.

Hamilton and his wife, Haven, had just received some other bad news. Their dog, Tugboat, was seriously ill. The nine-year-old golden retriever had had an allergic reaction to some medication, and further examination had shown the dog was suffering from cancer. He'd received a blood transfusion but hadn't fully recovered. He was moving more slowly, and had trouble with stairs.

"If anything happens to Tugboat—" Haven said, not finishing the sentence. "Ty is so attached to him. I mean, it sounds silly to say, but he is like our child."

A week before the Tour, Hamilton visited Cecchini for the last time. His weight was perfect: like Armstrong, he aimed to drop a kilo between the Dauphiné and the Tour. His watts were solid.

"I've studied all I can," Hamilton said. "Now it's time to take the exam."

At his apartment in Durango, Mayo tried to deal with the storm of adulation caused by his Dauphiné victory. He turned off his telephone, avoided going to the grocery. He did not reply to the five-figure offer from *Interviu*, the racy Spanish magazine, to pose nude. He rode alone or with a few friends in the hills of his childhood, hoping to maintain his form.

The teams named their Tour riders, each choosing four or five climbers to handle the steep profile of the last week. T-Mobile replaced Vino with a fellow Eastern Bloc goombah, Sergei Ivanov, and talked up the chances of slender twenty-nine-year-old Andreas Kloden, Ullrich's friend and alum of Berlin's Dynamo sports school, who'd just won the German championship.

Disappointing conspiracy theorists, Landis was chosen for Postal, after all, along with usual suspects Beltran, Azevedo, Rubiera, Padrnos, Hincapie, and the ancient Eki. There was one surprise: Noval, the strong and shy first-year rider, was picked over Tour veteran Victor Hugo Peña.

Phonak followed the same formula: Hamilton would be supported in the mountains by an Iberian quartet, and by hardbodies in the flats. He made the last cut himself, calling up Cyril Dessel to inform him that he hadn't made it. "I felt terrible," Hamilton said. "But it was only fair that he hear it from me."

The Basque Euskaltel-Euskadi team gathered in the Spanish city of Derio for a send-off. The team sat in sweltering heat beneath a tent, in matching suits with orange pocket squares and matching brown shoes. They were blessed by a Catholic priest, who sprinkled holy water on them. Then a group of white-clad Basque entertainers, called *dantzaris*, performed a fast-spinning dance.

"I aspire to do my utmost," Mayo said as he watched the dancers whirl.

A few hours after the Discovery announcement, which went fairly well, despite the unwelcome doping question, Armstrong flew back to Europe. Before the book controversy, he and Ferrari had planned on doing one long test on Alpe d'Huez. The long test before the Tour was a crucial part of the Armstrong template—half an hour or more at threshold, to see if he was truly ready. But after the stress of the press conference and the travel, the test was canceled.

"[The test] wasn't going to make us any wiser," Bruyneel said. "The only possible result would tell us what we already knew. We had to work."

Instead, Armstrong headed for the Pyrenees. He brought a handful of teammates: Eki, Landis, and Hincapie, along with Michele Ferrari. They rented bungalows in the town of Puigcerda, and started their last training session. The thinking went like this: since the Tour's mountains came in the third week, it was necessary to climb as much as possible just before the Tour, to avoid any letdown.

They rode La Mongie three times. They rode in Andorra and Bonascre and the entire stage 13, the Tour's hardest, which took them seven and a half hours. They practiced the team time trial, a day which pleased Bruyneel to no end.

"I could see then we were very strong, and Lance was very strong," he said later. "That day, I started to get a good feeling."

Other signs showed themselves. One day, the team was training in a single paceline with Matt White, a former Postal rider now with Cofidis, who happened to be in the region. Armstrong was leading up the last climb, talking on the phone, when White was dropped.

"How strong is that?" Bruyneel asked later. "Lance was not only leading, but he was talking on the *phone*? And he drops a Tour rider? Unbelievable."

"He was making all of us look like idiots," Landis said. "He was stupid strong."

Sheryl Crow stayed for a few days, then left on a brief concert tour in the States. Armstrong was alone in the bungalow. He took most meals alone. He occasionally snuck down to the Internet café in town to check how the Walsh story was playing out. Armstrong weighed himself every day. He thought often of the paper Bruyneel had showed him back at the Dauphiné. With every ounce he lost, with every hunger pang endured, he drew closer to Mayo and Hamilton.

Just before the Tour, Armstrong did one last threshold test with Ferrari, doing repeats on a one-kilometer climb just as he had in February at the golf course. Armstrong watched as Ferrari drew his lines on the graph paper, hoping for 500. He came in just shy, at 493 watts.

He stepped on the scale: 163 pounds—74 kilograms on the nose. Which meant his magic number was 6.66, a hair short of Ferrari's desired 6.7 level. Calipers revealed 6 percent body fat.

"Good numbers," Ferrari said. "He has been stronger, for sure. But this should be enough."

Armstrong's confidence, which was shaken on Mont Ventoux, was revived. When his picture appeared on the cover of *Sports Illustrated,* some in his agent's office expressed concern about the magazine's so-called cover jinx, the famous phenomenon of subjects suffering upsets after appearing on the cover.

Armstrong, whose knowledge of mainstream sports culture contains a few holes, hadn't heard of the jinx. Someone started to explain it to him—*see, when you're on the cover* . . . He cut them off.

"I don't give a fuck what it is," Armstrong said. "None of them is gonna beat me."

CHAPTER 20

PROLOGUE

JULY 3, LIEGE, BELGIUM

They arrived one by one, riding spaceship buses and gleaming new cars. They floated through the sooty grandeur of Liege, past the great pyramids of food and equipment in warehouses and churches, through the tangy mist of cigarettes and beer and *frites*. Past the feverish ant-brigades assembling the portable city with the barbershop, the bank, the portalets with gold-trimmed faucets. Past the luscious, retro-babe curves of the Credit Lyonnais podium girls, past the scurrying, crablike hordes of 2,200 working press. Past the leathered-up S&M boys of the motorcycle brigade and the twitchy-moustached gendarmes who guarded the entrances to the team areas. Past the ebullient Belgian drunks and grim, tidy Belgian children. Past the acid-tripped fantasia of the publicity cavalcade, with its giant teacup and sausage rickshaw and motorized mice and twenty-foot-tall plush lion and the rest of the characters in the supporting cast of the world's largest annual sporting event. Armstrong, Ullrich, Hamilton, and Mayo passed through all of it, unseeing, ready, nervous for today's prologue, the short time trial that kicked off the Tour.

"He-ere we go," Armstrong said as he got out of the team car and walked toward the bus.

Along with the rest of the contenders, Armstrong had already performed his assigned duties in the pre-Tour theatrical: meetings, team presentations, a physical examination in which their lung capacity, weight, and hearts were earnestly measured. At every turn, they were poked and prodded and asked magnificently inane questions: Who will win? What will be the toughest stage? How do you feel?

For the contenders, the real trick was to make it through three or four prerace days without feeling sick. This was not an easy task. If a misanthropic scientist set out to design the perfect hothouse for infectious disease, he could do a good deal worse than the Tour: thousands of people coming from all over the planet to form a gauntlet of handshakes, hugs, and unwelcome contact. Always concerned about their health, riders now crossed the border into wholly appropriate paranoia. They were one poorly washed hotel fork, one meteorite of spittle away from a Tour-sized problem. Things were not made easier in the prerace physical, when the ever-observant Landis noticed that race doctors were reusing the white plastic mouthpieces on the lung-capacity tester.

"Did you see that?" he told Armstrong afterward. "They were rotating three of those plastic things, and they had somebody wiping them down with a rag to get the spit off. Swear to God."

"Oh that's great," Armstrong said dryly. "I really needed to hear that."

Hamilton took no chances with the mouthpiece, curling his lips protectively around his teeth to avoid saliva contact. Ullrich was more relaxed, hamming it up for the photographers, donning a stethoscope to play doctor to his teammates, seemingly intent on proving himself the loosest. What use was tension anyway? After all, most of it was on Armstrong, wasn't it?

L.A. Confidentiel was climbing the bestseller list in France (by mid-July it would rise to #2; by summer's end it would sell 65,000 copies); Walsh's face was fast becoming a regular feature on French television, along with the milkmaid visage of Emma O'Reilly. The tension had peaked at Armstrong's eve-of-Tour press conference, at which the media trolls assembled in full cry. Armstrong's entrance into the hall turned into a perp-walk frenzy as crews threw themselves in front of the walking Armstrong to create the shot they wanted: the champion on the edge, under siege.

Armstrong took a seat on stage. In the front row, twinkly and genial, sat the inquisitor himself, David Walsh. In sport jacket and khakis, Walsh looked every inch the headmaster; his white hair shone angelically in the television lights. Whispers went around the room, fingers pointed, cameramen raced to get the angle. The story was perfect, and set up as all truly good ones are: along family lines. Walsh would play the stern father, Armstrong the defiant son.

Armstrong walked to the front table, and Walsh locked eyes on him, wanting a connection. *Just tell the master what you did.* Armstrong refused to look at him. *You ain't my dad.*

Armstrong took a deep, slightly quavery breath and began by thanking the media for the thoughtful messages of support he'd received in this difficult time (at which point many of the journalists exchanged slow, incredulous double takes).

"I'll say one thing about the book, especially since the esteemed author is here," Armstrong continued. "In my view, I think extraordinary accusations must be followed up with extraordinary proof. And Mr. Walsh and Mr. Ballester worked for years, and they have not come up with extraordinary proof."

Everyone listened intently. *Extraordinary allegations deserve extraordinary proof.* An interesting statement, partly because of what it was not: namely, the sort of aggressive categorical denial Armstrong had issued in the past. Fact was, most Europeans didn't regard Walsh and Ballester's allegations as remotely extraordinary—a fact underlined just two days earlier when Armstrong's friend, world time-trial champion David Millar, admitted taking EPO after French police discovered two used vials in his Biarritz apartment.

So what did Armstrong's words mean? Were they his acknowledgment that yes, maybe this book had something in it, but on balance, not all that much? Was it also a smart way of exploiting this Euro-American divide, a knowing nod toward Europe while maintaining innocence to a more credulous America?

When Armstrong exited, the media swiftly stickle-bricked itself around Walsh, calling out questions. Walsh calmly held forth for ten minutes, laying out his case in neat bricks: *Emma O'Reilly. Stephen Swart. Pills. Syringes.*

In the corner, Johan Bruyneel observed the proceedings with a huge, sweating smile on his face. He phoned Bart Knaggs, to tell him that Walsh was here, speaking to the press. When Walsh finished (or, actually, when Tour officials hustled him from the room), Bruyneel called to the Irishman.

"Congratulations, Mr. Walsh," he said in a loud, sarcastic voice. Walsh looked up.

"Congratulations," Bruyneel repeated more loudly, his smile widening. "You must be very proud to do such work."

If Walsh heard, he pretended not to. He turned away, and walked into the cavernous press room. A moment later, Bruyneel followed.

"Let's see who else is talking to our friend," Bruyneel said, leaning in, carefully noting names and faces. He phoned Knaggs a moment later to file another report. The game was on.

The following day's papers and television reports brimmed with the story. But as time passed, Armstrong's response seemed to take hold: Walsh and Ballester's book, intriguing though it may be, lacked a smoking gun. It was interesting, yes, perhaps even fascinating. But it was not proof. The media gave a collective shrug. Time to let the real race begin.

As if to reinforce the transition, Hamilton walked into the room barely an hour later, every inch the Boy Scout. His smile took on a cat-and-canary glint when he unveiled his new time-trial bike, built by BMC. It was a showstopper, a sexy black blade of a bike, with a pièce de résistance: a one-piece headset-fork combo formed from a single piece of carbon. It looked about a second-per-mile faster than the bike Armstrong would be riding, Scott Daubert of Trek later estimated.

A tribe of aero geeks gathered and marveled at the bike, and, moreover, at Hamilton's timing. He had let Armstrong talk all spring about his top-secret bike (which Armstrong wasn't riding), then showed up toting the hottest thing on two wheels. The time-trial bike was only half of it. Hamilton, like all the contenders, planned to ride a special superlight bike for the uphill Alpe d'Huez time trial. Rumor was that BMC had built him five different superlight bikes to choose from, and that he'd tested them all on his Alpe d'Huez recon.

"Five bikes!" Giro's Toshi Corbett said incredulously. "Nobody tests five bikes!"

That wasn't all. Hamilton let it be known that he and his team had done their homework, spending two weeks reconning every mountain stage, plus all the stages in the Massif Central (which Armstrong had said he didn't do), plus the team time-trial course, plus the cobbles of stage 3 (which Armstrong had said he did by car). Hamilton raised his eyebrows meaningfully. "There are some tough stages," he said. "Anybody who didn't look at them all is going to be surprised."

Then it was Ullrich's turn. He strolled in and doffed his sweatshirt to reveal a level of skinnyness no one in the press room had seen in years. Seven years, to be exact, since he won the Tour. The rumor was that he weighed 166 pounds, four less than last year.*

Ullrich showed the press the same face he wanted to show Armstrong: calm, impassive, mildly entertained at all the fuss. Ullrich played up the contrast, smilingly referring to Armstrong as a bit of a *schauspieler,* an actor. He spoke of the Besançon time trial on the Tour's next-to-last day, the day he'd targeted so many months ago. "It could come down to just a few seconds," Ullrich predicted, reminding people of his last-gasp win in the Tour of Switzerland barely two weeks earlier.

The crowd thrilled to his words. Let the yucky doping allegations go away; this was what they wanted, heat-sculpted asses and sexy-hot bikes and last-second comebacks, the properly epic ending to the Tour's script. Everyone departed on a high.

But during that night, something happened. In days afterward, Ullrich said he'd picked up a bug from his infant daughter, but that was what everyone always said. The truth was, you could never know when it happened, only that it happened. An amoeba, a para-

---

*As with heights of basketball players, cyclists' official weights are subject to strategic manipulation—Armstrong, who weighs 163 pounds [74 kilos], is usually listed at 71 kilos, while Ullrich, who usually weighs 169 pounds [77 kilos], is listed at 74 kilos.

mecium, a squirming, cilia-fringed bacterium had somehow made its way into a warm universe named Jan Ullrich, and was now replicating itself. The truth was, a different sort of race was beginning.

Ullrich woke up the morning of the prologue feeling a little funny.

In tactical terms, the Tour prologue resembled the old carnival strength game that involved a sledgehammer and a bell. The course was barely six kilometers long, space enough only for a quick, over-the-threshold explosion. Time gaps would likely be so narrow as to be symbolic—which was precisely why the prologue mattered so much to Armstrong. Last year, he had finished seventh, seven seconds behind the leaders, a result that had opened the door for the attacks of the following days. This year's prologue was Armstrong's first opportunity to correct the situation.

In a light rain, teams set up their encampments along Boulevard d'Avroy in Liege's Pittsburgh-like downtown. According to Tour protocol, the team area was restricted to people wearing authorized badges. Which, by the looks of it, was pretty much everybody. Mullet-headed, bouquet-toting German teens chased podium girls; mink-swaddled doyennes skidded on spike heels; heavy-breathing bike geeks photographed framesets as if they were Playboy models; goggle-eyed fans hero-spotted (There's Induráin! There's Hinault! There's Merckx!), receiving the blessing of their steely impassiveness. A million cobble-faced Belgians drank, smoked, shrugged, and whoofed. Occasional Americans wandered through the melee, smiling, waving a flag in an attempt to get a football-style chant going, but they were lost in a fog of secondhand smoke, their Lance-whoops tending to peter out in desultory coughing. Cyclists picked their way through, pushing their bikes with one foot, like kids on scooters, not bothering to ass-check each other, because they knew this was the one race when everybody was on the razor.

Amid this roiling sea, most team compounds strove to become islands of calm. Phonak had arranged itself with jaunty Swiss perfection, its kitchen of love whirring happily along, with one major difference. They had set up the team's stationary rollers so the bikes faced the bus, away from the crowd. Instead of the frantic wave of humanity, the riders saw only old Ferdi Kubler staring happily at them from the spotless white backdrop of the bus. The message was clear: Tour or no Tour, they had a job to do, and they desired no distraction, no unnecessary stimulation.

The same could be said for Mayo's Euskaltel team and Ullrich's T-Mobiles, who were united in their desire to re-create some semblance of peaceful normality. After all, it didn't serve to get too amped up, to waste energy. This was the prologue. The Tour wouldn't be decided today, or probably any time during the first ten days. The goal was to be conservative, to avoid any big mistakes. No crashes, nothing stupid.

"You can't win the Tour in the first week," Hamilton had said. "But you can definitely lose it."

Over at the Postal compound, however, something else was happening. The bus and truck were parked in the customary Belgian power rectangle, but within its space whirled a new level of activity, as it was transformed into something like a clubhouse, the members of which were now being welcomed inside, a new one every few minutes.

There was Mr. Magic, aka Jeff Spencer, the team's chiropractor. Balding, bespectacled, and softspoken, Spencer toted black cases containing his formidable quiver of healing tools: cold lasers, H-wave frequency generators, thermal-imaging cameras, microcurrent generators, carbon gloves, and all manner of top-secret devices that he's not allowed to tell you about. Spencer gave Armstrong daily chiropractic treatments and served as a one-man MASH unit against tendinitis, sickness, and other injury. He was also confident: "Short of a broken leg," he said, "I don't think there's anything here we can't handle."

Next to him stood the mismatched set of bodyguards. On Spencer's right was Serge, the scowling, bullet-headed Belgian cop who used his vacation time to drive Air Force One, the unmarked, tinted-windowed Subaru that served as Armstrong's getaway vehicle (for speed's sake, Armstrong never rides the team bus during the tour, though he goes there before stages). Serge enjoyed his work, never more so than when he got to tackle someone or blast through fervent lines of Lance's fans. His approach to driving was similar. "Hey, I haven't killed anybody," he said. "This week."

To Serge's right stood Erwin, whose full title was Mataas Na Guro Erwin M. Ballarta, of the Pekiti-Tirsia School of Kali martial arts. Like most trained killers, Ballarta radiated the menace of a kindergarten teacher. He worked as George W. Bush's bodyguard when Bush governed Texas, and now taught martial arts to cops. He favored baggy clothing, and said things like "Guns are redundant," though it was unlikely that Christian and Frederic, the two plain-clothes gendarmes provided by the Tour, would agree. ("Those two are sharpshooters," Armstrong told me later. "Badasses.")

There was Elvio, Postal's Italian *soigneur*, chatting up some of the lovelies near the ropes. Elvio, a tall, high-cheekboned twen-tysomething, was known for his social skills with the podium girls; in fact, it was Elvio who had helped broker the meeting between George Hincapie and his now-girlfriend last year. This year, Elvio was looking to set a record of his own. "Five," he said, pushing his sunglasses back. "Lance's record is five, and my own record is also five. So, you see, we both are making history."

Gliding through the mix were the guys from Capital Sports & Entertainment and Tailwind Sports, the joint companies that owned the team and represented Armstrong. The CS&E boys, as they were known, emanated an effortlessly casual vibe that is only possible when young, confident people come into contact with deep rivers of money and power. They were easy to spot. They wore large, complicated watches, drapey sport shirts, and identical blue Nikes. They addressed everyone, including the heads of multimillion-dollar corporations, as either "Bro" or "Dude"—not out of disrespect, but out of honor. Here, inside the gravitational field of Planet Lance, there *were* only Bros and Dudes (especially women). How else can you signify the marvelous tin-gle of fraternity you felt by being part of Armstrong's crew at the Tour? The math itself was inspiring, staggering: each time Armstrong rode the Tour, his story was told anew; his logoed image was seen by billions; and sales went up. Plus, there was the cancer work, to which every

company here contributed generously and which added to the rare
feeling of being part of something, the kismet of golden American
hope. But the buzz of being a Bro wasn't about money or good causes,
rather it was about being. They were young, good-looking, and they
could feel the pleasing tickle of vast subterranean rivers of money rush-
ing just beneath their feet. They felt lucky, so deliciously chosen, as if
they'd accidentally discovered a secret room that held all their best
friends! Here in freaking Belgium! With Lance! *Dude*! (And beneath it
all vibrated the ghastly, unspoken gut-fear that if Armstrong got sick, or
crashed, or, sweet Jesus, tested positive, this fabulous clubhouse, and,
more important, this feeling would vanish like a mirage—*poof*.)

But enough about that—there's Toshi from Giro and Burke and
Zap from Trek and all the OLN Bros (who might be a television network, sure, but they're Bros first, and team sponsors to boot), and a
steady rotation of Nike and Oakley Dudes, most of them bearing
new shoes or wheels or sunglasses with MP3 players built in, lined
up like magi to offer some new Shit, and to exchange knowing
pleasantries with Sheryl Crow, aka Juanita Cuervo (who's looking
positively glam in a belted white overcoat, a regular *dame blanche*).

Presiding over this clubhouse was the man who was generating
that river of money. Armstrong rode the stationary trainer, concentrating but also watching what was going on around him, ambush-
ing people with a friendly wink or a nod, enjoying the feeling of
each element slipping and locking into place, like the blades of a
Swiss Army knife. Unlike his rivals, Armstrong did not wish to shut
out the Tour's million-footed animal energy—to the contrary. He
wished to match it, to create a tool to correspond with each of its
dangers, each of its distractions. Armstrong rode, feeling his body
warm up, feeling his heart rev. He felt good. He felt . . . normal.

Here, then, was one advantage Armstrong held over his rivals.
He was the only one for whom the Tour, in all its frantic, fantastic
craziness, bore resemblance to everyday life.

Five minutes before their appointed start time, each of the contenders went to a holding pen just behind the start ramp. As Hamil-

ton launched, Armstrong entered the pen and encountered Krohme, Ullrich's physiotherapist. She wished Armstrong a good Tour. Armstrong responded by beaming her The Look.

"He stared at me as if he wanted to eliminate me," Krohme said later, her eyes wide with indignation. "Why? This is not Rome, we are not gladiators. We do not have to kill anyone."

When Krohme saw Armstrong aiming The Look at Ullrich as well, she took Ullrich's arm.

"Pssssh," Krohme whispered dismissively. "This is all American stuff. It's nothing."

Ullrich nodded calmly. It was nothing to him now, distant static. He had his talent, he had his form, he had his Walser narrow bike. He walked the bike to the start house, a silver, inflatable, clamshell-looking apparatus that was meant to invoke the mythological scallop on which the goddess Venus came to earth, but which, in fact, looked like an exploding packet of hot dogs.

The starter counted down. Ullrich breathed, and the muscles in his abdomen twitched, snakelike. He cleared his throat. He had gotten a report from a teammate, Ivanov, who had nearly fallen on the course's turnaround. Ullrich suddenly looked nervous.

Ullrich launched, and a minute later, to a smattering of cheers and boos, Armstrong chased. They raced along the twisty streets of Liege; Ullrich churning his big gear steadily, Armstrong flashing the more emotive violence of his high cadence. The best time had been set earlier in the day by a big Swiss twenty-three-year-old named Fabian Cancellara. Ullrich rolled through the intermediate check ten seconds down on Cancellara. He reached the U-turn where Ivanov had almost fallen. "Go slow, go slow," his team director, Mario Kummer, reminded him.

Behind Ullrich, Armstrong was gaining. He passed the timecheck only two seconds off Cancellara's time. He glided around the U-turn and headed for the line, his teeth showing, Bruyneel shouting in his ear that he was close, close, close. Armstrong flew across the line, missing Cancellara's time by two seconds, and visibly pissed off.

His anger soon abated. Armstrong had put fifteen seconds on Ullrich, sixteen on Hamilton, nineteen on Mayo. Small margins, perhaps, but they were achieved in barely six kilometers. Back at the bus, the Dudes and Bros high-fived. Armstrong returned for his customary half-hour warmdown on the roller, looking happy and relieved. He laid a smooch on Juanita, then held court as he did his warmdown. In London, the bookies lengthened Ullrich's odds to 2.8:1 from 2:1. Armstrong's odds were shortened from to 1.6:1 from 1.9:1. The bell had been rung.

"The important thing is, how does it feel?" Armstrong said. "I was very comfortable. I felt strong, and that feels good. For all the people who said, 'I don't know about Lance Armstrong'—you know, I was also one of those. I had serious doubts the night of Mont Ventoux. I was also at home thinking, what the hell happened? So I don't blame anybody for thinking that. It was huge to have a big ride."

Bruyneel elaborated. "The point is not only how it makes you feel, it is how it makes them feel. To lose so much time in a short prologue, to finish tenth in front of everyone. They think about this a long time."

Postal's Belgians had a gesture they used to signal when Armstrong did something big. They would hold an invisible jackknife in their fingertips, then casually slip the blade into the invisible victim's ribs, giving the handle a parting twist. Now, back at Postal's bus, radiantly smiling Belgians stabbed one another with enthusiasm; the clubhouse party rolled on.

The contenders pretended not to feel the cut, of course. Each issued nearly identical statements—a few seconds don't matter, the Tour is three weeks long, etc. But privately, they felt differently. They had hoped to do better, and when those hopes went unanswered—when they were stomped out by Armstrong—something changed inside them.

"This touches Jan deeply," said former teammate Jens Heppner, who used to room with Ullrich. "He does not show it, but it does."

Michele Ferrari was not one to believe in metaphysics, but he did believe in math. Watching the prologue from his favorite chair in Italy, Ferrari was pleased, but also puzzled. Not at Armstrong, whose performance ranked as normal, but at Ullrich. Fifteen seconds over six kilometers? More than two seconds per kilometer?

"It should have been closer," Dr. Evil said, sounding almost concerned. "Perhaps there is something else going on."

That night, Ullrich's cold worsened. Krohme prepared one of her patented remedies: a dish of Chinese mint oil and chamomile tea, heated by candles. Ullrich inhaled the steam from beneath a towel. He said he felt better, but later that night, Krohme heard Ullrich coughing.

Concerned, T-Mobile's doctors huddled. A cough might mean an infection, and an infection meant performance would go down. They had the option of killing the infection with antibiotics, but then again, antibiotics would also cause a more lasting dip in performance, possibly for three or four days, maybe longer.

After some discussion, the doctors decided to hold off on antibiotics. The mountains where the Tour would be decided were still almost two weeks off. By then, maybe, his immune system would have taken care of things.

Though perhaps they would have been less worried if they had witnessed an event that took place at the Postal bus just before the prologue. Because Sheryl Crow had sneezed.

Not a big sneeze, to be sure, half-concealed behind the swift white curtain of her coat sleeve. But a sneeze, an indisputable *a-choo*, and when she sneezed, several Postal *soigneurs* raised their heads with the slow alertness of gazelles who just heard a lion rustling in the brush. Nobody said anything, of course. But the sneeze was noted, along with a new scratchiness in that Grammy-winning voice, a wet shine in her lovely eyes. The Belgians cut glances at each other and shrug-whoofed. There could be no disputing it: Juanita Cuervo had the sniffles.

When Crow kissed Armstrong after the prologue, one of Postal's *soigneurs* winced.

CHAPTER 21

BELGIAN TOOTHPASTE

"A crash is much more than a crash."

—MICHELE FERRARI

Bike racers know mud. Riding in all weather, pelted in wheel-wash, racers learn geography by taste: the reddish, grainy gruel of Spain, the pale, salty grit of Brittany, the rich muck of Provence. During the first two rain-spattered days of the Tour, Iban Mayo's elegant face wrinkled with disgust as he was treated to his first taste of Belgian toothpaste.

"Belgian toothpaste" is the cyclists' name for the distinctive brown ooze extruded by the lowlands when it rains, which is often. It is neither mud nor dirt, but rather a tangy mix of rain, diesel, fertilizer, and million-year-old glacial silt, a primeval petrochemical butter that coats the roads and rims the curbs and makes the lips faintly numb. Belgian toothpaste is hated for many worthwhile reasons, but the main reason Mayo hated it was that it apparently hated him.

The toothpaste was everywhere, defiling the gleaming frame of Mayo's orange bike, spattering in his delicate curls, flying up his aquiline nostrils, showering him with such a jet blast of slime that it seemed as if the earth itself were sneezing. To defend himself against the onslaught, Mayo swathed his skinny body in legwarmers, armwarmers, caps, and jackets. It didn't help. Unlike some of the bigger riders, Mayo lacked the body fat to stay warm. Worst of all, however, was how uneasy the toothpaste made his bike handle, almost as if he were drunk. Tires skidded unexpectedly. Routine turns had the feeling of adventure.

All around him, riders were crashing. The first happened even before the race began, when the unlucky Matt White skidded on a wet cable-cover and broke his collarbone. But that was just the overture to what would be a one-week symphony of toothpaste-lubricated crashes, the sound of which became familiar: a nervous rattle, the papery crumple of expensive carbon, and the soft sound of bodies hitting wet pavement. Thud—Gian Matteo Fagnini breaks a collarbone. Thud—Frederic Bessy tweaks a knee. Thud—Alessandro Petacchi breaks a rib. Postal's rookie, the doe-eyed Benjamin Noval, decorated both hips with a macrame of road rash and hematomas. By the third day, Kurt Asle Arvesen's limbs were wrapped in so many white bandages he looked as if he'd been poorly mummified. The real problems, of course, happened afterward. Crashes threw joints out of whack and caused hormonal imbalances. Energy had to be diverted to regrow skin, heal ligaments, and repair muscle. Ferrari had it all calculated: a hard crash lowered threshold by around 10 percent for a few days afterward. Birdlike climbers, of course, paid more.

A fast, nervous race, the commentators murmured. It was fast because all the contenders and their teams wanted to be in front to avoid crashes. This meant Postal, Phonak, T-Mobile, Euskaltel, and a few others. But since the road wasn't wide enough to hold all of them, riders were forced to go faster—cycling's version of fluid dynamics. The speed created crashes, which, in turn, created more speed, as teams tried ever harder to avoid the crashes. By the end of the first week, the Tour was averaging a dozen crashes and one broken bone a day, and was 8 percent faster than last year's race, which had been the fastest in history.

Thanks to the cruel magic of physics, that relatively small increase in speed meant a huge increase in effort.* Going 8 percent

---

*Not to get too mathematical, but here's why: velocity has one dimension, while air, possessing volume, has three. Increasing speed by a factor of two (say, from 15 to 30 mph) means pushing eight times the amount of air ($2 \times 2 \times 2 = 8$) and thus spending eight times the energy. Which is why a sixth-grader can ride 15 mph on a flat road, while only certified badasses can reach 30 mph. This is also, incidentally, why pro bikers are so impressed by seemingly tiny differences in prologue times, since they represent much larger differences in raw power.

faster meant pushing 25 percent more air, thus doing 25 percent more work, burning 25 percent more energy. The cold and rain increased the workload. All of which added up to perhaps the most energy-expensive first week in Tour history.

"It's insane," said Swedish rider Magnus Backstedt, who had won this year's Paris-Roubaix, generally considered the toughest one-day race. "People are struggling just to hang on to a wheel. It can't keep up like this."

Each contender wanted to be in the front and avoid crashes, but each took a different approach to staying there. Ullrich, with baby-duck humility, simply rode behind Armstrong, tethering himself to the American's wheel. *If he crashes, I crash,* seemed to be the thinking. Hamilton and Mayo, on the other hand, used their teammates to carve out space in the front, and to make a point. They would not simply bow before the god of kilowatts; they would ride their own race.

The morning of stage 3, Mayo was relieved to see blue skies. This was the stage he'd been fearing, the 210-kilometer run from Waterloo to Wasquehal. While the media spent most of its energy weaving Napoleonic metaphor, the real reasons for Mayo's and every other rider's concern were two cobbled stretches of the course. They weren't long, about 4 kilometers in all. But they were cobbles, and cobbles, as any cyclist knew, had a way of turning into tombstones.

"Kinderkopke," the Belgies called them—the children's heads. These particular children had been arranged in an especially unruly pattern, the road edges sunk by years of oxcart wheels, the central spine elevated by frost heaves, forcing riders to go single-file, balancing on the slippery central hump. One German rider had calculated that racing across cobbles was exactly equivalent, energy-wise, to racing up an Alp. But energy didn't concern Mayo or the others so much as crashing. To crash on cobbles, or to be caught behind a crash would mean losing time, lots of time. The roads were narrow; the team car couldn't get to you quickly. A feeling began to grow: this would be a day for culling. But who would be culled?

At the start in Waterloo, nervous riders gathered according to nationality—a klatch of Eastern Bloc boys detachedly comparing scars; a few Italians soothing their nerves with a round of girlspotting, the Germans adjusting their shorts to prevent any disorderly tan lines. The Basques of Euskaltel-Euskadi huddled in a tight orange circle, front wheels pointed in as if around an invisible campfire. They yammered brightly in their indecipherable tongue. They'd made it through the first two stages without incident. The team had been strong, riding near the front, despite having lost one rider, Gorka González, just before the Tour, when his hematocrit exceeded the 50 percent limit. But that was ancient history. They chatted, gesturing at the perfect Basque-blue skies, and at God who would now permit His justice to be done.

Like every other team, Euskaltel had a strategy for the cobbles, starting with the bikes. They would ride heavier wheels and thicker tires. They would stay near the front at all costs as they approached the cobbled stretches. They would ride in two groups, one containing Mayo and the other Haimar Zubeldia, the team's other talented climber, to minimize the odds of losing both in a single crash. In addition, Mayo would keep close to Iker Flores, who was roughly the same size. In case of a mechanical problem or a crash, Mayo could grab Flores's bike and ride on.

Standing amid a green bloom of Phonaks, Tyler Hamilton was worried. This stage reminded him of the key moment in the 1999 Tour, a crossing of the Passage du Gois, a beach road that was periodically submerged by the tide. The road had been slimy with algae and kelp; the peloton was nervous. There'd been a crash, and several contenders were caught behind it and lost six minutes on the day.

Hamilton had spoken to the team on the bus, fixing each of them with his green eyes, laying it out. This was their first big test, he said. He told them about the Passage du Gois; he reminded them how Tours can be lost in a single instant. They would not be caught behind, not today; nor would they simply ride behind Postal. He took a sip of his lucky water. He checked his jersey for his vial of lucky salt.

Forty kilometers before the cobbles, the race started speeding up. Postal, Phonak, and T-Mobile put on testing surges. Each group of leaders fought to the front. Elbows were thrown, saddles pushed. The speed increased to 25, 30, 35 miles per hour—small increases in velocity, gigantic increases in effort. The pack's fishlike shape lengthened and stretched. They reached 40 mph, a full sprint.

"There were guys going left and right, guys yelling and screaming," Armstrong said later. "I've never seen anything like it at the Tour."

Nine kilometers from the cobbles, the road straightened into a broad highway that cut through some wheatfields. Postal seized the lead, led by Padrnos, Ekimov, and, on the front, Noval, who was trying to make up for his falls of the first two days. Mayo, perhaps seeking a respite, drifted back and left. There was a brief moment of relaxation as Postal took control, a sense of natural order asserting itself.

Then, on the right, Phonak launched a savage acceleration. Led by Oscar Pereiro, Hamilton surged past the Postals as if they were standing still. Watching Pereiro go by, Noval dropped his head and shook it dispiritedly. He was cooked; he could not match this. The rookie pulled out of line and drifted back and left as if he'd tossed out an anchor.

Behind them, the peloton flexed and moved, as if hit by a jolt of adrenaline. As the exhausted Noval fell back, the peloton flowed into the space Phonak had vacated on the right. Noval suddenly found himself next to someone in orange. Handlebars touched.

A bright crumple of metal, a thudding of bodies. Seven riders on the clean French pavement, scattered in various postures of surprise. In a ditch to the left, a big Italian named Marco Velo lay on his back, bewildered, touching the growing red stain on his shoulder. He'd fractured his collarbone and fallen on a broken bottle, opening a gash that would require eighty stitches. To the right, held up by the crash, stood the yellow jersey, Norwegian Thor Hushovd.

Next to Noval, Mayo stood up shakily, checking his body for injuries. His shorts were torn on the left side, a burn mark on fish-pale skin. Mayo stood for a moment, disoriented, his mind slowly accepting the reality of the crash.

Ahead, Bruyneel was already shouting the news into his team's ear-pieces: Mayo's down, Mayo's down. Though traditional race chivalry dictated that the leaders slow so that the yellow jersey can catch up, the leaders kept going, surging toward the cobbles, increasing their speed.

Mayo moved shakily. A teammate helped him put his chain back on, and he pedaled off, shaking his head. His team dropped back to help, including Zubeldia, who'd avoided the crash. Euskaltel's strategy of dividing the two contenders was abandoned—this was an emergency; they needed every watt to propel Mayo back with the front group. The team dropped into a disciplined line, leading the several dozen riders who'd been gapped. They were a minute down; getting back would be hard, but they would do it. They were Basques, after all. They upped their speed to 30, then 35 miles per hour. Their director, Julian Gorospe, spoke to them calmly. "*Sangre frio*," he said. "*Venga venga venga.*"

Mayo rode with blind intensity, taking his turns in the lead. He could see the dust up ahead as the lead group hit the first stretch of cobbles. He could imagine what was happening: Hincapie and Eki leading Armstrong onto the first section, with Ullrich right behind and Hamilton not much farther back.

They chased. For half an hour, an hour, the Basques led the group. Up ahead, they could see the helicopter, the distant rumble of the crowd. Up ahead, the Phonaks and Postals and T-Mobiles were still fighting for the lead, pushing the pace higher and higher. Each time check showed the Basques falling back. Now 1:15, now 1:25.

On the second section of cobbles, twenty-five kilometers from the finish, Mayo's pedaling lost its elegance. The adrenaline from the crash gone, his toes-down style devolved into a Neanderthalish churn. His shorts were wet with blood, his face twitching and grimacing, his tongue wandering. He was six hundred miles from the Pyrenees. He looked hungry and cold and alone.

They rode the last kilometers without speaking.

Mayo crossed the line 3:48 behind Armstrong, Ullrich, and Hamilton, a full minute lost in the final ten kilometers. Four minutes was too much time to make up in the mountains, given Mayo's likely losses in the time trials. His hopes for winning the overall were gone, and for that he and the Spanish press blamed Armstrong and the other leaders, who rode so hard after the crash.

"That was unfortunate for [Mayo] to crash at that time," Armstrong replied. "Had it been thirty kilometers before that? I am sure it would have been no problem. He would have made it back and started the cobbles near the front and stayed and not lost any time. But ten kilometers before a critical section in any bike race, nobody waits."

Other riders expressed sympathy for Mayo, particularly Hamilton. What a shame, they said, to work so hard for a year and have it all go away in the twitch of a random crash. Even if, deep down, it wasn't random at all.

Everybody knew it. Mayo had lost concentration, hadn't forced his team to stay on the front, hadn't anticipated Phonak's aggression, had allowed Noval (who was at that moment the most dangerous of riders, an exhausted rookie) drift too close. No matter how you cut it, Mayo had screwed up. What had anyone expected, after all? That a skinny Spanish climber would come to the north country, that some flamenco dancer could ride cobbles with the hard men, eat Belgian toothpaste and like it? The cycling nation gave a collective shrug-whoof.

At first Mayo complained about being left behind, blaming Armstrong, who surely could have slowed things down with a word, a gesture. Then he gradually understood. Mayo vowed his revenge, spoke of reloading his shotgun. He would attack in the mountains.

"The Tour doesn't forgive," Mayo said.

Left unspoken was the second half of his sentiment: Neither do I.

Armstrong's daily mood during the Tour could be gauged by examining the expression of his Belgian bodyguard, Serge. When things were normal, Serge's face tended to assume its natural scowl. But when things were nervous, Serge smiled and joked. As Armstrong climbed out of Air Force One in Cambrai's main square for the stage 4 team time trial, Serge's face was cracked with a huge, manic grin.

"Hey-ho," Serge said, looking at the threatening sky as Armstrong stalked wordlessly to the bus. "Beautiful day today, eh?"

The crashing and the bad weather were taking their toll, both on the team and on Armstrong. The cobbles had gone well, but the race remained dangerously unstable, with ten days to go before the mountains. Here, in the part of northern France that most resembled Nebraska, Armstrong would try to pick up where he left off in the prologue.

Complicating things, Armstrong had a slight cough—his usual hack, he called it. The *soigneurs* watched him closely, looking for signs of sickness. They saw none; Sheryl Crow, too, had seemed better since her sneeze.

"Everyone is good, very healthy," said Postal *soigneur* Freddy Viane. "Very, very good and healthy and totally perfect."

Stages 4 and 5 formed the strategic linchpin of Armstrong's first two weeks. In stage 4, the team time trial, Armstrong would try to win the yellow jersey. In stage 5, a conventional flat stage, he would give it away.

If the second part sounded strange, it was due to the nature of the Tour. To defend the yellow jersey meant to lead the peloton, and to lead the peloton meant to spend energy. Postal was strong, but not even the god of kilowatts possessed the strength to control a race for three weeks. Therefore, Postal wanted—no, needed—someone else to win the jersey, someone whose team could shoulder its burden, take the glory, and do the accompanying work. The trick was finding someone who was strong enough to wear yellow for a few days, but not so strong that they were a threat to win the race.

First, however, came the matter of winning the jersey. When Postal rolled together off the start line in Cambrai, the rain, which had been falling steadily all morning, started to pound. In the start area, the podium girls huddled together beneath a small tent in the middle of a rising lake. Outside town, wheatfields hissed and rolled in oceanic waves.

Eki led the team out, in the order they'd practiced in the Pyrenees. On the radio, Bruyneel reminded them of their strategy. Progressive, he kept saying, which meant to make a slow start, and speed up as they went along. Going last, a privilege earned by having the most top riders in the prologue, Postal would know where they stood at all time checks. No surprises.

The team time trial was a specialty event: all nine riders racing as a unit, all riders who finished together given the same time. It was one of Armstrong's favorite events, made more so by the fact that it usually yielded nice time gains on his rivals. The previous year, the team time trial had given Armstrong forty-three seconds of his 1:01 winning margin over Ullrich and a whopping 3:22 on Mayo and his team of skinny Basques. The Tour de France organization, desiring to lessen that advantage, took the extraordinary step of socializing the event for 2004. The second-place team, regardless of where they finished on the clock, would lose only twenty seconds to the first-place team. The third-place team would lose thirty, the fourth-place forty, and so on. The event, in some ways, would be less a chance to gain time and more a chance for top teams to demonstrate strength (or, as some pointed out, for weak teams to effectively take the day off).

The wind picked up; the rain blew horizontal. Ten kilometers in, Postal hit the first time check. Bruyneel's voice came over the team headsets, low with concern.

"We are twenty-seven seconds behind T-Mobile, twenty-seven seconds behind T-Mobile. Come on boys, come on."*

Up ahead, however, almost every other team was having concerns of their own. The weather was causing a string of crashes and punctures. Riders were being dropped, which slowed each team down since there would be fewer riders to share the work. T-Mobile lost Ivanov, their goombah. On a seemingly harmless turn, three CSC riders hit the deck, skidding and spinning comically, still attached to their bikes. But nobody was having a worse time than Hamilton's Phonak team.

This was supposed to be Hamilton's day, the day for his team to show their strength. However, Phonak had a handicap. Every other team was running wider, twenty-one-millimeter tires to handle the weather and the debris washing over the road. But when Phonak's mechanics tried to put the safer tires on their sleek, new time trial

---

*In-race quotations come from two sources: Interviews with Bruyneel or, more often, a tiny camera and microphone that was mounted in Postal's team car for planned use in *The Lance Chronicles*. For a variety of reasons, the program never aired, but OLN and Bruyneel granted me access to the tapes.

bikes, the rubber came dangerously close to rubbing against the top of the fork. The bike had been designed to run with thin-walled, nineteen-millimeter high-pressure tires, and nothing wider. The Swiss had outdone themselves. As the team rolled out, one of the mechanics made the sign of the cross.

What happened next sounded like popcorn popping. Phonak's first tire blew at the thirteen-kilometer mark. The second and third followed shortly after, forcing the team to decide whether it would be worthwhile to wait for the unlucky riders. Chaos ensued. Another tire blew. When Santi Perez's handlebars worked loose, Phonak's director, Alvaro Pino, ordered the team to go on; Hamilton, fearing they would not finish with the required five riders, yelled at them to wait, then came to a near-stop on the road. They were not yet halfway through the race.

"Phonak's only six guys," Bruyneel radioed his team. "We're going to make up time [on them]."

After the first time-check, Postal accelerated. Noval, still shaken from his crashing of the first few days, was dropped; the team did not look back. They drove hard through the storm, Armstrong taking long pulls at the front. The god of kilowatts showed himself, riding smoothly, obediently, powerfully.

"We're going unbelievably good, boys, we're going fucking fast!" Bruyneel shouted. "The blue train is rolling."

By the time they crossed the line, they'd gained 1:19 on T-Mobile and 1:07 on Phonak. Though the gains would be reduced by the rules, the impact remained. The most visible part of it was the yellow jersey being placed on Armstrong's back at day's end, proof that part one of their strategy had worked.

"If twenty seconds is what we get, that's what we get," Armstrong said. "I think the only consolation is that we had by far the strongest team."

Hamilton, though disappointed, located the silver lining. His team had a nightmare day, finished with the minimum five riders, and still finished second. He added up the delays—thirty seconds here, forty-five seconds there. What had they lost by?

"You do the math," Hamilton said, raising his eyebrows. Plus, there were other signs that their fortunes were starting to shift. The previous day, Hamilton's bike had blown a tire moments after he'd crossed the line. Examination revealed a slit in the tire's sidewall, a slit that could have given way during the race, perhaps even on the cobbles. If the tire had blown there, Hamilton's chances, like Mayo's, might have ended.

"Pretty lucky, huh?" Hamilton said.

The first half hour of the following day, stage 5 from Amiens to Chartres, resembled a Broadway casting call. From the gun, riders raced out of the peloton, auditioning for the breakaway that would likely carry a new yellow jersey holder. Bruyneel squinted into the television monitor in the team car, swatting the riders away by ordering his team to chase down any that he deemed too dangerous, too big, or too unpredictable.

Finally, after ten auditions, Bruyneel found what he wanted: a tidy break of five, neither too big nor too small, which contained no contenders, no scary climbers, and whose highest-placed rider was a twenty-five-year-old Frenchman named Thomas Voeckler, from the Brioches la Boulangerè team, who had recently won the French championship.

"It was an ideal scenario," Bruyneel said. "Young guy, French champion, from a strong French team. Also a team looking for a sponsor for next year, wanting to show itself."

Bruyneel had no way of knowing how perfect Voeckler and his BLB team would prove to be. Sure, Voeckler was young and handsome and well spoken, but the next few days would show that beneath his pleasant exterior lay a true hard boy, one of the brotherhood. French-born, Voeckler had been raised in remote Martinique, the son of a sailing family. Even better, he possessed the requisite family tragedy (father, ocean-crossing, body never found),* and had

---

*After one has watched a lot of bike races, it becomes clear that there's a strong correlation between family tragedies and epic performances. As the dark joke goes, a rider doesn't need to train so much as he needs to have a loved one die at the proper time. Examples in the 2004 Tour would include stage 5 (Stuart O'Grady—grandfather), stage 10 (Richard Virenque—grandmother) and stage 12 (Ivan Basso—mother's cancer diagnosis). One of the more famous recent examples was provided by Armstrong, who won a stage in 1995 after teammate Fabio

come to France as a teenager, to race bikes, to dream of the yellow jersey. He may have looked ordinary, but he rode with sharp teeth.

That's the one, Bruyneel said, and ordered Postal to back slightly off the pace. The knowledge passed through the peloton: the break had gone. The lucky ones had made it.

The rest of the stage, however, wasn't quite so ideal. The crashing started again almost immediately, as four Postal riders—Rubiera, Azevedo, Beltran, and the seemingly cursed Noval—slammed to the pavement at kilometer 101. Two hours later, Beltran went down again, and the breakaway's lead grew to fourteen minutes—too much, by Bruyneel and Armstrong's estimation.

Bruyneel ordered the Postals to the front, promising them that it would be the last work they would have to do for a week. By the end, the lead was down to a still-substantial 9:35 over Armstrong, who was now in sixth overall, thirty-six seconds up on Hamilton and fifty-five seconds ahead of Ullrich.

After the stage, Bruyneel was pleased: part two of their strategy was accomplished, the yellow jersey had a new owner, and Postal had an opportunity to rest before the mountains. When asked about the crashes, he loosed a series of shrug-whoofs. Beltran? Oh, he touched the floor, but he was fine. Rubiera? Fine. Noval? Looking stronger all the time.

"No bandages," Bruyneel said. "So bad news for the Germans."

In truth, there were bandages; plenty of them. Rubiera's calf bristled with nineteen stitches, courtesy of a chain ring. Beltran's elbow was similarly decorated; his crash would so weaken the normally strong climber that he'd be among the first riders dropped when the race reached the mountains. Eki was limping around the hotel with a bag of ice on his leg. Noval, who had broken down in tears after the team time trial, looked like a victim of shell shock. The hotel resembled a MASH unit in triage mode, as Mr. Magic beamed his lasers and electrodes and applied his carbon healing gloves.

Casartelli was killed in a crash. Another was Bruyneel, who lost his father in a biking accident a few weeks before the 1993 Tour, then broke away to win what was then the fastest stage in history. "He rode in a trance," his brother Alain said.

The next morning, weary of crashes, Bruyneel and Armstrong changed their strategy. Rather than contest the finish and risk a crash, Armstrong would try to ride about fifty riders back from the front. The sweet spot, they called it, the sugar being the extra microsecond of reaction time in the event of a crash.

Armstrong had other reasons to be cautious. In 2001, after Armstrong had won his third Tour, he had approved a bonus system for his Tailwind contract that called for escalating payments on each Tour win. The bonuses had been $3 million in 2002, $6 million in 2003, and stood to be $10 million in 2004. (This would be in addition to the bonuses built into his contracts with Nike, Trek, and Oakley.)

"The stakes were very high," Armstrong said later, referring to the bonus. "Nobody knew how high; and it was on my mind for 365 days, aside from trying to make history. And regardless of whether money means anything to you or not, $10 million is a lot of money. I don't need it, but just having that out there, I thought, God, what if I fall over and break my collarbone. I'm lying there and thinking, I just lost $10 million."

Ironically, Armstrong had his first crash the following day. He was riding next to Voeckler eight kilometers from the start when riders fell in front of him, victims of leftover Belgian toothpaste. He braked, then went over at low speed, cutting his leg and arm slightly. Not a hard crash, but it didn't matter. Armstrong leapt up and chased the peloton, his face grim, his legs churning with fury.

"Things are perfect," Armstrong said.

The first week of racing ended with a flat stage along the Loire Valley, capped by an uphill sprint finish in Angers. As the peloton approached the final kilometer, Tyler Hamilton spun along near the front, his head up, alert. It had been another fast, slippery stage, windy and rainy, and he'd be relieved to have it over with.

The peloton came in fast down the Rue de Maine, all eyes rising toward the inflatable blue arch at the one-kilometer-to-go line. The arch, from which hung the traditional red pennant, marked the boundary of the most dangerous spot on the Tour landscape. Here was where the sprinters took over in all their primal, telegenic, crash-filled glory, each of them aware that victory here would make their season, next year's salary, to say nothing of their career. Here was bike racing at its purest: a group of poor, superstitious small-town boys fighting for money and immortality. So pervasive was the accompanying danger that the Tour had adopted a special rule: riders who crashed inside the one-kilometer mark were not penalized but given the same finishing time as the group leaders.

Ahead, several gendarmes stood nobly at the footings of the blue arch, as if guarding them. To accommodate the arch, Tour organizers had scooted the steel barricades one foot into the blacktop on either side. The road, normally twenty feet wide, now contained a choke point eighteen feet wide. From their post, the gendarmes leaned out into the road as the riders approached, pleased at their fine vantage.

Armstrong was riding in accordance with his new conservative strategy, about forty riders back, behind teammate Hincapie. Ullrich trailed him, as usual. Hamilton rode closer to the front, four teammates deployed in front and behind him. Hamilton glanced around, checking on Armstrong and Ullrich, seeing the arch, feeling the frenzy begin.

People drummed on signs that hung on the barricades. Overhead, the television chopper thwocked. The sprinters moved up to the front, darting and shifting, fighting for space, a chance. A thought slipped through Hamilton's mind: *Somebody's going to crash.*

To Hamilton's left rode a big Austrian sprinter named René Haselbacher, of the Gerolsteiner team. Haselbacher was a flamboyant personality with a history of causing crashes. He'd done it at last year's Tour, somersaulting down the barriers and shredding the seat of his shorts. Two days earlier, he had stayed at the same hotel as Phonak, drawing Hamilton's eye as Haselbacher walked across the lobby for breakfast. Hamilton had smiled, as most people did when Haselbacher walked past—or, rather, strutted past, his bleached hair piled high, his pirate earrings dangling, his musketeer mustache freshly trimmed, his swashbuckling, death-defying, sex-god mojo radiating. He sure was a character, that Haselbacher (and, just as surely, a poor, ambitious kid from some podunk town).

A second before they reached the arch, Haselbacher moved up and accelerated, followed by teammate Danilo Hondo. The right was jammed, but the left looked open, or at least more open. This was Haselbacher's chance. He saw a space, a few inches of daylight, and dove into it. The gendarmes raised their hands.

The sounds came first: A dull clang as Haselbacher's body hit the barricades, followed by a rolling crunch, the harsh rip of tearing carbon and bending aluminum, the firecrackers of exploding tires, the soft percussion of bodies. Viewed from the front, it was as if a cannonball passed through the peloton, sending up a spume of atomized fabric, metal, and flesh.

Hamilton saw it coming and braked hard, knowing it was too late. His front wheel hit something solid. His next awareness was of being in the air, upside down, seeing his wheels spin against gray sky. Forty miles per hour of velocity was efficiently converted to rotational momentum, whipping his 130 pounds up, around, and down onto his lower back. He skidded a few feet along the pavement and then lay there, stunned. When he moved his head, his helmet made a crackling sound. His left foot was still clipped in its pedal.

A few yards to Hamilton's right, on the fringe of the impact zone, Armstrong managed to stop on top of the fallen Hincapie, who was unhurt. Hincapie alertly pointed up to the red flag—no penalty. Just to be safe, Armstrong hitched up one leg of his shorts, so that any watching official would think he had crashed. Ullrich, who was safely to Armstrong's right, made it through similarly unscathed.

The pack trickled grimly across the line. Beyond generous helpings of road rash and hematoma, the initial toll was considered rather mild: Gilberto Simoni suffered a mild concussion, Jens Voigt compacted his neck, Robbie McEwen suffered percussion fractures to two vertebrae, Mayo severely bruised his elbow, Christian Vande Velde was slashed by a chain ring, Oscar Pereiro and Paulo Bettini dislocated fingers, Bobby Julich injured his hip and lower back, and

Nicholas Jalabert bruised his testicles. Haselbacher's panache was rewarded with three doubly fractured ribs, a broken nose, and kidney and liver injuries. He would remain in an Angers hospital for three days, unable to be moved. He was the ninty-ninth rider to crash in the first week of the 2004 Tour, and the twelfth to abandon.

Armstrong's anger showed immediately, directed at race organizers. "The barriers were really tight and everybody's going forty miles per hour," he said. "I don't know what the hell they were thinking."

Hamilton rode wordlessly across the line accompanied by three teammates, his face a dark cloud. He kept his composure as he put his bike away, unbuckled his helmet to examine the cracks. Head down, he mounted the steps of the Love Bus.

Later, Hamilton would troop gamely before the press and his team, trying to convince them and himself that this was nothing, a little scrape. Just a spot of bad luck, one that could've happened to Armstrong (who was only a few feet away) but which had happened to him (again). He would smile politely and raise his eyebrows knowingly, and everybody would be reminded of last year's broken collarbone, of the teeth ground down to their nerves, of a man who let his legs do the talking—this was Tyler the Tough, after all, the king of pain. "It's nothing I can't handle," he would say.

But right now he could not do that, could not be that. He grabbed his helmet and threw it across the fucking bus.

CHAPTER 22

POINT OF STRESS

I like a look of agony, because I know it's true.

—EMILY DICKINSON

The sound was beastly, a slurping, gnashing, glugging noise that traveled through the hotel's glass door, wafting out into the warming air and making small French children look nervously about. In the lobby, Bruyneel lifted his head to listen and smiled.

"They're eating good, eh?" he said. "Good appetite means a good day."

The Postal team was gathered at their table at the Novotel hotel in Limoges, fueling up for the coming day, the longest of the Tour. They were a bit banged up, but their appetites were good. A Tour rider needs to eat up to nine thousand calories a day, the equivalent of twenty-eight cheeseburgers. By the sound of things, the Postals were well on their way, working noisily through two boxes of bran flakes, one box of Special K, one box of muesli, one box of Golden Grahams, two baskets of bread, several dozen single-serving yogurts (half plain, half fruit-flavored), two pitchers of fruit juice, nine large bottles of water, and four jars of honey, not to mention the vast quantities of eggs, pancakes, oatmeal, and pasta that were disappearing down their gullets.

It was a sound to warm Bruyneel's heart, for it meant energy into his bank. Having more energy meant that Bruyneel could spend it at a rate the other teams could not match, having his team churn away at the front, slowly wearing down the opposition.

Armstrong was hungry, too, in his own way. Now that the race had stabilized, he'd taken to drifting around the pack, showing himself. Armstrong would let himself float near the back, then power back up to the front, riding in the wind. It was the cycling equivalent of flexing a bicep, and it was noticed.

"It was definitely impressive," said Christian Vande Velde, a former Postal who was riding for Liberty Seguros. "When you see someone doing that, the question you always ask yourself is, could I do that right now? And he was doing stuff all the time, very casually, that most of us couldn't imagine doing."

Today marked the Tour's halfway point as well as its first true climbs. It was thus a day for what the French call the *petite lessive*, the little wash that reveals who is on form and who is not. The cleansing would be done by the course, a nasty 238-kilometer journey over the Appalachian-type topography of the Central Massif, the high point of which was a 5,243-foot extinct volcano called Col du Pas de la Peyrol.

The race had stabilized somewhat since Postal had given away the yellow jersey. Young Thomas Voeckler had proven himself worthy of the role, and more important, his Brioches team had risen to the occasion, riding strongly to chase down breakaways, allowing Postal to gain some rest. Today, however, would likely bring a shift. Bruyneel told his team to expect attacks. Armstrong had taken a different strategy the previous day, warning the peloton against riding too hard.

"There will be a lot of people going home tomorrow if we start like we did today," he'd said, referring to stage 9's breakneck pace. "I think these three days you just stay up there, stay out of trouble, and wait for Friday and Saturday [in the Pyrenees]."

Others disagreed. "The day requires boldness," French rider-turned-commentator Laurent Jalabert said. "Even a little insanity."

The pack rolled out, and attacks began. Postal rode at the front, chasing down break after break, until finally they found one to their liking, containing Axel Merckx, son of the great Eddy, and sultry, bandy-legged, thirty-four-year-old French hero Richard Virenque, who was gunning for a record seventh king of the mountains jersey. Virenque, whose skill on the bike was only surpassed by his skill as a thespian, had endured a seven-month ban earlier for doping while riding for the infamous 1998 Festina team (after denying it for two years, he tearfully confessed in court). Virenque's status as a French hero was undimmed, however, and now, on the French national holiday of Bastille Day, he moved onstage.

Merckx and Virenque gained five minutes, then ten. Behind them, the peloton rode up the first climbs in what had become its customary formation: Armstrong gliding behind Hincapie and Landis. Mayo rode off to the left, looking around alertly. Hamilton tilted his head back, as if he were trying to see over everyone's head. Ullrich took up his usual post on Armstrong's wheel, cruising with an aquatic stillness, his mouth open. He did not seem to breathe as much as filter-feed, the pink mollusc of tongue stirring sleepily.

After three hours of steady up and down, they rode onto the slopes of the Peyrol, which held a secret. In the race bible, the handbook given to all the racers, the climb was listed at 12 percent. In fact, as Phonak and a few others knew, it exceeded 17 percent for brief sections. A perfect setting for an attack.

Be ready, Bruyneel told Armstrong.

Ullrich was miserable. He was still sick, sick enough that he'd been put on antibiotics after the team time trial, sick enough that he was bundled up on a sunny day, and, worst of all, sick enough that he was now coughing.

They heard him, he knew it. Ullrich saw Postal heads turn when he coughed, saw them note the fact he was wearing two layers when everyone else wore one, saw them stare at the cold sores on his lips.

"Jan is sad," Birgit Krohme said, pursing her lips. "The weather in the time trial made it worse. So he takes the antibiotics, which compress his system. There is no other choice."

The last few days had been difficult for him, feeling the sickness spread inside his body, feeling himself weaken. It was made more difficult by the fact that his sickness forced Ullrich to do something he despised: to pretend.

I'm fine, he kept saying over and over, his words believed only by the person he didn't want to believe them: T-Mobile manager Walter Godefroot, a former Belgian champion who proceeded to employ the most trusted form of home-country motivation: unmerciful public criticism.

"Armstrong's lead [of fifty-five seconds] is too much at such an early stage of the race," Godefroot told the newspapers. "Jan has often been poorly placed and perhaps lacks a bit of power compared to his rivals. Armstrong has no weaknesses."

Armstrong, on the other hand, kept up a gushing stream of admiration for Ullrich's ever-dangerous talent.

"Lance's angle on Jan is to praise him," Jeff Spencer explained. "Lance understands that what Jan doesn't like is pressure. If you want to get into his head, praise him to the skies. It starts a seed of doubt—if I'm so talented, then why haven't I won? What's wrong with me?"

Halfway up the Peyrol, Armstrong dropped back a few places, letting Ullrich take the lead. Ullrich accepted. He rode in front, his face immobile, as Armstrong moved behind him, watching. He felt the American's eyes on him. He rode harder. The two rose in matched cadence.

Ullrich had fooled Armstrong before. Last year, Ullrich was so sick with fever during the first week that he'd actually made plans to drop out. He'd continued only when revived by a couple of aspirin a teammate had retrieved from a race doctor and surreptitiously slipped him. A week later, Ullrich had dominated Armstrong in the time trial at Gaillac. Things can change.

"He is the sphinx," Ferrari said after the stage. "He looks strong. But we shall see."

The peloton snaked its way up the peak, riders dropping off the back. This was a preview, a first cut. Some twenty-five riders remained, among them some surprises. Andreas Kloden, Ullrich's teammate, looked skinny-assed and strong. So did young Italian Ivan Basso of CSC, who'd finished seventh in last year's Tour. So did Francisco Mancebo of Ileas Balears. Mayo was in the back, his bad luck continuing. He'd had a mechanical problem, then whacked his knee on his handlebar, and was now fighting to get to the front. Only one guy was missing. His team was looking for him, in fact, turning confusedly in their saddles, their eyes asking the question.

Where was Hamilton?

Hamilton wasn't sure where he was at that moment. The Angers crash had reshaped his world, the map of which was freshly drawn on his slender back.

The deeper chunks of flesh were taken from the bottom right side of his spine, atop the fin of bone that approaches the skin's surface. His left ribs were similarly marked. He had a long rip along the top of the left shoulder blade, road-rash on both elbows, and a cut below his eye. Also, in the center, a smaller red mark from his vial of lucky salt.

"Meat," he said later. "I'm missing meat."

The problem, however, was invisible. The impact had caused severe bruising and swelling in his lower back. Around the injury, his body was trying to preserve itself by locking up muscles, fixing itself into a nature's version of a bodycast. Hamilton had broken his back once, thirteen years earlier, in the mountain-biking accident that had brought him to cycling in the first place. The Angers crash felt familiar.

"This isn't an injury," he told his wife, Haven, over the phone that night in Angers. "This is damage. I'm going to feel this the rest of my life."

He rode the next three days with the lead group. Nights he spent with team physiotherapist, Kristopher. On the bike, however, he felt strange, detached, as if the signals from his brain to his legs were getting blocked.

Still, Hamilton knew the routine. He'd been smiling a good bit these last couple of days, trying to persuade the media, his team-mates, and himself that he was okay. He rode conservatively. No more attacks, just safety and maintenance. Baby steps, he kept reminding himself.

Then, at the moment when it couldn't get any worse, it got worse. Three days after the crash, Haven called: Tugboat, his beloved dog, was dying of cancer. She would bring him up to say good-bye.

"He hardly stopped crying all afternoon [of the rest day]," team-mate Oscar Sevilla said. "We were all trying to help him get over it."

His tears were for the dog, but when his wife arrived, she saw that they were also for something more. "You could see it in his eyes," Haven said. "An ugliness, a stress. He didn't look like himself."

That night, when Tugboat arrived, Hamilton and Haven lifted him into Tyler's bed. (Haven, in obedience to cycling custom, stayed in a separate room.) The morning of stage 10, Hamilton hung Tug-boat's tags around his neck. Haven departed for the vet's, feeling sad but optimistic. Tugboat's death would be tough, but it had the potential to be positive motivation, help her husband through the injury. Give him wings, she thought.

But now, as the leaders crested the Peyrol, Hamilton was still climbing. He chased, and eventually caught the leaders. But the finish would hold another portent. Alert to Hamilton's condition, Arm-strong put on a burst on the final uphill section, and Hamilton couldn't keep up. The resulting pack split cost Hamilton seven seconds, which pleased Bruyneel to no end.

"It is not the time," he said, echoing his feeling from the pro-logue. "What matters is how Tyler feels. To come into the finish line, to have everyone watching, to go to bed that night. It has an impact, a big impact."

When it was over, Hamilton spoke to the press. He smiled and said a few of the usual things. A hard day, a good day, let his legs do the talking.

Then he said, "I think a lot of people were watching each other, but there's still plenty of time for the shit to go down."

Pens stopped moving. Reporters looked up from their note-books to make sure they were still talking to the same guy. "Shit to go down?" Not the kind of thing Hamilton would normally say. No question, he was not his usual self. Maybe Tugboat's death was affecting him, they thought.

That night, Hamilton called Haven. Tugboat had gone easily, she told him, put to sleep. She'd given him some sweets in the park beforehand; he'd eaten so happily, she said, it was as if he already were in heaven.

They talked about the day. He said all the things Haven was expecting to hear—*We'll get them tomorrow, I'm feeling better every day*. Then she said her usual things—*You can do it, Ty, I know you can*. Then, just as they said good-night, he blurted it out.

"My legs aren't working," he said.

It took a moment for her to hear. His voice sounded strangled.

"I can't push," he said.

"Did you talk to Cecco?" she managed.

He had. Cecco had been his usual self, comforting, understand-ing. It would get better. But it wasn't.

"It'll get better," she said, not knowing what else to say, how to respond to this. "It will, it will."

He didn't say anything.

The trolls had been quiet since the press conference with Walsh, but the following night, Armstrong saw that it had just been a tactical retreat. Now he watched, unsurprised, as they crept out again on the eve of the Tour's arrival in the high mountains. Not just one or two trolls, either: it was a crawling, heaving, sticky-fingered horde, arriving from all angles, emboldened by each other's presence, attacking him one after another. The Night of the Trolls.

The first arrived in the form of fellow American Greg LeMond. In an interview with *Le Monde*, the three-time Tour winner spoke about the allegations that Armstrong may have used performance-enhancing drugs. "I want to see the truth when I watch the Tour," he said. "Lance is ready to do anything to keep his secret, but I don't know how long he can convince everybody of his innocence."

Armstrong's negative drug tests left LeMond unimpressed. "Everybody says that. But neither had David Millar tested positive, and he now admits he took EPO. The problem with Lance is that [if you raise the doping question] you're either a liar or you're out to destroy cycling."

It wasn't the first time LeMond had expressed doubts about Armstrong. In 2001, after LeMond was informed that Armstrong was working with the notorious Ferrari, he said, "If Lance is clean, it's the greatest comeback in the history of sport. If he isn't, it would be the greatest fraud."

At the time, Armstrong had rung up LeMond, and the two had what could politely be referred to as an animated discussion. Trek, which also manufactured LeMond's signature line of bikes, was displeased at the dispute between two of their athletes, and attempted to encourage LeMond to keep his criticisms to himself. But LeMond hadn't stayed completely quiet, Armstrong knew. LeMond's wife, Kathy, had provided an account of the 2001 phone conversation between her husband and Armstrong to David Walsh for his book.

"It's sad," Bill Stapleton said. "Before the Tour, Lance and I had even talked about burying the hatchet with Greg. And now this?"

The morning the LeMond story broke, Armstrong noticed a television crew from the France 3 network loitering around the lobby. He knew them, of course; they'd been trailing the team around for some time, just like that television crew did back in 2000, when they surreptitiously followed a team car and rooted through the team's garbage bags. This time, though, Armstrong heard that they were buttering up the clerk, attempting to gain access to Postal's vacated hotel rooms.

"They show up and ask sporting questions to our face, but as soon as we leave they're digging in the rooms and looking for dirt," Armstrong said. "The scary thing is, if they don't find anything and get frustrated after a couple of months, who's to say they won't put something there and say, 'Look what we've found.'"

To top it all off, the Tour de France organization chose this moment to start proceedings to eject Pavel Padrnos, one of Armstrong's most powerful teammates. Worried about its image after a scandal-filled season, the Tour had embarked on one of its periodic cleanup kicks, deciding to boot any rider who was involved in any kind of doping investigation (a rule that, had it been in effect in 2001, would have prevented Armstrong from riding). In 2001, while riding with another team, Padrnos had been investigated for using Mannitol, which is banned when injected. But in Padrnos's case, the Mannitol had been swallowed as an ingredient in a vitamin supplement. The case was bogus! But here they came, a clot of French trolls in white shirts and ties, led by race director Jean-Marie LeBlanc, trying to kick Armstrong's guy from the race.

That night and the following day, Armstrong watched the trolls come at him. He observed the usual protocol: He issued a statement expressing disappointment and dismay at LeMond's words; he checked to see which wire services picked up the hotel-snoop story (Reuters didn't—he'd remind them of that later); he protested the Tour's treatment of Padrnos (who would remain on the team, thanks in part to the intervention of the UCI) and gave LeBlanc the silent treatment when he showed up at the team bus.

Mostly, though, he got angry.

LANCE ARMSTRONG'S 2004 RACE RESULTS

Tour of Algarve, Portugal (February 18–22)	5th
Tour of Murcia, Spain (March 3–7)	23rd
Criterium International, France (March 27–28)	3rd
Tour de Georgia, U.S.A. (April 20–25)	1st
Tour of Languedoc-Roussillon, France (May 19–23)	6th
Dauphiné Libéré, France (June 6–13)	4th
Tour de France (July 3–25)	1st

"It's attack until they crack, or I do": Armstrong the night before the Tour began.

(Casey Gibson)

Tyler Hamilton, Armstrong's ex-teammate and upstairs neighbor in Girona, Spain. "Somewhere deep inside he's got that edge, that urge to kill," says a former U.S. Postal rider. "But Tyler buries it very well."

(Daniel Coyle)

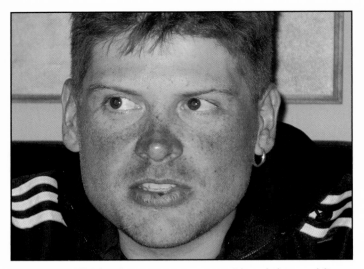

Jan Ullrich of East Germany, considered the world's most gifted and enigmatic rider. Ullrich had finished second five times in the Tour de France, and promised it wouldn't happen again. It didn't.

(Daniel Coyle)

Alexandre Vinokourov, Ullrich's wingman who made it out of bleakest Kazakhstan, but never made it to the start of the Tour.

(Phil O'Connor)

Iban Mayo, the Basque who came back from a horrific car crash to become the best pure climber in the world.
(Phil O'Connor)

Floyd Landis, an ex-Mennonite whose biblical toughness made him invaluable—and occasionally infuriating—to Armstrong.
(Daniel Coyle)

Controversial Italian Dr. Michele Ferrari *(smiling)* leaving the Bologna Tribunal after his doping conviction on October 1, 2004. Later that day, Armstrong officially ended his nine-year relationship with Ferrari.

(Nico Casamassima/AFP/ Getty Images)

In October 2003, Sheryl Crow walked up to Armstrong at a charity function and asked, "Would you take me for a bike ride sometime?" She would soon be sporting a new nickname: Juanita Cuervo.

(Tim de Waele)

British sportswriter David Walsh worked for three years on his book *LA Confidentiel: Les Secrets de Lance Armstrong* with French journalist Pierre Ballester. "I got the sense [from Armstrong] that any people who wanted to get into this doping question were the enemies," Walsh says. "And I was going to be the enemy."

(Philippe Ledru/Deadline/ Polaris Images)

Armstrong and the ill-fated $250,000 narrow bike during its last set of test runs in March on Tenerife, an island off the coast of North Africa.

(Scott Daubert/Trek)

Officially in town for training, Armstrong surprised everyone—particularly American Chris Horner *(in green)*—by outsprinting the field to win the Tour de Georgia's stage 3.

(Michael Pugh/Dodge Tour de Georgia)

Mayo *(in yellow)* dominated Armstrong in the Dauphiné Libéré, a critical tune-up just three weeks before the Tour.
(Tim de Waele)

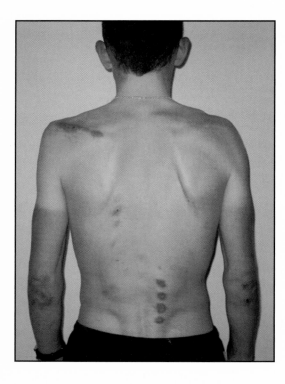

Hamilton after his crash at Angers on stage 6 of the Tour.
(Geoff Hamilton)

Ullrich cracking on La Mongie, stage 12.

(Casey Gibson)

Italian hope Ivan Basso and Armstrong ascending La Mongie, stage 12. "Armstrong is unbeatable," Basso said afterward.

(Tim de Waele)

Due to the death threat against Armstrong, police sharpshooters rode in the team car on Alpe d'Huez. "We were terrified," Postal director Johan Bruyneel said.

(Doug Pensinger/Getty Images Sport)

The night before the celebration in Paris,
Armstrong was already thinking about
number seven.

(Daniel Coyle)

CHAPTER 23
BURST

"First week you feel good. The second week you lose
strength. Third week, fucked."

—PER PEDERSON, TOUR RIDER, 1993

"The ideal Tour de France is one in which only one rider
finishes."

—TOUR FOUNDER HENRI DESGRANGE

It may come as a surprise, but the characteristic sound of the Tour
de France is not the velveteen purr of a well-oiled bike. Nor is it the
happy shout of the crowd, nor the elegant clink of wine glasses. No,
the sound of the Tour is the guttural roar of an internal combustion
engine.

Thousands of engines, actually, in thousands of lacquered, toy-
bright cars and trucks that make the Tour possible, most of them
vehicles shined and glossed within an inch of their lives for the
occasion, and driven by immaculately dressed, large-bellied men in
their forties and fifties who approach their job with the dead-eyed
panache of military test pilots. They may spend eleven months a
year as mild accountants or salesmen, but put them behind the
wheel during the Tour and they form a mad peloton all their own,
obsessed by some long-thwarted French dream for speed and glory,

zooming into corners, blasting the horn, revving that motor until the sound echoes from Paris to Marseille.*

On the morning of stage 12 in Castelsarrasin, Johan Bruyneel stood amid the revving cars, wondering about the condition of Armstrong's engine. Specifically, he was wondering—along with the other 167 riders remaining in the Tour—whether Armstrong would have his fifth gear today.

"I think he will be good," Bruyneel said. "Probably not great, but good, for sure."

Fifth gear was what Chris Carmichael called Armstrong's signature high-revving attack, also known as The Burst. Ferrari, of course, thought of it in terms of numbers—500 watts for thirty minutes—but it was simpler to describe it as the tool with which Armstrong had won his first four Tours.

He typically used it on the last climb of the first day in the mountains. First, Armstrong had his team set a fast pace, burning off as many riders as possible, each of Postal's climbers driving at the front, then falling away in turn. Then he attacked, building an unbridgeable gap and, more important, extinguishing any notion that he was vulnerable. It was as subtle as a baseball bat to the stomach: No tricky strategies, no romantic early attacks, no sticky alliances.

"Armstrong takes the wind out of your sails with his attacks on the final climb," said Phonak's Sevilla. "You hope you can carry on, but it's demoralizing when you're already behind after the first mountain stage."

---

*Tour-organization officials don't wear uniforms, exactly, but the highest-ranking ones wear special pants. Specifically, flat-front, beige, wrinkle-free trousers that serve the same function as medals in the military: When you see the pants (and these are, as pants go, exceptionally nice pants), you know you're dealing with somebody truly important.

During the Tour, I was caught breaking numerous rules—blundering into off-limits areas, lending my credentials to friends so they could dine at the press buffet—but none of my transgressions inspired half so much terror as the time I jumped a barrier and my shoe accidentally brushed against the pristine fabric of a Tour official's pants. The official whipped around, especially pissed off. I ran.

It worked like this:

- 1999, Sestrieres: Four-minute gain in six kilometers
- 2000, Hautacam: Three minutes in three kilometers
- 2001, Alpe d'Huez: Two minutes in thirteen kilometers
- 2002, La Mongie: One minute-plus in four kilometers on all but Joseba Beloki, who was distanced the following day on Plateau de Beille

Armstrong had lacked The Burst in 2003, and it had made all the difference. Whether he had it in 2004 was up for debate, one heightened by the fact that, unlike in other years, Armstrong had not subjected himself to one of Ferrari's long tests.

"I think he will be good," Ferrari said, back in Italy. "But races, they can be strange. There are many factors."

The upshot was, everyone knew Armstrong would attack on La Mongie. The feeling was so strong that Armstrong tried to quash it, saying that the stage, which held two moderately long climbs at the end, was better suited to an explosive climber like Mayo. His denial, however, only strengthened the buzz. Of course Armstrong would attack.

The night before, however, Armstrong and Bruyneel decided they would not attack. Armstrong would play defense.

"We wanted no gaps," Bruyneel said later. "The plan was not to do a big attack, no full-out efforts. If they attacked, we would follow."

Armstrong was also concerned about Thomas Voeckler, who'd acquitted himself admirably for the past week, keeping himself in the yellow jersey by riding with the lead group, keeping pace on the climbs of the Central Massif. Seven days in yellow, and Voeckler's 9:35 lead on Armstrong remained intact.

"Lance mentioned several times, maybe we shouldn't have given [Voeckler] so much time," Bruyneel said later. "And yes, nine minutes, it can be a lot."

"This Voeckler," Ferrari said musingly. "He is young, eh? He is strong. No one knows his limits. He could be dangerous, if he can keep up."

That morning, on the mountain, people walked up the road with their picnic baskets, bikes, loaves of bread, beach umbrellas. They trudged in a long line, grandfathers and children and teenagers carrying flags. The day held a feeling of quiet ceremony, though whether a wedding or a funeral was difficult to say.

Back at the start in Castelsarrasin, Ullrich was feeling loose. "I will see where I am," he said. At the very least, he was enjoying the heat. After almost two weeks, a proper summer day had arrived, with temperatures in the nineties. Ullrich breathed it in. He had a history of doing well in the heat; he had no idea why, but it seemed to loosen up his system. Armstrong's track record was the opposite: averse to heat but good in the cold and wet.

Hamilton looked subdued—still mourning poor Tugboat, everyone figured. His team looked loose enough, however; Sevilla pretending to drive the team bus, Santiago Perez making faces.

Mayo hung near the back, wearing his orange cap and an expression of quiet consternation. For all his Basque heroism, he carried an unpatriotic secret: He didn't actually like riding in the Pyrenees. He said it was the terrain, but it might have also been the knowledge that 80,000 of his countrymen stood ahead, preparing themselves for an ecstasy that depended in large part on him. His knee ached where he'd hit it on the handlebars; his hip still burned from his crash. He shook his legs questioningly.

Armstrong looked alert. In the area before the start, he moved about, watching, gliding, chatting, always one beat ahead. An Italian rider drank a cup of espresso; Armstrong leaned over and took it, sniffed it, handed it back, his nose wrinkling.

"They gotta start getting some good coffee here," he said.

On paper at least, Armstrong had a few reasons to worry. Beltran, one of his key climbers, was banged up from crashing and would probably be of little help today. Armstrong was not overly fond of La Mongie ("I have suffered [there] more than I do on other mountains, and I don't know why," he said later). Tour historians eagerly noted that La Mongie also happened to be where Bruyneel's career had ended in 1998, when he'd abandoned the race due to injury. But those thoughts, in the unlikely event that they crossed Armstrong's mind at all, evaporated an hour or so into the stage when he spotted a dark smudge on the horizon ahead.

"It's going to rain," he told Hincapie.

Hincapie looked around. It was still hot and sunny. The clouds were miles off. Hincapie laughed at the idea.

"You're crazy," he said.

When the first lightning hit two hours later, the temperature had already plummeted to fifty degrees Fahrenheit. The rain pelted down; the road turned into a river. The riders blasted through it, amphibious, hissing. Heads were lowered into the rain. Chechu Rubiera found his way over to Armstrong.

"What else do you want?" he shouted. "This is perfect."

With Postal in the lead, the pack of fifty riders approached the first climb, the Col d'Aspin, twelve kilometers at 6.5 percent. They fought for position, a scramble similar to that before the cobbles, attacks coming left and right. Then came the moment just before the climb began, the deep breath. Some riders muttered quick prayers; some joked with doomed bravado. Most riders went quiet, preparing to lose themselves in the sensations of the climb.

Riders began to get left behind. Fifty men, now forty-five, now forty. The riders dropped away in twos and threes. The smart ones accepted their fate and ratcheted back to their own tempo, knowing that cracking, like drowning, goes easier if you don't struggle too much. Along the roadside, a boy of about twelve opened his mouth wide and tilted his head back, letting the mist and grit settle on his tongue.

Ullrich unzipped his vest so that it billowed like a superhero's cape, not remotely aerodynamic, but he didn't care. Armstrong rode near the front, his legs spinning easily, his face hawklike. Hamilton and Mayo were further back, watching.

The storm increased. The stream alongside the road began to swell. The surviving group flowed up the pass, nostrils flaring, cheeks reddening, faces showing the microscopic signs of cracking. Landis rode too close to Armstrong, and Armstrong put his hand on his teammate's back and shoved him away like a running back straight-arming a tackler. Landis swerved six feet across the road, recovered. Armstrong's face tightened.

As they crested the Aspin, the attack came. Ullrich, Mayo, Kloden, and a few others accelerated unexpectedly, performing the rare move of attacking on the descent. The lead built—100 meters, 200 meters, a half-kilometer. The contenders rode hard, cutting corners with daring panache, feeling their tires skid. Behind them, Postal rode cautiously, not willing to risk a crash.

Eighty thousand Basques rejoiced—this was it. Mayo's triumphant arrival in the Pyrenees. In the T-Mobile team car, excitement grew. Ullrich had been feeling good that morning, he seemed recovered from the cold completely now. No cough, no sniff, nothing. The heat had woken him, and now he was himself again. He would beat Armstrong to the foot of La Mongie, the final climb, and he would keep pace, perhaps even defeat the American.

The lead grew to five seconds. Ten seconds.

In the Postal car, Bruyneel alternated between urging caution and aggression.

"Come on boys, chase it down, eh? Chase it down," he said. Then, a second later, "No risks, eh, no risks. Eleven seconds, no risks."

Postal waited until the descent flattened, then they started to chase in earnest. Up ahead, the escapees took stock. They had a fifteen-second lead and two kilometers to go before the climb. They were faced with the choice between reasonable tactics and irrational hope: to keep riding alone, possibly wasting energy for a few seconds' gain, or to drop back into the shelter of the peloton and start the climb all even. They chose reason.

Forty riders passed through the picturesque Ste-Marie-de-Campan at the bottom of La Mongie. They made a hard left-hand turn and saw the climb lit up by the returning sun. Sixteen kilometers, 7.6 percent. Not a huge climb by Tour standards, but enough.

Armstrong was midway in a group of five Postal riders, riding behind Hincapie and Landis. Hincapie bobbed slightly, near his limit. Landis was grim and focused, a picture of Old Testament determination. Behind them rode the remains of the peloton, including the yellow jersey, Thomas Voeckler.

"Lance, pay attention for the attack of Mayo here," Bruyneel warned.

Bruyneel did not mention Hamilton, who had been riding near the back of the lead group. Hamilton, in Bruyneel's mind, was no longer a threat, not today, anyway. At least three Phonaks were stronger than Hamilton, anybody could see that.

When one of his Phonak teammates met Hamilton's eyes, he nodded and raised his eyebrows. He was okay. He was going to make it. His teammates believed him. His face was red but he didn't look like he was hurting.

He wasn't hurting; that was the problem. His legs still felt detached, numb; his back felt as if it were wrapped in steel. He wasn't suffering, because he couldn't go hard enough to make himself hurt.

Hamilton downshifted, tried to ride a higher cadence. He'd fallen behind during the last Tour, when he had the cracked collarbone. It had been early in stage 16; he'd been dropped. Some of his teammates had come and helped him back. He'd recovered, broken away on the steepest climb, and gone on to win the stage, the best moment of his career, not for the victory but for how it embodied who he was.

The road steepened, perhaps a half-percent. A few more feet of rise, a fractional increase in strain transmitted through the chain to the pedals, legs, heart, mind. He dug harder.

Hamilton had a trick he did when he was at his limit, where he tipped his head back and relaxed into the pain. That was the key, not to fight it but to let it become a part of him. Strange, how hardness and softness were so close. He would almost close his eyes, make it all go away.

Now Hamilton tried it, tipping his head back and pushing harder, but this time hoping to feel pain. It felt like a dream, like he'd been cut in two. His legs were right there, spinning away, perfect and undamaged, awaiting only the awakening microburst of electricity that would turn things back to the way they should be, must be. He closed his eyes.

Only later would he give this feeling a name; only later would he say that he felt like he'd been cheated. Cheated because he'd been riding at the front, near Haselbacher. Because Haselbacher dove left instead of right. Because the barriers narrowed the road. Because Tour organizers had to fit their precious arch. Because it was the Tour, and because he was Tyler Hamilton, the nice guy who had hard luck.

He opened his eyes to see riders disappearing up the road, riders whom he could beat easily if he were healthy. He heard his coach's voice in his ear.

"*Allez, Tyler, allez.*"

Allez, Tyler. The same words his parents painted on the banner back home in Marblehead. The same words he'd heard for the first time when he was a teenager, words that sounded so exotic and cool that he was surprised to learn that they just meant "Go."

He saw the eyes of his teammates.

"Go," he told them. "Don't wait."

Hamilton moved to the side of the road, near a small stone wall. He closed his eyes again. He would not quit until the following day. But this was when he knew.

In the Postal team car, Bruyneel glanced at the television screen.

"Hamilton dropped," he reported, his voice businesslike, almost bored. "Hamilton is dropped."

Armstrong dipped his head and went harder.

Jan Ullrich leaned into the Col d'Aspin, low on the handlebars, head down. He hadn't been happy about the rain, it was true. But it wasn't the rain that bothered him so much as its manner of arrival, the slow unfolding of a small horizon smudge into a storybook, mountain-dwarfing, lightning-tongued fury. For Ullrich, believer in portents and mystery, this did not feel like a summer storm. It felt like a memory.

The worst day of his career had been like this, cold and wet. It was 1998, the year after he'd won the Tour, on a stage to Les Deux Alpes. It had been a spectacular crack; Ullrich's body had stopped working, his muscles had seized up. On the Galibier, he'd lost nine minutes and the Tour to Marco Pantani; his face had swelled in the effort, showing the puffy eyes that would become the trademark sign of the Ullrich crack.

Other rainstorms, too, other memories. In 1993, Ullrich was preparing for the amateur world championship event when he heard a familiar voice calling him. He turned to see his father, whom he hadn't seen in fourteen years, standing at a steel barricade. They spoke, and his father said how proud he was. Could they see each other again? His father wrote his phone number on a scrap of paper, which Ullrich tucked carefully in his jersey pocket. But the rain fell throughout the race, and when he pulled the paper out, the number was unreadable. His father did not try to contact him again.

The rain blasted. Ullrich kept his stoic mask, but he felt that cold water soak in, chilling his muscles. Ullrich knew too well how cold can block the muscles, reduce circulation, rob efficiency. No one cycled well when the temperature dropped, least of all someone on antibiotics. His system was down, he knew, and this was going to depress it further.

Unless he could jump-start it. Unless he could do something half-crazy and aggressive, something that did not make sense but that might work anyway—in short, something Ullrichian. He raced off on impulse, throwing himself into the turns, revving his great motor to its limit. He hoped to feel a change. But it didn't come.

At the bottom of La Mongie, his teammate and sports school friend Kloden pulled alongside. Ullrich asked how Kloden felt.

"Good," Kloden replied. "I can keep up with these guys today. You?"

Ullrich shook his head. "The legs are stiff," he said. "The feelings aren't good."

Four hundred miles away in Italy, Michele Ferrari watched with interest as Ullrich shifted to a larger gear. Ferrari knew this was something Ullrich sometimes did before a crack, as if trying to propel himself to the top in one great, irrational push. Ferrari leaned into the television, clinically interested. He'd been grateful for the rain, for it forced Ullrich to remove his sunglasses. Ferrari looked into the eyes, looking through the pixilated distance, trying to see.

Ullrich kept churning. His grip on his handlebars tightened. He drifted back a few inches, then forward. His teammate Giuseppe Guerini glanced, wondering. "[Ullrich] didn't understand what was happening," Guerini would say later.

The big gear felt good for a moment. Ullrich felt his muscles working against it, pressing down in that familiar heartbeat rhythm. Pain comes in different flavors, and this was what he wanted: white, fresh pain. "Awakening the muscles" his coach Rudy Pevenage called it, and Ullrich's muscles weren't the sort to be awakened by a kindly jostle. They needed a big alarm bell, and when they woke up, they would take to this big gear like they were made for it. But it didn't work, not today. Ullrich felt his muscles stiffening.

Up ahead, Kloden was riding comfortably with the remaining twenty or so riders.

The question came over Ullrich's radio from T-Mobile's director, Mario Kummer: "Should Kloden wait for you?"

Ullrich listened. The real question was not whether Kloden should wait. The real question was, can you do it? Can you keep up with Armstrong?

Ullrich hesitated. When the answer came, his first words were not about himself; they were about his old friend, his neighbor.

"Klodi should ride," he said. "Giuseppe is with me."

With 6.5 kilometers left, the crack began to open. Even in distress, Ullrich's body revealed little: his pedal stroke was still steady, his body did not bob and weave, like some. A slight slowing of the legs, an infinitesimal pause at the top of each pedal arc. A few inches lost, then regained as Ullrich dredged up bursts of energy to keep himself close. Ten times. Fifteen. Knowing he would run dry.

Only his face seemed to absorb the strain. The head receded, turtling into the shoulders. The eyes puffed slightly. His head tilted forward.

He began to slide back.

It would have been smart to shift to a smaller gear. But Ullrich did not. He kept it in the big gear, feeling the pain, feeling his legs slow, the blood run to his face. His face swelled, his eyes looked wasp-stung, his brow thickened, his mouth twisted. Some spectators would fail to recognize him as he passed.

Still six kilometers to go. He pushed harder, knowing how bad it was, knowing that this was all he could give, trying to retrieve honor through the magnitude of his pain. Still believing in that mystery, that, somehow, despite everything, it would be okay.

"Ullrich dropped!" Bruyneel's voice had boomed with genuine surprise. "ULLRICH DROPPED! ULLRICH DROPPED!"

When he was younger, Armstrong would occasionally celebrate these moments by making his finger into a gun and blowing pretend smoke from its muzzle. Now, he just kept riding.

He was down to one teammate, Azevedo, with eleven riders left. Mayo rode at the tail of the small group. A thousand Basques screamed, pleading for an attack. *Gora, gora!* But Mayo couldn't. He'd felt it since the bottom of the climb, when Postal had accelerated.

Armstrong looked behind. Saw Mayo's clenched face, protruding jaw, labored cadence. Five weeks and one day after Ventoux, Mayo looked like Dead Elvis.

One by one, they cracked, flashing their own death grins. First Azevedo pulled off, having given his boss his all. Then Santos Gonzalez, who had gone ahead at Hamilton's urging. Then Mayo, gritting his teeth. Then another Phonak, Oscar Pereiro, staring down at his legs, and Ullrich's teammate Kloden, and the Spaniard Mancebo, his head tipping epileptically to the left, then Carlos Sastre of CSC, who tried an attack only to have Armstrong chase it down.

Then there were two: Armstrong and Ivan Basso, the twenty-five-year-old Italian from CSC. They tunneled together into the flag-snapping core of the crowd.

Basso, the son of a butcher, looked calm and ecstatic at the same time; the face of *salto de qualità*. He'd been almost invisible during the first stages, never showing himself at the front, always riding in the shadow of the contenders. Basso led Armstrong onto the high mountain; Armstrong looked slightly labored but was strong enough to make a brief attempt to get away. Basso followed with ease, then took the lead.

"There were moments when I remember thinking to myself, 'I wonder if he can slow down a bit,'" Armstrong said later. In the car, Bruyneel said little except informing Armstrong of the most important number.

"Forty-five seconds on Ullrich," he said. "Good job, Lance, stay on the wheel, good job."

They climbed together in matched strokes. Armstrong had long singled out Basso as a future Tour winner; in fact, tried to sign him for Postal prior to this season. Basso, however, signed with Bjarne Riis at CSC. He looked like a seminarian, but he was a hard boy, a disciple of the notorious Cecchini, as everyone else on Riis's team. Those looking for an emotional edge would point to his mother's recent cancer diagnosis, about which Basso had sought Armstrong's counsel only three days earlier.

As they came to the line, Basso was a picture of elegance; his face relaxed, his cadence smooth as he accelerated in the last five hundred meters. Armstrong spun along behind, his head slightly down, his face deeply creased, his teeth showing. It wasn't the Dead Elvis grin, but it was close, and made more dramatic by Basso's youthful effortlessness.

Basso beat Armstrong easily to the line and pointed to the heavens. Armstrong didn't stop at the finish, but cycled slowly further up the mountain, continuing to his rendezvous with the ecstatically scowling Serge and Air Force One.

Armstrong took a drink of water and squinted down the mountain, where riders were limping over the line, the price of the first eleven days carved in their faces. Mancebo crossed the line and nearly vomited. Armstrong looked drawn, hollowed-out by the effort. But his words were easy, almost casual.

"The race isn't over," Armstrong said. "Ullrich's never good in the first mountain stage, but we'll see what happens tomorrow. I think they'll get better."

"A collective shipwreck," *L'Equipe* called it.

"A black day," T-Mobile's Mario Kummer announced.

"Armstrong has been the only one who didn't crack," Mayo said after finishing ninth, 1:03 back. "Everyone else cracked today and the Tour might be over for all of us."

Basso chimed in: "Armstrong is unbeatable."

"I will work for whoever is strongest on our team," Ullrich said, before departing to spend the night, appropriately, in Lourdes.

At the Postal bus, the Belgians stabbed one another in celebration. In Italy, Ferrari pronounced himself moderately pleased. Armstrong's numbers had been solid, but not good: 460 watts for the last five kilometers. Ten percent off his maximum capabilities. He had not had The Burst, after all.

"But when there's no one left," Ferrari said, "you do not need to go so fast."

The overall standings looked like this:

- (1) Thomas Voeckler 51 hours, 51 minutes, 7 seconds
- (2) Lance Armstrong at 5:24 behind
- (5) Andreas Kloden at 6:33
- (6) Ivan Basso at 6:33
- (16) Jan Ullrich at 9:01
- (20) Tyler Hamilton at 9:46
- (51) Iban Mayo at 12:06

CHAPTER 24

NORMALITY

In 1957, Dr. C. P. Richter of the Psychobiological Laboratory of Johns Hopkins Medical School carried out an experiment that attempted to measure the motivational effect of hope. The experiments involved placing rats into cylinders of water thirty inches deep and eight inches wide. After a short time, half of the rats were momentarily rescued—lifted out of the cylinder for a few seconds, then put back into the water. The other half were not. The group that was given hope swam for more than three days. The other rats drowned almost immediately.

The morning of stage 13, The Dude and Bro Clubhouse was expanded to include children. These were not ordinary children, of course. They were Dude-Kids and Bro-Kids, the progeny of clubhouse regulars. They toddled out into the Saturday sunshine in Lannemezan, bidden by some coded signal that Armstrong had the race well in hand, which looked to be true. Armstrong's rivals had all lost big chunks of time at La Mongie. Voeckler, the French boy wonder, had finally showed himself mortal, losing half of his nine-minute lead. The remaining half, most observers figured, would evaporate today. Things were good. So good, in fact, that the area in front of the bus had been transformed into a playground presided over by den mother Juanita Cuervo.

"And what's your name?" Sheryl Crow asked one shy Dude-Kid

of about eleven wearing a Postal hat and a yellow jersey that fit him like a kimono.

"Davey."

Crow leaned over, friendly aunt style. Davey looked up. She was dressed in a sleeveless baby-blue tank top and flared jeans with buckskin laces up the sides of the legs.* The Dude-Kid stared down her shirt. Crow didn't seem to notice.

"Whaddya think of all this?" she asked.

Davey stared.

"It's really cool," he said.

Crow gave a beneficent smile and tousled Davey's hair. They were here on the leading edge of a perfect Tour de France day, sunny and hot, in yet another picturesque gingerbread French town—or at least they could imagine it was picturesque somewhere beyond this parking lot jammed with sweating French people and packs of sticky-fingered media trolls. But that was okay, because the clubhouse was about imagination.

All around, invisible and marvelous things were happening, signs were appearing. Jack Black, the actor, might be flying in, along with rap impresario Dr. Dre. Will Smith was due at some point, along with Perry Farrell, the rock singer. Clubhouse regular Robin Williams would parachute in any second now, along with

---

*This might be a good time to hold forth on that vital question: what is Sheryl Crow like?

For starters, she's oddly difficult to recognize—she's tiny, and she rarely wears makeup, so when you see her, you're never quite sure if it's her or her less glamorous sister. In addition, Crow is skilled at being normal and down-homey, at least to the extent that any celebrity can be normal and down-homey while surrounded by worshipful strangers—a skill she shares with you-know-who.

Seeing Crow with Armstrong, I occasionally was struck by the feeling that they never would be together if it weren't for the thrill of their jock star/rock-star chemistry. In other words, the *idea* of Armstrong and Crow dating was just as intoxicating to them as it was to the rest of us, and therefore the buzz was destined to wear off. My other reason for doubting their relationship's future was that Crow, despite her evident sportiness, is fundamentally a quiet, reflective, artistic type—something which Armstrong most definitely is not. Then again, I could be wrong. Last summer, I bet my wife that they'd never last to the 2005 Tour, and at last check, I still owe her dinner.

Julian Serrano, the chef from Bellagio in Ls Vegas, and Frank Marshall, who was producing the Armstrong bio-movie, the same guy who did *Seabiscuit*. More Americans were showing up, with flags and ballcaps and yellow bracelets, ready to howl and shout and taste history. Elvio was lounging in the start village, chatting up another podium girl—after a bleak spell in the first two rainy weeks, he was at two and counting. Lance wasn't in the yellow jersey yet, but anyone could feel it would happen soon. It was flowing, all the fame and heroism and subterranean rivers of money, and it felt . . . really cool.

It felt even cooler when Armstrong strode down the steps of the bus, looking fresh and alert. He went right to the kids, did some handshaking, did a quick interview, and then set about eyeing his seat, adjusting it by a micrometer as Crow and Davey looked on. A kiss for luck, and he was Batmanning through the hordes, ushered by Erwin and Serge. There was a lightness to his manner, a casualness that the pantomiming *soigneurs* knew meant one thing: this was a day of the knife.

Physically, this would be the Tour's nastiest day, 205 kilometers from Lannemezan to a mountaintop finish at Plateau de Beille, with three vertical miles of climbing spread out over seven categorized climbs. Armstrong's goal was to make it the nastiest psychologically. To do so, Postal decided they would ride in front the entire race, sheltering Armstrong until his signature attack on the final climb. Of course, Basso, Ullrich, and every other contender would be similarly sheltered, but that was not the point. Only Armstrong had control over the god of kilowatts, only he could dictate the pace, while the others would be spending the race watching, reacting, knowing all along that if they showed weakness, Armstrong would bring the whip down. On La Mongie, he had defeated their bodies. Today, Armstrong would try to take their minds.

Three riders managed to escape early on. Voeckler's teammate, Sylvain Chavanel, took off with Michael Rasmussen of Rabobank and Basso's teammate Jens Voigt. But their escape gained them a mere five minutes, while Postal ground away behind according to the game plan they'd sketched out on the bus: Pavel and Eki, the Eastern Bloc goombahs, would take the valleys and flats. Triki and Noval, banged up but recovering, would take the early climbs. Hincapie and Landis would lead up the latter climbs, leaving Rubiera and Azevedo for the big one, the sixteen-kilometer, 8 percent haul up Plateau de Beille.

"Keep things normal," Bruyneel instructed, not seeming to notice how abnormal, even outrageous, it would be for one team to control the race, start to finish, on the Tour's toughest stage.

They rode in tight formation, no other teams contesting the space on the road. They set the pace high, not looking back. Behind them, the peloton was unduly quiet; the clatter-thud of the first week had given way to quieter sorts of crashing. On the radio, Bruyneel laconically described the damage they were causing. Fabian Wegmann abandoned at ten kilometers, then Haimar Zubeldia, Mayo's teammate who finished fifth last year, abandoned at seventeen kilometers. Fifteen minutes later, Dennis Menchov (eleventh in 2003), then Gerrit Glomser. World-class riders, breaking apart like Chinese motorcycles.

Just before the first big climb, Tyler Hamilton drifted to the back of the peloton. The night before, after La Mongie, Phonak's director, Alvaro Pino, had suggested to Hamilton that it might be time to consider quitting. Hamilton had said no—he'd gut it out, he'd finish, he'd never quit. Then Hamilton talked to Kristopher, his physiotherapist.

"Be honest with me," Hamilton said. "Is my back fucked?"

"Your back is fucked," Kristopher said.

Pino approached Hamilton again, and assured him that the team would support any decision. Hamilton agreed to see how it felt, and if it wasn't better, he would stop. As the peloton approached the first feed zone, Pino asked Hamilton if he was any better.

"No," Hamilton said.

"Stop," Pino ordered.

"Are you sure?"

"One hundred percent," Pino said.

Still Hamilton hesitated. He sought out teammate Nicholas Jalabert and asked him what he thought. Jalabert was a good sounding-board; a veteran Frenchman, brother to the famed Laurent Jalabert, and a practical-minded lifer who had seen the race from all sides.

"In the end, Tyler, it's just a bike race," Jalabert said.

"I took Nic's words to heart," Hamilton said later. "After that, I wasn't afraid to stop."

Hamilton stopped pedaling. He stood by the side of the road and saluted his team as it went past, then stepped into the team car without a word, bound for Girona.

Exactly two hours later, it was Mayo's turn. The Postals were blasting up the Col d'Agnes, and the Basque rider had been dropped with the rest of his team. As they rode together, trying to catch up, Mayo suddenly stepped off the bike and stalked disgustedly to the side of the road. His director ran to him and persuaded him to keep going, but the truth was clear: Mayo was broken, cracked, finished. A hundred thousand Basques stood farther up the road, wondering what had happened to their hero, the man who had defeated Armstrong.

Postal rode on, trading the lead according to plan. In best Armstrong form, they kept it casual. They may have been hurting, but they made sure their rivals only saw an easy manner, an occasional joke, the easy flip of a water bottle from one rider to another. On one steep section, riders stared as Hincapie casually rode no-handed while he fiddled with his sunglasses.

"I tried to escape, but the Postal Service was like a giant train that you couldn't escape," Mancebo said. "I was hoping some other riders would join me, but they were scared after they saw the effort I made for nothing. No one would risk it."

"On the climb of the Agnes, it was unbelievable," said Levi Leipheimer, an American who rode for the Dutch Rabobank squad. "I counted twenty-two riders in the group, with seven U.S. Postal guys in front. I've never seen anything like that."

"Christ, the Postals were strong," Australian rider Michael Rogers said.

The final climb of Plateau de Beille was a clinical application of brute force. First, Hincapie and Landis drove the peloton a kilometer or so, then pulled off. Then the ever-gentlemanly Rubiera, jersey unzipped to reveal a pale chest, applied more impolite pressure, reducing the group to eleven riders.

With twelve kilometers left, Rubiera finished his turn at the front and Azevedo took over. After a hard acceleration, eleven riders had been reduced to four. Then Ullrich slid off. Azevedo kept going, his face delirious, until the race had been distilled to yesterday's essence: Basso and Armstrong, tunneling through the orange throng. It soon became evident that yesterday's crowd antics had been merely a warm-up for Mayo's Basque fans, who still blamed Armstrong for leaving their hero behind on the cobbles. The Basques had already been busy key-scratching the Postal spaceship and emblazoning the OLN truck with the name of ETA, the Basque separatist organization. Now was their chance for more personal revenge, and they took it eagerly, screaming, gesturing, splashing beer and water on the American. Armstrong rode, grim-faced, his tires rolling over the letters: *LANCE PIG. LANCE-PO.* Armstrong let Basso lead through the chaos, Bruyneel's voice sounding in his ear, keeping him posted on Ullrich's slide—one minute, two minutes— and keeping up a stream of talk.

"Lance, drink water. Lance, let Basso pull. Lance, talk to him. Lance, push it. Lance, regulate."

The two rose into the last kilometer; yesterday's faces having switched. Armstrong looked comfortable, even serene. Basso, on the other hand, looked strained.

"Lance, you must win this stage," Bruyneel said.

With half a kilometer left, Armstrong zipped his jersey and moved his hands lower on the handlebars. He sprinted for the line, crossing a few meters in front of Basso, teeth gritted, into a wave of cheers and more than a few boos. He punched the air.

The loudest cheer sounded five minutes later, when young

Thomas Voeckler heaved himself into view, wearing the yellow jersey he'd earned nine days earlier. He'd been dropped several times during the stage, and each time had come back, wrenching the bike back and forth beneath him, his legs stiff as a marionette's, his eyes closing with effort. As he came closer, he saw the clock over the finish line, and his face cracked into a woozy, triumphant grin. Voeckler had kept his lead over Armstrong by a mere twenty-two seconds. He would stay in yellow for one more day.

"Le courage, l'humanité," the French murmured. *"C'est le Tour."*

An hour later, after the solemnity of the podium presentation, Armstrong and Crow walked across an open pasture toward a waiting helicopter, encircled by twenty or so arm-linked Clouseaus. A crowd followed, teenagers mostly, shouting what sounded like taunts. Among them was a Basque boy, a skinny, shirtless kid, maybe sixteen years old. The boy hopped alongside the gendarmes, waiting for the right moment. Then, when the gendarmes turned, the boy leapt over their linked arms and made a grab for Armstrong's black baseball cap. The boy started to lift it off, but it was tight, and as he lifted, Armstrong made a grab for the boy's arm, but the boy was too fast. He pulled again and the cap came off. The boy ducked, then danced off in triumph, waving his trophy, and the crowd shouted.

An hour later, an elite crew of Bros and Dudes played a game of touch football while they awaited their helicopter. The CS&E boys were there, along with Perry Farrell, Tom Dolan, CEO of Bristol-Myers Squibb, and Billy Campbell of the Discovery Channel. It was an epic moment in Bro and Dude history: there on the Olympian mountaintop, with all of Europe stretched before them, with the sweet images and stories of Armstrong's win streaming invisibly from the press tent to the waiting world. The Bros and Dudes had one hell of a game. They ran and dove and yowled in the empyrean mists, while the Basque people gazed from their greenwood campfires, staring with the dull eyes of the conquered.

The Basques watched the football arc through the air, watched an end-zone dance.

"What is this game?" an older man asked in halting English.

"It is American," another explained.

"You know what's funny?" Chris Carmichael was telling me. "Lance hardly talks at all about six Tours. Getting six isn't at the motivational core of the guy. It's more like, I'm just going to go to the Tour and kick the shit out of everybody.'"

Carmichael was standing in the OLN mobile studio atop a trailer at Villard de Lans, the finish of stage 15, the first day in the Alps. He was preparing for his analyst role, and had just asked announcer Al Trautwig if it would be okay if he worked in another plug for his new nutrition book, when a piece of surprising news came in: Ullrich had broken away.

"Ullrich?" Carmichael turned. "How much time does he have?"

Thirty seconds, the answer came.

Carmichael located a monitor. He crossed his arms and bit his lip.

"Nervous, Kid?" OLN commentator Bob Roll asked with a grin. Roll was a former cyclist and author, a friend of Armstrong's, and one of the sport's more subversive and entertaining characters.

"No," Carmichael said, leaning in to see the monitor. "It's under control."

On the little screen, a five-inch-high Ullrich surged away from Postal, opening up a gap of a minute with sixty kilometers to go. He blazed past other riders, his face alight. Behind him, Armstrong was down to only two teammates, Landis and Azevedo. Around the trailer, the crowd buzzed.

"Nervous, Kid?" Roll asked again.

"Lance has got, like, seven minutes on Ullrich," Carmichael said. "No way Ullrich can get even. No way."

Carmichael leaned in until his nose was inches from the screen. To this point the day had gone well for Armstrong. Mayo had quit this morning after he couldn't keep up with a team practice ride on the rest day ("Iban's problem is mental, not physical," said his manager, Miguel Madariaga). The stubborn Voeckler had been dropped by Ullrich's acceleration, which meant Armstrong would likely end the day in yellow. Now Carmichael watched Ullrich pull away, blowing past the day's early breakaway riders as if he were on a motorbike. It was a spectacular display of raw power; precisely the kind of surprise attack for which Ullrich's fans had been hoping.

"Too far out," Carmichael said. "Too far to go."

Landis led a furious chase, assisted by Basso's CSC teammate Jens Voigt, who dropped back from the breakaway to help. The sight of CSC helping Armstrong infuriated many of Ullrich's German fans, serving as proof of their suspicion that CSC had given up Basso's chance of winning, and were now content to scrap with Ullrich over second place. (Conspiracy theorists were heartened by the sight of a white envelope being passed between the Postal and CSC team cars. The dull truth—a mechanic passing his phone number to another mechanic—wasn't half as interesting.)

By the time the race entered its last climb to Villard de Lans, Carmichael had calmed considerably. Ullrich was caught with fifteen kilometers to go. ("When you don't win, you're always wrong," Ullrich said afterward.) The culling began. With three kilometers to go, Azevedo rode on the front of a group of ten. With two kilometers to go, the group went to five, including Ullrich, then to four. Armstrong and Basso, Kloden and Ullrich. Kloden led for much of the final stretch, trying to set up Ullrich for the win.

"C'mon, Lance," Carmichael said quietly. Behind him, on-camera, Al Trautwig and Roll commentated the finish.

Basso attacked. Armstrong reacted instantly, moving up on Basso. The last kilometer was tricky, with a tight left corner just before the line. Armstrong picked his moment and dove. He accelerated into the corner, cut it sharply, and flew to the line for the victory. Another sprint, another fist in the air, another yellow jersey.

"Lance Armstrong!" Trautwig boomed. "Laaaaance Armstrong!"

They tallied Armstrong's gains: He would pick up eight seconds on Basso (stage winners received a twenty-second time bonus, second place received a twelve-second bonus). He would pick up an additional fifteen seconds on Ullrich. The first Alps stage had been a perfect demonstration of team and individual strength. And something else, too.

"Did you see that?" Carmichael said to Trautwig during commercial break.

"See what?" Trautwig didn't look up.

"Lance knew that turn," Carmichael said. "He knew that left-hand turn, and that let him cut inside Basso."

Trautwig looked up blankly. Carmichael tried again.

"He knew the turn," Carmichael repeated slowly. "He was here this spring. He reconned it."

The word "reconned" did it. Trautwig snapped to full alert. That Armstrong won was not news, not anymore. Exactly how he won, however, remained as mysterious to Trautwig as it did to anybody else—after all, the sport was basically a bunch of guys pedaling along. But reconning?

"Get me a telestrator!" Trautwig boomed to his producers. "We're going to show that on the replay. He knew the turn! He reconned it!"

The studio buzzed with activity as the replay was being prepared. Trautwig scrawled some notes; producers scurried. Over in the corner, a Cheshire-cat grin was spreading slowly across cyclist Bob Roll's features.

"So he reconned the finish, huh Chris?"

"Yes," Carmichael said.

"He reee-conned it," Roll repeated with relish. "Lance reee-conned that last left-hand turn."

"Yep."

Roll turned and aimed a long, meaningful look at the roiling seascape of trailers and people that stretched to the horizon. He turned back to his colleague, immensely entertained.

"So let me get this straight." Roll's smile grew wider. "You are telling me that Lance Armstrong came here back in May, in the snow."

Carmichael nodded, his face blank.

"Before any of the trailers or barricades or anything was here," Roll continued, "and he found out exactly where the finish line was going to be, and he remembered that."

"Uh-huh." Carmichael's face stayed deadpan.

Roll smiled and shrugged.

Then Trautwig was bellowing to the producer, getting the telestrator online, preparing to deliver the story. It would not matter that later Armstrong would say that the corner's sharpness had caught him by surprise. It would not matter that twenty kilometers from the finish line, before he'd even caught Ullrich, Armstrong had said to Bruyneel over the radio, "Just have the Ace (Azevedo) keep it together. I'm going to win this stage." It would not matter that the real reason Armstrong won was closer to what Carmichael had said earlier—that Armstrong just plain liked to kick the shit out of every-body at the Tour. For now, the camera's red light blinked on, and millions of viewers were treated to a vivid, in-depth illustration of how Armstrong had won the stage, way back in May, when he had the icy-cool foresight to recon the finish.

Ullrich was now 6:54 down. Basso was second at 1:25, which was not as close as it seemed, since Basso himself estimated that he'd lose three minutes to Armstrong in the final time trial in Besançon. Barring a crash or an act of God, Armstrong had the Tour won, and since Armstrong didn't believe in God, only a crash could stop him. But truth was, he was just getting started.

CHAPTER 25
ALPE D'HUEZ

> Road racing imitates life, the way it would be without the corruptive influence of civilization. When you see an enemy lying on the ground, what's your first reaction? To help him to his feet?
>
> In road racing, you kick him to death.
>
> —TIM KRABBE, IN HIS NOVEL, *THE RIDER*

A mountain of people, that's what it looked like. As if the rock and turf had been scooped out and replaced, starting from the bottom, by geologic layers of humanity. The stout-calved Germans, the lanky Dutch, the gimlet-eyed French, the big-bellied Luxembourgers, the tight shorts–wearing Danes, all combined to form a hot, heaving pile of sunbroiled, stippled flesh, the citizenry of Europe having set aside their cultural and geopolitical differences to commune in the service of a shared belief, the core of which was painted on the black pavement in large, carefully edged white letters: FUCK LANCE.

Also *LANCE SUCKS, EPO LANCE, GO HOME LANCE,* and *ARMSTRONG PIG,* along with a few less gentle sentiments that sought to express the feelings of the half-million people who had come here to the stage 16 time trial on the legendary Alpe d'Huez.

By purely objective standards, Alpe d'Huez should not be a legend. At fourteen kilometers, it lacks the tortuous length of some

Tour climbs; at a consistent 8–10 percent grade, it lacks vicious, drama-creating upturns. But Alpe d'Huez qualifies as a legend, because, like the Tour itself, it is carved from pure romance. It's a hairpin road to nowhere, the site of sacramental victories that started with the hallowed Coppi in 1952 and moved through Hinault to Pantani to Armstrong, who won here in 2001. The Alpe captures and compresses the Tour in the folds of its road, distilling its frenzy to a potent essence, the pure human spectacle of half a million souls gathered on a slab of rock to watch a race.

It looked quite different now than it had back in late May, when my son and I had come here to do a recon of our own. We'd ridden the first few hairpins together on mountain bikes, an experience that confirmed the mountain's steepness and its lethality, particularly on the third turn, when we passed an ambulance and a group of bored-looking paramedics zipping up a bodybag containing a sixty-year-old French cyclist who'd suffered a heart attack.

"Oui, il est mort." A paramedic shrugged when I asked. *"C'est l'Alpe."*

At this moment, as it happened, Armstrong had good reason to be thinking about mortality, namely the death threat he'd received the night before. Armstrong had learned of it from Stapleton, who'd been told by Tour organizers, who'd notified French authorities. Death threats were nothing new—Armstrong had received one last year, too, in Toulouse. They'd dealt with it the usual way, a slight variation on the Batman method: Serge and Erwin, linked-arm rings of gendarmes, a speedy helicopter evacuation from the finish. But today was different. This was a time trial, each rider alone against the clock. Everyone on the mountain knew to the minute when Armstrong would depart. Every troll, if they so desired, could get close enough to touch.

The Tour has a rich history of fan overparticipation. The race's early days featured nail-strewn roads, carefully timed roadblocks, sawn-through handlebars, and, in one case, covert sprinkling of itching powder in a rider's shorts. Fans were particularly busy in 1911. After top contender Paul Duboc was poisoned, his rival Gustave Garrigou had to don a disguise to evade a revenge-minded lynch mob in Duboc's hometown of Rouen.

As fate would have it, fans had played a key role in scuttling two previous attempts to win a sixth Tour. In 1975 a Frenchman punched Eddy Merckx in the kidney on the Puy de Dome. Merckx finished the stage, but the medicine he subsequently took may have contributed to his crack the following day on Pra Loup. In 1966 another fan poured a bucket of water over Jacques Anquetil before the long, fifty miles per hour descent of Grand St-Bernard. Anquetil caught a chill on the way down and withdrew the following day, suffering from bronchitis.

Thus far, on this year's Tour, Armstrong had been lucky. Even so, teammates still reminded him to stay in a group. "Never, ever be alone," they told him. "If anybody's going to do anything, it will be then."

Naturally, the death threat was kept secret, or as secret as possible, which wasn't very. Truth was, this was completely expected. "Lance spends a lot of time thinking about security, but the bottom line is that there isn't much that he can do when he's on the bike," said Chris Brewer. Brewer, a testicular cancer survivor who runs Armstrong's Web site, worked eighteen years in the Air Force's Opposition Forces division. His specialty was infiltration, finding holes in secure zones. "If someone wants to get him bad enough, there are many ways they could get him. And Lance knows that."

At the start, in the village of Bourg d'Oisans, Armstrong warmed up on the stationary rollers, looking relaxed, chatting with the gendarmes. His mood tightened when he learned Sheryl Crow might have to give up her seat in the follow car for a security agent. But then, another plan: there would be two extra motorcycles, with more security agents aboard, and another next to Bruyneel in the car.

"We were terrified," Bruyneel said.

On the mountain ahead, the mass of humanity shifted restlessly. Many had been waiting for several days, wedging campers and tents along the steep roadside; others opted for the less elegant, sleeping-bag-on-the-pavement approach. All of them had spent a long, hot morning defending their space from the arriving hordes as the mountain swelled and grew. The sun slammed down, alcohol flowed, cigarettes flared. When the race began, the crowd contented itself by lazily torturing Armstrong's teammates, and by early appearances, they were in rare form. Rubiera reached the top looking as if he might break into tears. Voigt of CSC received special treatment for his role in helping Armstrong chase down Ullrich the previous day (*JUDAS*, many of the signs read). His later pleas that he was helping his team captain, Basso, were dismissed as immaterial: he was helping Armstrong, and so he was guilty.

They didn't all hate Armstrong, of course. In fact, many European fans admired the American; they commonly greeted his passing with respectful applause. Armstrong had made efforts to improve his image, speaking more French and expressing respect for the tradition of the race. But no amount of diplomacy could change the brute fact that he, an outsider, had come to dominate Europe's biggest race at a time when American influence was seen as something less than a good thing. It would be easy to chalk this up to an extension of anti-Bush, anti-American sentiment, but, in fact, the war in Iraq was almost never mentioned. Nor had the latest doping allegations created a wave of resentment. Most Europeans shrugged: everybody knew that they all doped anyway, right?

No, the truth was that Armstrong offended because he would not give European fans what they desired from their sports heroes: pain, vulnerability, suffering, humanity. His recovery from cancer, the inspirational touchstone for many Americans, was regarded by Europeans with mild interest: a feat of medicine and discipline, certainly, but that was what, eight years ago? Wasn't the treatment fairly brief, a matter of months? It was impressive, yes, but hadn't plenty of other cyclists overcome extraordinarily difficult circumstances? After the Tour, Armstrong would rank third in a French survey of most-hated sports stars. What they wanted was a man wrestling fate, not obliterating it.

"I think they genuinely hate him," said Andreas Kloden. "He comes across as so impenetrable. If Armstrong has a difficult relationship with the public, then he has only himself to blame. Perhaps that even motivates him."

First Ullrich rode off, then Kloden, then Basso, all of them helmetless in the heat. At the last minute, Armstrong considered donning his helmet to fend off any bottles or rocks. He decided not to, figuring the helmet might, in fact, encourage contact. He mounted the start ramp wearing a blue Postal hat turned backward. In the car, Crow bit her nails.

He had good legs, he'd told her that morning. He could feel it when they hit the floor, the familiar strength and springiness that foretold a good day, maybe a great day. But first he would need to get to the top in one piece. The bottom two-thirds of the climb were unbarriered. For nine kilometers, nothing would stand between himself and the people; about twenty-four minutes of what the military-minded Brewer termed "major exposure."

The first two minutes were flat, a gentle rise from town, a quick zip through the crowds. Then a hard left, the road tilted upward, and he was inside them.

Troll mouths screaming, blasting him with sour breath. Flags snapping like whips. A shaking forest of fists inches in front of his wheel. It seemed as if he was riding down some endless collective throat, a peristaltic dive into some unseen belly. Armstrong stared at the motorcycle's wheel, felt something warm on his leg. Troll spit.

"It made me sick," Crow said later.

He rode, his legs firing out the familiar high cadence. All strategy was reduced to one reflex: if I go faster, they can't get me. The crowd reacted, red-faced men stepping into the road for a crouched, clenched scream, then falling out of the way at the last second. On their motorcycles, the security agents swatted and pushed, trying to clear a path. A roadside gendarme tackled two threatening-looking men; only to have them replaced by more. They threw beer and water; they spat. They were aiming for his face, but most hit his jersey, providing Armstrong a desultory jolt of satisfaction: he was going faster than they'd anticipated.

Bruyneel drove the team car close behind, snowplowing sluggish trolls out of the way. He would draw an official sanction from Tour officials for blocking television-camera motorcycles, but Bruyneel didn't care: the car's presence shortened the trolls' window of opportunity. Bruyneel read the splits, kept up the encouraging talk, as if his voice might block those other voices out.

"Very good, Lance, very good."

Armstrong marked his progress by the numbers of the turns (signposted in reverse order, from 21 to 1) and the church steeples of the two small hamlets along the road. He moved past the smiling Dutchmen from Maastricht at turn 18, past the Belgian guy at turn 8, who'd parked his camper three weeks ago, and the sad Basques who'd hiked up with their bedsheet signs. Past the German technopop groovers and the other Dutch guy with the microphone, shouting, "Show me your titties!" He rolled over the GO ULLRICH and GO BASSO messages, over the elaborately detailed penises, and over a sign that said RIP THEIR BALLS OFF, LANCE!

Yes, Americans were here, too, in huge numbers. In their yellow baseball caps and Uncle Sam hats and and Postal jerseys, their arms swathed in yellow bracelets, waving Texan and American flags and sending out the whooping, ringing call of the American sports fan. There weren't just a few, either. There were dozens, hundreds, thousands of bright-eyed, ecstatically sober Yanks on that mountain (twenty-five thousand of them, it was estimated), people who didn't give a damn about Eurofate or history, people who had come across an ocean and who were now receiving the birthright that every American desires and demands: a miracle.

"Whoooooooooooooooooo Lance!" they shouted as Armstrong rode past. "Whoooooooooooooooo!"

He rode furiously. Up ahead, Ullrich had set the day's top mark at the intermediate time check, besting the previous time by a whopping thirty-three seconds. Armstrong came through, wanting to hear his number, wanting the proof. He listened as Bruyneel read it: he'd beaten Ullrich by forty seconds.

Forty seconds! Atop the mountain, a group of German fans

blinked at the number on the screen, openmouthed. One turned away in disgust.

Armstrong rode through the last of the crowd and on to the relative safety of the barriered road. Up ahead, at turn 3, he could see Basso, who was having a bad day. He'd trained here in May, but now his legs would not turn the same-size gear. Basso was straining, his grace evaporating, his seminarian's face etched in pain. Armstrong surged past without a look.

He sprinted for the line, low and hard, fists clenched, teeth bared, an image of freshly peeled ferocity. Some of the crowd shouted, but many more stared. After 156 riders, 156 different exhausted faces, they were seeing something different, a face that did not ask for applause or love or understanding or anything except the animal respect due a superior force.

Armstrong crossed the line and Batmanned to the safety of the trailer, accompanied by Serge and Erwin.

"Got 'em," he said.

That night, contendedness reigned atop Alpe d'Huez. At a lovely chalet near the airfield, the Dudes and Bros gathered to celebrate Robin Williams's birthday with a Julian Serrano-prepared feast of quail and salmon. Armstrong couldn't come, but sent Williams a yellow jersey as a present.*

A few hundred yards away, at the Club Med hotel, Postal, T-Mobile, and a few other teams settled in for the night with the

---

*Williams is a passionate recreational cyclist (he owns sixty bikes) who comes to the tour every year, attends corporate team events, and occasionally rides with Armstrong. Because they're both celebrities, and because Williams is, well, Williams (i.e., alternating between unbearably manic and cloyingly saccharine), it's impossible to tell just how close their friendship is. But here's something weird: there were times when Armstrong's sense of humor reminded me of— horrors!—Williams. Armstrong is uncannily good at imitations, and lightning-quick with the out-of-nowhere, stream-of-consciousness joke. Once, on a training ride, Armstrong passed a fellow biker who happened to be wearing a turban. Half a second went by, then Armstrong spoke: "Hey, it's Osama Been Bikin'!"

usual routine: massage, dinner, sleep. As the riders went to bed, the hotel bar filled with *soigneurs,* coaches, and various insiders who formed beery circles to rehash the Tour and compete in their own Shrug Olympics. On a cramped stage, a five-foot-tall bald lounge singer belted Queen covers. On the stairs, Jan Ullrich was chatting quietly with his brother, Stefan, who was informing him that their mother would be coming to watch tomorrow's race. In a corner, the ever-smiling Erwin was demonstrating the Kali death-grip to the exuberant amusement of the Cutters, a group of die-hard Armstrong fans. Elvio was text-messaging a podium girl, planning a rendezvous at a club. Everybody, to one extent or another, was relaxing. Almost everybody.

Upstairs in his room, Floyd Landis was pacing. He knew he was supposed to have his feet up, supposed to be resting, supposed to be saving his energy for the next day, but he couldn't. He was angry, working himself into a full, unfrozen Mennonite rage over Johan Bruyneel's joke.

They'd been sitting around after dinner that night when Bruyneel leaned back in his chair and smiled that big Belgian smile and said, "Hey Floyd, twenty-first place today—not so bad for going easy, eh?"

Then he smiled again and everybody laughed knowingly.

"I did go easy," Landis replied. "Just like you told me to."

"Right," Bruyneel said, smiling hugely. "Twenty-first out of one hundred fifty-six, eh? Pretty good."

Landis tried to respond good-naturedly. "Hey, I can't help if I'm in good shape," he said. But Bruyneel wasn't listening.

"Twenty-first!" he said. "Twenty-first!"

Bruyneel's message was clear: I told you to go easy and you didn't. Consciously or unconsciously, you showed off, and in showing off, you spent energy that should have been reserved for the team. You broke the unbreakable rule: you put yourself above Armstrong. Bruyneel had ample reason to make the point. A *domestique*—not even a climber, coming in twenty-first while going easy? Impossible.

There was one hitch to Bruyneel's theory: it was wrong.

"I tried to tell him, but he wouldn't listen," Landis said later. "I went easy. I kept it below my limit, I didn't burn any matches. I have never, ever saved anything for myself on this team, ever, I have always done the maximum I could do. Why would he say that?"

The tension Landis had felt back in June had never really disappeared, and, in fact, had increased when a Dutch newspaper printed the rumor that Landis was thinking of signing with Tyler Hamilton's Phonak team.

"There's a weird vibe around Floyd," Toshi Corbett of Giro said during stage 4. "The sponsors are worried. Floyd's the next American, the next big guy, maybe a Tour winner. For him to leave Lance now, what does that say?"

Landis, however, was not concerned about vibes, or sponsors, or appearances that might fall short of the marketer's ideal. Like others before him, Landis felt hemmed in by Postal. What they wanted were docile horses who didn't ask questions, who didn't rock the boat. That wasn't him.

"They try to tell me it's a privilege to ride for 40 percent less than what other teams offer?" Landis said. "That might be fine for other guys, but not for me."

"Postal tries to act like it's one happy family, but it is a business, period," Landis's agent, Mike Rutherford, said later. "Floyd's a huge talent, and he wants to win big races. Armstrong is like a black hole. He sucks in everything."

Bruyneel's joke was given added edge by the fact that some of Postal's riders were hurting. Azevedo had fallen sick with chills and fever during the rest day before the Alps, and Rubiera was suffering the effects of his earlier injury, which meant Landis moved up in the rotation, given the responsibility of protecting Armstrong on the last climbs. Landis, who was not known as a climber, had ridden outstandingly well in stage 15, leading the chase of Ullrich and pruning the pack to a handful, a performance impressive enough that Armstrong deemed him "player of the day." But as Landis thought about his role on the team, and about next year, the core issue remained.

"The question is, do you need to be like Armstrong to win?" Landis told me in May. "I don't think you do. I think there's another way to do it."

Tonight, in the darkness of the hotel room, it all came back. The more Landis thought about Bruyneel's joke, the angrier he got. The angrier Landis got, the more certain he became: there was only one way out of this, one way to prove Bruyneel and Armstrong wrong, one way to escape the Postal team and show his loyalty at the same time. As luck would have it, that way passed directly through familiar territory: hell.

The heat rose from the road in waves, reflected off the rocks, poured from a thousand car exhausts, laid itself in a great shimmering track up the Col de Croix Fry, the last true climb of the 2004 Tour. It glowed like an unwelcome mirage at the end of a long, delirious day, 205 kilometers of riding, five categorized climbs, 17,000 feet of climbing, the second-toughest day in the Tour. Until this point, Postal had done their job with now-customary efficiency, pruning the peloton down to an elite twenty, an all-star team including Basso, Kloden, Karpets, Simoni, and Virenque. Landis moved to the front.

The situation was straightforward: Landis's job was to ride tempo, to chase the lingering breakaway, to keep things stable. Landis, however, had more in mind. He was not wearing argyle socks today, but he may as well have been. His face seemed to squish up on itself. The big gear began to whir. The scenery blurred into colors, faces. A Mennonite kid from Pennsylvania started to ride.

His family had been there a couple days earlier, standing by the side of the road. They'd come from Farmersville, their second time on an airplane, his mom, Arlene, and his father, Paul, and his sisters Charity, Priscilla, and Abigail, the women in their long dresses and prayer veils, standing straight and tall and a little nervous amid Europe's devilry and sex and craziness, holding out their response, a hand-lettered sign of Mennonite clarity: WE SUPPORT FLOYD LANDIS.

They brought photos, too, pasted to a piece of cardboard, which they showed anybody who asked. Photos of Farmersville and of young

Floyd on his bike standing next to their small brick house. Passers-by stopped, people from everywhere, and the Landises showed them the photos, too. It was the strangest thing, chatting with complete strangers on a road in the middle of France about their son, about themselves. But they did it. Landis was a bit embarrassed by the attention. But he liked it, too. He hadn't thought his family could be so open, so comfortable with strangers. So proud of him.

He kept riding. Now there were fifteen riders left. The climb moved into a high valley, through a granite-rimmed amphitheater, the sort of landscape that's always described as a cathedral. Landis sometimes rode with his hands folded. Riding was prayer, it had its own mysteries, its sacrifices. As with prayer, the question was, to whom were you praying? For what end was the sacrifice intended?

Halfway up the climb, the slope eased to five percent. Behind him, riders perked up, hoping for a break. Landis gave them none, and when the road rose to 10 percent, he pushed harder. More riders fell away.

"Good job, Floyd," Bruyneel said. "Very good job."

Seeing riders drop, the television commentators hesitated, trying to figure out what was happening. Attacks they understood, but this? This was a *domestique* riding tempo, yet the Tour's top riders were getting blown out of the back like so many tumbleweeds. Landis's speed became apparent when the day's breakaway was swept up in a blink, not caught so much as trampled.

Behind Landis, the faces showed signs of cracking.

"I was on my limit just trying to stay there," Levi Leipheimer said later. "Everyone was hurting. Kloden was yo-yoing, so I went around him. I could see that Ullrich was low, that Lance was getting lower, and that Floyd was still strong."

Ullrich stood to keep up, as did Basso. Landis accepted a large bottle of water from a spectator and poured it over his head, then turned to offer some to his captain. Tight-faced, Armstrong declined, his hands gripping his bars.

Landis was in full reverie, moving toward something: a new team, a new place, working himself into the state of mind when a rider is most dangerous, when his ride tells a story. Landis was telling his story with each rider dropped, a story for the doubting Bruyneel, for his parents, for other teams, and for Armstrong, a message that was both proof of his loyalty and, though Landis would never say so, also the subtlest provocation that grew in emphasis with each rider that fell away: *I could drop you, too.*

Landis and Armstrong crossed the summit, followed closely by Ullrich, Kloden, and Basso. Armstrong put his hand on Landis's back and asked if he could go downhill fast.

"Real fast," Landis said.

"Ride like you stole something, Floyd," Armstrong said.

Landis took off. Ullrich chased, however, shutting down Landis's chances. Armstrong caught up, and for a moment the three of them rode, Ullrich gesturing angrily. Why wouldn't they go? If the three of them worked together, they could get to the finish; one of them would surely win the stage.

Armstrong said no. Basso and Kloden rejoined the three, and five of them came into the outskirts of Grand Bornand. After Landis tried again to escape, and Ullrich chased him down, Kloden launched a powerful attack with one kilometer left, opening up a football field–sized gap.

Landis chased, Armstrong on his wheel. With three hundred meters left, however, Kloden had the stage sewn up. He still had forty meters on Armstrong, too far for anyone to catch. In commentary boxes, heads started to nod: it would be a deserving victory, proof of Kloden's fine Tour, a touch of redemption for Germany and T-Mobile.

Armstrong whipped around the exhausted Landis, head down, wrenching his bike from side to side with effort. He shot forward, the gap with Kloden closing with uncanny rapidity. Still, the distance seemed too great. He couldn't possibly.

Armstrong checked behind him, made sure Ullrich wasn't lurking on his wheel. Then, with Kloden only a few dozen meters from the line, Armstrong took thirteen pedal strokes, thirteen unmatchable bursts. Kloden, sensing something, tried to respond, couldn't. Armstrong's last pedal stroke pushed his front wheel a few inches in front of Kloden's. Armstrong's arms spread like wings, his face open in raw astonishment.

"Nothing personal," Armstrong whispered to Kloden afterward.

"Perfect," Hinault told Armstrong on the podium. "No gifts."

The sages contemplated Armstrong's feat: yet another sprint win; four mountain stage wins in a row; something beyond Hinault, beyond Merckx, beyond anyone.

"He has expanded his repertoire again," said Tour historian Jacques Augendre. "Now he has become a sprinter. It is crazy."

Afterward, Italian rider Gilberto Simoni was asked if Armstrong's win was the sign of a new Cannibal, Merckx's nickname. "That's not the act of a cannibal," Simoni said. "That's the act of a piranha."

Other riders expressed similar sentiments, but not Landis. "[The T-Mobile riders] were bummed they didn't win. But what do they think this is, a Christmas party?" he asked. "I trained six months for this too, man."

Despite the finish-line drama, the sages agreed that Landis was the story of the day. He'd proven himself Armstrong's most valuable teammate, a talent worthy of leading another team. Right now, however, Landis only wished to straighten something out with Bruyneel, who was now clapping him on the back, speaking in his big Belgian voice, telling him good job, Floyd, good job.

Landis smiled. "I tried to tell you," he said.

CHAPTER 26

THE SOURCE

I've never had a single conversation with my mother about
[my biological father]. Not once. In 28 years, she's never
brought him up, and I've never brought him up. It may
seem strange, but it's true. The thing is, I don't care, and my
mother doesn't either.

—LANCE ARMSTRONG, *IT'S NOT ABOUT THE BIKE*

Her presence was felt in the clubhouse long before she arrived. At the
Besançon time trial, two days after Armstrong's sprint at Grand Bornand, the Dudes and Bros shifted alertly, scanning the crowd.

"She's here."

"Where?"

"Flew in this morning."

They exchanged grave, professorial nods, un-Dudelike seriousness being the only preparation for the imminent arrival of the only
person who might possibly hold more power than Armstrong: his
mother, Linda.

She still surprised them, trotting through the crowd on cat feet,
a tiny, blond fifty-year-old woman in a blue top and black Capri
pants. She worked her way toward the bus wielding her elbows and
her eyes, which flickered sharply around. She had a loaf of banana
bread in one arm, and a thickset, bewildered-looking man in a golf
shirt on the other. She may have been looking for her son—who was
due to arrive any second for his warm-up—but she saw everyone.

"Hi hi hi guys," Linda Armstrong called as she ducked under the rope, pulling the man through behind her.

"Mo-om!" the CS&E boys cried. They greeted her with full Dude and Bro honors, hugs, kisses. They greeted the golf-shirt man, too— Linda's husband, her fourth or fifth, the CS&E boys thought. Mr. Four/ Five stood politely. From the team car, Bruyneel watched warily.

But Mom was already past them, having spotted someone. "Hi hi hi!" she called in a piping twang, greeting familiar faces in the crowd, working the ropeline. They were all familiar faces, it seemed, pulling her over, wanting to chat, to share in the glow of this moment, and if they weren't familiar just yet, they soon would be.

"Jiminy crickets," Linda said to one well-wisher. She put her hands on her hips, taking in the scene. "Isn't it something? It is something, isn't it?"

Around her, sprinkled by an intermittent rain, the circus of the Tour carried on in slightly dampened glory, a glory that at the moment was wrapped up in a question created the previous day by stage 18, a question Linda Armstrong could perhaps help answer: What more did her son want?

Yesterday was supposed to have been an uneventful day, a smooth run across the flats that separated the mountains from the last time trial. It began as exactly that, when eight riders broke away at the ten-kilometer mark. The plot line was clear: After a week of Armstrong dominance, this was a day for one of the other riders to find victory. The plot line changed, however, when a troll named Filippo Simeoni quietly slid up to the front.

Thirty-two-year-old Simeoni was a troll because he'd testified against Ferrari in the notorious doctor's 2002 trial. Actually, as Armstrong took pains to point out, he had testified several times, providing varying accounts of his relationship with the good doctor, admitting to using dope himself (he'd received a four-month ban), and eventually coming around to the story that Ferrari had provided him with EPO and instructions on how to avoid getting caught. When Armstrong called him "an absolute liar" in *Le Monde,* Simeoni had sued the American for defamation of character in an Italian court, vowing to donate any award to charity. At Postal's prerace meeting on the morning of stage 18, Simeoni's name had come up.

"Don't let Simeoni in the break," Armstrong told his teammates. "He'll try to do something and then mouth off."

In fact, Simeoni had been allowed in a break during stage 9, and had come close to winning the stage. But now, with the race in control, Armstrong wasn't going to let it happen again. When he saw Simeoni pass, Armstrong jumped onto the Italian's wheel, expecting his team to follow. Caught off-guard, they didn't. Within seconds, the two were gone up the road. Postal was left scratching their heads along with the rest of the peloton.

"We didn't know what the hell was going on," Landis said later. "By the time we did, it was too late, and what were we going to do, chase our own guy down?"

Once he and Simeoni were alone, Armstrong had to make a choice. He could back off, let Simeoni go, then order his team to chase. Instead, Armstrong upped the ante, not only staying with Simeoni but leading him up to the breakaway, showing his superior strength.

When the two reached the break, the eight riders turned in rank disbelief. The yellow jersey trying to break away? Armstrong pointed at Simeoni.

"If he stays, I stay," he said.

The eight riders knew that if the yellow jersey remained with them, the peloton would surely chase them down. Several of them pleaded with Simeoni to drop back, which he did.

Armstrong and Simeoni drifted back together, talking. Simeoni later recounted Armstrong's words for an Italian newspaper. "[Armstrong] said, 'You made a mistake to speak against Ferrari, and you made a mistake to take legal action against me. I have money and time and lots of lawyers. I can destroy you.'"

Armstrong rejoined the peloton in a high mood, laughing and miming a zipped-lips gesture. Several riders shouted at Simeoni, who rode with his head down at the rear of the peloton, his humiliation complete.

While most of the peloton supported Armstrong—or, to put it more accurately, kept their mouths firmly shut—the Tour's sages were nearly unanimous in their condemnation of Armstrong's move.

"A moment revealing all of the champion's cunning and ruthlessness, that will forever color memories of his career," intoned *Procycling* magazine.

"It throws light on his split personality," said *L'Equipe*.

"Vindictive and disingenuous," said former British great Chris Boardman.

"The ugliest side . . . of the race's grandest champion," said *Bicycling* magazine.

"I was protecting the interests of the peloton," Armstrong said. "He's not a rider that the peloton wants to be in the front group. All he does is attack cycling and say bad things about the other riders and the group in general. All he wants to do is destroy cycling, to destroy the sport that pays him."

"I am surprised by what Armstrong did today, but he showed in front of the whole world what kind of person he is," Simeoni said. "It's a sin."

"Lance made his point," Landis said later. "He's like that; if he thinks something he has to let it out. If somebody fucks with him, he makes it clear that they shouldn't."

Beneath the elms of Besançon, Linda Armstrong visited with the crowd, posed for a few photos. When Air Force One pulled up a few moments later she was ready, banana bread outstretched.

"Now *this* is the good stuff," Armstrong told a nearby Dude, giving a relishing sniff to some more Shit That Will Kill Them. "I'm talking about the best."

Mother and son chatted. There was no lingering embrace, no sentimentality; just the cordial briskness of two people who speak every day. Mr. Four/Five watched politely. So did American fans, who had seemingly tripled in number since Alpe d'Huez. They stared at her tiny body, at the quick movements of her limbs, at her fine, vaguely hawkish features, the intensity of her blue gaze. They felt the Freudian buzz of being in the presence of the latest in the series of great American mother-son relationships. Long before Lance had given anyone The Look, he had watched his mother give it to the world on his behalf.

"She was fifteen when she had him," one woman stage-whispered, missing the number (Linda was seventeen) but nailing the essence: Lance Armstrong had come from the womb of a child. A single mother, daughter of a Vietnam veteran, a hard-scrapping Texas girl from the housing projects—perfect! There was a father, of course, a no-good abandoning father, the most no-good thing about him being how good he seemed at first, before his true colors showed.

It started with Linda's first husband and Lance's father, Ed Gunderson, who, a few years after their bitter divorce, signed a paper that renounced his rights to his son, in order for Lance to be legally adopted by Linda's new husband, Terry Armstrong.

And if the story was perhaps a little more complicated than that, too bad. If Gunderson later told a reporter for the *Austin American-Statesman* that he was afraid not to sign the papers because he'd fallen behind in his $20-a-week child-support payments and feared he'd be jailed, well, that was too bad, too. If Gunderson, who lived near Dallas, still carried a photo of Lance in his wallet and had two children who'd never met their half-brother, that was also too bad. And if Gunderson's mother, when she found out her grandson had cancer, had led a special prayer service for Armstrong every Sunday at Four Mile Lutheran Church, and if she still wrote letters to Armstrong, letters that were never answered, well, that was too bad as well.

After Gunderson and Terry Armstrong came John Walling. All of them showed their true colors, one by one. Linda showed hers, too, rising from the registers at Kentucky Fried Chicken to become an account manager at a telecommunications company, with a real-estate license to boot. When her twelve-year-old son showed interest and ability in swimming, then triathlons, then cycling, she put that ferocious energy behind him. Make every negative into a positive, she said.

Mother and son lived together inside a capsule of forward

momentum, never looking back. When Armstrong was fifteen, he became friends with Rick Crawford, who at the time was the nation's third-ranked triathlete. They met when Armstrong leapt into a pool and started swimming alongside Crawford and another top triathlete, Mike Pigg. "Can I train with you guys?" he asked.

Crawford, who'd just moved to Dallas and was recently divorced, taught Armstrong how to train, lent him gear, and over several years became close to mother and son (Crawford's ex-wife and Linda were friends). There was some tension between Crawford and the young Armstrong, most often when the two traveled alone together to various triathlons. Armstrong, never the most obedient child, tended to run wild. On a trip to Bermuda, Armstrong rented a moped in Crawford's name and didn't return for hours, leading to a police search. That night at dinner, Armstrong was horsing around and broke some expensive dishes and crystalware at the house where they were staying, which was owned by a friend of Crawford's. Fed up and embarrassed, Crawford shouted at Armstrong, at one point holding him against a wall. "Fuck you," Armstrong yelled back. "You're not my dad." And that was it: Crawford was out.

"She's queen of the universe, and she holds him in such reverence," Crawford said. "He was real fragile, just a raw nerve.

"When things were peachy, they treated me like gold, and we were like a family," Crawford continued. "But when that happened, it was over. I wrote Linda a note explaining and apologizing, saying I loved her son. But I was never in their house again. It's the anger they have, that's the bad thing and the good thing, because it's what created the whole package."

When Armstrong was twenty-one, he spoke about his mother's second divorce. "When you're growing up, you're fourteen, fifteen, or sixteen, and you're in high school or whatever, your friends' parents are getting divorced and the kids are falling apart. They start crying, they get upset, they gotta have counselors and they gotta have this, that, and the other. I'm looking around, seeing all of this, and my stepfather left. And I had a party, you know, because it's such a load off my back. I got confused because I thought, 'Well, man, what is wrong with you?' This tears kids up and yet we're kicking this guy out and [I'm] ecstatic.

"For a while, I thought maybe something's wrong with me but then I just realized how happy we both were. Actually, my mom wasn't that happy, because it is just like any relationship, you're miserable being in it but you don't want to end it. And so she broke it off and then she was lonely, and nobody's happy when they're lonely. But I tell you she was a hell of a lot better off than being miserable. And that's true for everybody. I don't care what the situation is, it's always better to be lonely, because you can always find someone else, and she has."

Lance and Linda chatted for five minutes. Over their shoulders, riders departed to the time trials, a fifty-five kilometer loop through the hills and dells around Besançon. Then it was time.

"I better get going, and you better too," Linda said. "I'll see you at the finish."

"Okay, Mom," he said.

Linda was already on the move, taking Mr. Four/Five's hand, walking toward the rope line, checking out the territory ahead, smiling at a new friend. Behind her, as if in a mirror, her son was doing something very much the same.

Armstrong rolled into the starting gate. Ahead of him, Floyd Landis had set the best time; Kloden and Basso were on the road, fighting for second and third. Ullrich was riding mostly for pride and doing a good job of it, bettering Landis's splits—this was, after all, where he was to have won the Tour.

The starter held the seat. To the side, some gendarmes tussled with a troll who was trying to spit on Armstrong. The American looked down, hardly noticing.

"He's going to be scary today," Chris the mechanic said. "He feels it."

Armstrong leaned on his bike. The road glowed.

Trois. Deux. Un. Partez.

In the stands at the finish line, Linda Armstrong began moving her legs in the rhythm of her son's.

In the car, Bruyneel stared. Armstrong was going out hard, far harder than he needed to.

Let's fly. That's what the Postal guys always say to him right before he goes. To escape, to leave it all behind, to explode out and up until he can look down over the curve of the earth. That's what he did, with no reason, no pressure, no rivals except the desire to feel that feeling, to get up there, now.

"I've never seen him ride like that," Bruyneel said. "We usually want to start time trials slowly and go faster as it goes on. But here, he was like a madman."

Bruyneel quickly got over his surprise, and settled down to guide Armstrong through the ride. He spoke in the usual way, which for Bruyneel was to pretend as if he were inside Armstrong's mind, an extension of his will.

Here is what Bruyneel said:

Very good, very good, very good.
Come on Lance, come on, very good, come on, come on, come on.
Come on Lance, kill those fucking motherfuckers!
Very good Lance, very good.
Stay in the middle of the road. Stay in the middle of the road.
Very good Lance, very good. Come on come on come on.
Come on Lance, come on come on COME ON!
Very good, very good, very good!
Come on come on come on come on come on.
Fifty seconds faster than Ullrich. Fifty seconds faster than Ullrich.
Find our rhythm find our rhythm find our rhythm.
Very good, very good, very good come on come on come on.
Come on Lance, come on come on come on!
Come on Lance, come on COME ON COME ON COME ON.
Come on Lance, come on come on COME ON!
Come on Lance come on come on COME ON!
Very good Lance come on GO GO GO GO GO!
Here we turn to the right on the big road.
Come on come on COME ON!

Come on Lance come on come on.

Three hundred meters uphill and then it's downhill. Come on!

Yes yes yes yes yes!

Come on Lance, come on, we can take Basso, we can catch Basso.

Basso is there, Basso is there in front of you.

Not too close to the people, not too close to the people.

Come on Lance, come on come on come on come on!

Still fifty seconds for Ullrich, fifty seconds for Ullrich.

Come on Lance! Come on come on come on COME ON!

Come on Lance! Come on! Come on! COME ON!

Come on Lance! Come on! Come on! 5k! 5k!

Come on Lance! Come on come on COME ON!

Come on Lance! Come on! Come on! Come on!

Come on Lance! Come on! Come on! 5k! 5k!

Come on come on come on!

Come on Lance! Come on! Come on! Come on! GO GO GO!

There's Basso in front of you, there's Basso!

Here we go left . . . that's it . . . come on come on.

No turns anymore, all straight. Come on! Come on! COME ON!

Come on Lance, two kilometers.

Come on man come on! Let's go for Basso! Come on come on COME ON!

Come on Lance very good very good very good come on push it! Push it! PUSH IT!

Come on Lance come on come on come on.

The last kilometer's easier Lance, the last kilometer's easier.

Come on Lance, come on! Come on! Come on!

Come on Lance! Come on! Come on! A minute on Ullrich, a minute!

Come on come on!

Great job! Great job!

GREAT! GREAT! GREAT! GREAT! GREAT!

A few minutes after the stage ended, Armstrong ran into Ullrich at the medical control tent. They stood for a moment looking at each other. For ten years they had been together at the top of the sport, ever since that rainy day in Oslo in 1993, when Ullrich had won the world amateur title and Armstrong had won the world pro title. Two men, forever defined by each other.

Armstrong reached out to shake the German's hand.

"Awwwwww, come on," Ullrich said, and pulled the surprised Armstrong into a friendly bear hug.

"Can you believe that?" Armstrong said later, still in disbelief. "He *hugged* me."

Result, 19:

(1)   Armstrong, 1 hour, 6 minutes, 49 seconds
(2)   Ullrich at 1:01 behind
(3)   Kloden at 1:27
(4)   Landis at 2:25

CHAPTER 27

INTO THE LIGHT

There is a quality of light that exists on the Champs Élysées on the final afternoon of the Tour de France. The sun angles in from the southwest, quartering past the Eiffel Tower and over the River Seine, outlining the angels and beasts frozen on grand rooftops, bouncing off the waxy leaves of the plane trees, glittering upward from chunks of mica in the cobbles until everything is bathed in an ethereal golden-white haze. Swept clean of traffic, capped by the Arc de Triomphe, the empty boulevard becomes the most beautiful stage in sport.

One hundred and forty-seven riders raced down it, a sinuous ribbon of color and speed. They rode around it again and again, and then one last time, a mad-dog sprint won by a tough Belgian kid named Tom Boonen. Armstrong crossed safely in the pack, and a few minutes later climbed the podium.

He stood on the top step, holding the blue porcelain trophy, the gift from the president of France that is given to all winners. He smiled and waved. The American anthem played, and he took off his cap and put his hand over his heart.

Nearest to the podium stood three reviewing stands sheltered by a yellow canopy. In the first two sat a royal array of governmental and corporate dignitaries. This European delegation sat straight-backed, sipping wine, united in their air of grim, churchlike determination, summoning centuries-deep reserves of discipline to try to ignore the unseemly commotion taking place in one of the stands to their left.

Across a narrow aisle, the clubhouse had set up shop in all its T-shirted, ballcap-wearing, cell phone-shouting, photo-snapping, Texas-size glory as they yelled and whooped and proved to the world that they were here, on the goddamn Champs, in that kick-ass light, with Lance (and Sheryl Crow! and Robin Williams! and Lance's mom!). Around them, in the barricades, thousands of their countrymen whooped louder, waving their signs (FRANCE: U.S. OWNED AND OCCUPIED SINCE 1999, read one), snapping their flags, enlarging the clubhouse until it seemed to stretch the length of the avenue, sending their voices out into that light, filling that holy stage with big, loud, irrepressible American happiness.

Whooooooo Lance! Whooooooo Lance! Whooooooooooooo!

All that remained was the lap of honor, the traditional journey around the Champs made by each team. They rode down the avenue waving and smiling, luxuriating in heavenly slowness, weaving like children around the empty street, pulling off their helmets and sunglasses to let the light warm their skin.

Here were the Basques, five lonely men in their orange, riding in a tight line. Iban Mayo was already back home in his Durango apartment, trying to figure out what had happened. He would soon be diagnosed with mononucleosis, which would help some to soothe his nation's questions, not to mention his own. He would not race again this year, instead concentrating on recovering. This had been a learning experience, he would say. He had peaked too early and fallen off the razor. He would know better next time.

Here were the Phonaks, with none other than Tyler Hamilton riding shotgun in the team car, smiling and waving to the crowd in his checked button-down shirt and clean khaki pants. He and Haven had come to Paris to support the team and show everyone that he was feeling better already. The examinations had shown no fractures or tears. He'd taken a week off the bike, but had started riding just the other day, with an eye toward competing in August's Athens Olympics.

"Life throws you a curveball every so often," Hamilton wrote on his Web site. "The trick is making the catch and hucking the ball back where it came from. I'm getting ready to do just that."

It was the nice thing to say, everyone agreed, but underneath, Hamilton's anger was growing. "I feel ripped off," he told me a few days later. "It was a dangerous, unnecessary finish. You train for a year for something and then it's gone, like that."

Hamilton was already working with Cecchini on a new training schedule, planning more transcendently dull training sessions on the NII strip. "I'm thirty-three years old," he said. "I don't know how many more grand tours I'll be able to do, and this is definitely my last Olympic chance."

Here was Ullrich, a giant grin pasted on his freckled face. He'd wound up fourth, completing his worst-ever Tour, and he looked thrilled. As he passed the podium area for the second time, he spotted an island of German fans and made a beeline for them, hopping off his bike and leaning over the barriers into a forest of welcoming arms, hugs, kisses. Someone handed him a giant magnum of champagne, and Ullrich swiftly popped the cork to the skies and showered the delighted crowd with white foam. Then he turned and squirted his friend Kloden, who had finished second, then the unsuspecting photographers. He took another drink, closed his eyes, and a dented tuba groaned to life, then an accordion. His teammates looked on; some of them started to leave. But Ullrich stayed. He began to sing along, swaying. Around him, some Americans in yellow looked on, a bit puzzled. Didn't that guy *lose*? So Ullrich blasted them, too, and laughed a deep, musical laugh.

Here was Ivan Basso of CSC, his face set in an enigmatic half-smile. He rode a few feet in front of his coach, Bjarne Riis, who had spent the morning thinking up ideas for next year's training camp. In a few weeks Armstrong would try to sign Basso to the new Discovery Channel team, but Basso would resist. "We have an appointment," was the way the enigmatic Riis put it. "We must prepare."

Finally, after a long delay, the cry went up. *Lance! Lance! Lance!* The Postals rode into view. Nine men, shoulder to shoulder, identical with their yellow LiveStrong caps and bracelets, Armstrong in the middle. The rookie Noval looked glazed, ecstatic. Beltran chatted away with Rubiera. Ekimov was impassive. The giant Padrnos smiled, and at the barricades, several small children moved involuntarily back. Landis rode on the edge of the group, his hat turned backward, his eyes quick and flickering.

Landis would go, he was sure of that by now. He would ride the tour of Spain for Postal, then sign with Hamilton's Phonak in the off-season. Postal had the right to match the offer, but they would not try. "If Floyd wants to go, then he should go," Bruyneel would say.

"They've been good and fair with me," Landis said. "It's just time to try something new."

Following the riders, crammed into team cars, came the staff, the *soigneurs* and mechanics and other residents of Little Belgium, leaning out, whoof-shrugging, waving champagne. Here was Elvio, looking weary but satisfied.

"Four again," he said, sighing. "Alpe d'Huez was good, for sure, but it was not enough." Then he brightened. "There is always tonight, of course."

Here was Serge, after hoping for weeks that someone would attack him, finally getting his wish. A troop of alert gendarmes, spotting the bodyguard's scowl but not his security credentials, wrestled the Belgian to the ground, much to the amusement of his countrymen.

Nearby, moving unrecognized in the crowd, walked Michele Ferrari, invited by Armstrong to come to the team's celebratory dinner for the first time. It would be the first time he'd been to the Tour in ten years. He would sit and watch this show with amused eyes, all these people in love with the beauty he had helped build, enjoying the irony only he knew: Armstrong had never hit his best this year. His power was good, but not great, and he had never attacked. He had simply worn them down, found new ways to win.

Here was Linda Armstrong, leaning over the rail, answering questions about her grandchildren, telling interviewers that little Luke was just like his dad, and that Grace was a daredevil, and yes, she was sure they were watching right now with their mom in Austin, so proud of their daddy. And if time would show that the kids hadn't watched one blessed minute of the Tour (as their mother would tell the *New York Times*), well, all that would be too bad. But bad things could be overcome, and if not overcome, then left behind.

Here was her son, his face bathed in light, his eyes focusing up the road. There were no trolls in sight, not today. As long as this golden light kept shining, the trolls would have to stay in the darkness where they were born, where they belonged.

The trolls would return, of course. Though *L.A. Confidentiel* had been turned down by eight English-language publishers (because of fear of legal action, Walsh said), it would spark other inquiries. In October, SCA Promotions, the Dallas company that had underwritten half of Armstrong's $10 million bonus, refused to pay, launching its own investigation based on the Walsh/Ballester book. "The book to us looked credible and brought our attention to matters we didn't know of prior," said SCA attorney Chris Compton.

In January, the French magistrate in Annency would announce that it has begun its own preliminary inquiry, flying Emma O'Reilly from Liverpool for an interview. An Italian court would launch an investigation into Armstrong's actions against Filippo Simeoni, attempting to determine if Armstrong should be charged with sporting fraud or intimidating a witness.

But right now, in the sunshine, the stormclouds were far away. Armstrong rode, bumping slowly along, catching the eyes of friends now and again, gracefully receiving the love the world wished to give. Six! Six! Six! the crowd chanted. Behind him, atop the glass walls of the Grand Palais, shone Apollo, the sun god and symbol of divine manhood, whose name comes from the Greek *apollymi*: to destroy.

At the team dinner the previous night in a chateau in Burgundy, Armstrong had surprised everyone by giving a thank-you present: a yellow jersey. Everyone—team members, mechanics, *soigneurs*, Mr. Magic, Willy the cook, everybody. They donned the jerseys and posed on a staircase, twenty-seven men in yellow, all holding up six fingers. Behind them, standing on the top step, Armstrong raised seven.

FINAL RESULTS, 2004 TOUR DE FRANCE:

1   Lance Armstrong (USA) U.S. Postal, 3,391.1 km in 83 hours, 36 minutes, 2 seconds

2   Andreas Kloden (Germany) T-Mobile, at 6:19 behind

3   Ivan Basso (Italy) CSC, at 6:40 behind

4   Jan Ullrich (Germany) T-Mobile, at 8:50 behind

5   José Azevedo (Portugal) U.S. Postal, at 14:30 behind

CHAPTER 28

DECEMBER

"Come on in," the voice calls. "We're over here."

It's late afternoon, and Armstrong is on his back porch in Austin, knocking a soccer ball around with his son, Luke. His daughter Isabelle scoots around wearing her new blue slippers, a gift from Sheryl Crow. The clouds glow with winter's pinkish light. I've come here at Armstrong's invitation, for a talk.

Armstrong introduces me to Luke, grabbing him and lifting him. The boy looks up, taking me in. He's five now, with straw-colored hair and a sharp blue gaze.

The other day, John Korioth had stopped over at the house and Luke met him at the locked gate. Korioth asked the boy to open it. Luke looked Korioth up and down.

"What if I don't?"

"Well, if you don't then that wouldn't be very nice, would it?"

Luke considered this notion. He didn't move.

"Open the gate," Korioth repeated.

"What'll you give me?" Luke asked.

"I'll give you some good advice," Korioth joked. "Open the gate before I call your dad."

Luke eyed him levelly—figuring out the angles, just like his dad would, Korioth later remembered. Then he opened the gate and ran.

Now Armstrong leaves Luke with the nanny and leads me inside. The house is big but not ornate, with high ceilings, rock

walls, and furniture that looks like it's from Pottery Barn, and
which gives me the faint feeling of being in an expensive but taste-
ful hotel. We walk past the stairs, past photos of Sheryl and the kids,
past where his yellow jerseys hang within frames.

We enter a denlike room in the front of the house. He leans into
a stuffed armchair and lays out his phone and BlackBerry on the
ottoman, arranging them like chess pieces. We chat awhile, and
Armstrong tells me about a news-alert service to which he just sub-
scribed. Whenever his search engine locates an article containing
the term "lance armstrong," the BlackBerry buzzes and chirps. It
lies there for now, waiting.

It's been a big week. It's Thursday, so he's got the kids (Armstrong has them Thursday afternoons and every other weekend).
Tomorrow is a board meeting for the Lance Armstrong Foundation,
plus training camp for the new Discovery Team. He's also got a new
satellite radio show to figure out, and is about to sign an endorsement deal that will create a line of Lance Armstrong Fitness Centers. He's sniffing, and his voice sounds dry and nasal. He's not sick,
though, he points out. Just a little hack.

Armstrong brings up David Walsh.

"You can talk about age, history, fate," he says, ticking them off on
his fingers. "Those are real things. Walsh is not a real thing. He's a very
small component of the press, and in my view, he doesn't get a lot of
support from the cycling press, unless they're bullshitting me.

"My defense is that I've been around a long time," he says. "I'm
thirty-three years old. I won races when I first stepped on the scene,
and haven't stopped. For an athlete to be at a high level for fourteen
years, to ride consistently from February, March, April, throughout
the year, dopers don't do that, all year, for a whole career. I don't
need to name names, but these fucking chumps you want to call
rivals, they don't race the bike until July. Well, maybe not Mayo, he
had a good spring, but I've had fourteen years at the top, not winning all the time, but *there,* not the first guy dropped, not in the gru-
petto, all through the year. Those are not the signs of a doper."

He leans back, satisfied. I'm supposed to ask another question, but I'm silent, thinking, did he just say *fucking chumps*? Armstrong realizes, and picks up the thread.

"Look at Ullrich today," he says, gesturing at the BlackBerry. "I read that he wouldn't ride outside because he didn't want to get a cold. He said that! So he's riding inside on the rollers for an hour! Give me a break! He's in there, and I'm up in New York doing three hours riding into a headwind along the Hudson River. Give me a fucking break."

For nearly two hours, Armstrong is what I've come to expect as his usual self: charming and funny and prickly, always a beat ahead. We go over key moments in the season, relive the Tour, talk about his rivals. He tells me about Tenerife and about how Ferrari's advice helped scuttle the narrow bike. He talks about Mount Ventoux.

"I thought it would be close. I didn't think Mayo would win by that much, that I'd be fifth, that I'd nearly be caught by Tyler. But they were flying. And getting my ass kicked in that time trial was a good thing for me. I'm always at my best when I'm pushed down, when I really feel threatened. At that point, I thought, uh-oh. This is bad. Then it came together."

We keep going through the season, talking about the last training camp, and then the Tour. He goes through the big moments, the ascent of La Mongie, Plateau de Beille, Alpe d'Huez, about Ferrari ("an incredibly misunderstood, brilliant man"). He talks in general terms about his divorce ("Kristin's a good mom, and I'm a good dad, that's what counts"), and then more specifically about Floyd Landis's recent signing with Phonak.

"Where do you start with that guy?" Armstrong asks. "I love Floyd, I really do. As annoying as he can be—and he can be really annoying, very uncomfortable in his own skin—aside from all that shit, the guy is tough. He's a scrapper, and he's talented. We knew he was getting close to Phonak, wanted to go to Phonak. And that's fine. We've lost guys before, and it's always worked out. Always."

He talks about fame, about the intensity of the public's reaction to him.

"You won't believe this, but I really don't look around a lot," he says. "If I looked around every day and saw the frenzy around me, that's a deadly thing. You see that every day with athletes—they get used to it, and when it's gone, they're lost. I don't really want to know what's out there."

Other kinds of frenzy, he does know about. There's an article in today's newspaper on the Lance Armstrong Foundation. A bar graph shows revenue growth, from $238,000 in 1997 to $45 million so far in 2004, and speaks of the new lobbying presence on Capitol Hill that helped Congress approve $900,000 for cancer survivorship initiatives. Thirty million bracelets had been sold so far for $1 each; they are going for $30 on eBay; they've been copied by a rainbow of causes ranging from anti-bullying to chastity, creating the best possible problem: they are in danger of becoming too popular.

"It's crazy," he says, shaking his head in pleasure. "Fucking crazy."

It's been two hours. It's nearly dark now, and our time is drawing to a close. In accordance with my earlier offer, I've brought along a draft of the book. I set it on the ottoman and Armstrong looks at it.

"Okay," he says. "What's in there that's going to piss me off?"

Before I can answer, he leans forward.

"The Walsh stuff is not going to piss me off if it's factual," he says. "Don't call him the award-winning world-renowned respected guy."

I outline what's in the book, mentioning that Walsh seems motivated, at least in part, by the memory of his dead son, who he said was his favorite.

Armstrong's eyes narrow. He cracks his knuckles, one by one.

"How could he have a favorite son? That guy's a scumbag. I'm a father of three . . . to say 'my favorite son,' that's fucked, I'm sorry. I just hate the guy. He's a little troll."

His voice rises. I try to change the subject, but it's too late. He's going.

"Fucking Walsh," he says. "Fucking little troll."

I'm sitting on the couch watching, but it's as if I'm not there. His voice echoes off the stone walls—*troll, casting his spell on people, liar*—and the words blur together into a single sound, and I find myself wishing he would stop.

You won, I want to tell him. *You won everything.*

But he won't stop; he can't stop, and I'm realizing that maybe this has nothing to do with Walsh, or with guilt or innocence or ego or power or money. This isn't a game or a sport. It's a fight, and it can never end, because when Armstrong stops fighting he'll stop living.

A birdlike trill slices the air; Armstrong's eyes dart to his phone. The spell is broken.

"Listen, here's where I go," Armstrong says after putting down the phone. "I've won six tours. I've done everything I ever could do to prove my innocence. I have done, outside of cycling, way more than anyone in the sport. To be somebody who's spread himself out over a lot of areas, to hopefully be somebody who people in this city, this state, this country, this world can look up to as an example. And you know what? They don't even know who David Walsh is. And they never will. And in twenty years, nobody is going to remember him. Nobody. And there are a million cancer patients and survivors around the world, and that's what matters."

He stands up, and calls into the kitchen to see if his daughter Grace is awake, and when it's determined she is, he says I should really meet her, she's a pistol. So we proceed into the bright kitchen. The kids look up, macaroni-and-cheese faces shining yellow.

"My favorite color," Armstrong says. "Hey hey, kiddos."

The girls get up from the table and start cruising around in their blue slippers. Luke stays, playing a handheld video game called Frogger. The object is to get from one side of the street to the other without being squashed. It's tricky. There are boulders and cars and monsters, and you have to pick just the right path, and stay alert all the time.

"He's great at it," his dad says. "Aren't you, Luke?"

Luke doesn't seem to hear. His legs are crossed on the chair, his face tipped toward the glow, the irises of his eyes dancing with the antic glow of the screen. A boy, playing a game.

Armstrong gets my attention and points to the garage, where a black car is faintly visible—a 1970 Pontiac GTO, which had been on television a few nights before. Armstrong loves this car. Sheryl Crow bought it for him as a present for winning the Tour, and then it had been covertly fixed up on a Discovery Channel program called *Overhaulin'*.

We'd talked about the car that afternoon. Armstrong had told me how he'd recently found out a rather ironic fact: his birth father, Eddie Gunderson, also drove a GTO.

So now we spend a long moment looking out the window at the car, shining and black and perfect. "Hell of a fast car," he says. *"Hell* of a car." Then it's time to say good-byes and walk into the night.

It's a cool, clear night, dew is starting to jewel the grass. The neighborhood materializes as my eyes adjust to the darkness. New stone houses built along old-fashioned lines, all gables and hedges and neatly edged lawns. Clean, brightly lit American houses, filled with people who work and live and who, if they should encounter some hardship, can lean on something special, something that can fill them with belief and the will to fight, something that is no less than magic: they live on Lance Armstrong's street.

As I'm getting in the car, the screen door creaks and a figure walks into the dark. It's Armstrong, hunched, scooting his slippered feet, carrying the trash can.

He sets it down with a gentle clatter. His earlier anger seems miles away. He pauses and looks up into the trees, and the stars beyond. Icy light and sweet-smelling leaves, and everywhere a silent struggle.

EPILOGUE

Twenty-four days after the Tour ended, Tyler Hamilton rode in the Athens Olympics time trial. In keeping with Hamiltonian tradition, the race was marked by an unexpected hitch. The ninety-degree heat melted the tape affixing his radio inside his helmet. Feeling it come loose, Hamilton tore it away and flung it to the roadside, the wires dangling tantalizingly near his spokes for a second. He rode the rest of the 48-kilometer race in silence, not knowing how he was doing. He crossed the line, looking around as friends and fans frantically waved, trying to communicate the amazing news: he'd won gold.

A few moments later, the audience was treated to the sight of Hamilton, gritty, hardluck Tyler, mounting the podium to receive his crown of olive leaves, placing hand on heart as the anthem played, raising his eyebrows in that modest way of his, showing Tugboat's tags, which he'd carried with him. Sure, Armstrong had skipped the Olympics, but his absence didn't diminish the achievement one iota: this was the happy ending for which they'd waited so patiently. The crash had been a blessing in disguise: abandoning the Tour had allowed him to recover, and now he was in possession of something not even his upstairs neighbor had achieved.

"This is the best feeling in the world," Hamilton said, squeezing the medal. "This is the biggest day of my life."

Energized, Hamilton decided to ride September's crown jewel, the Tour of Spain. The three-week race started well enough. Hamilton was among the leaders for the first few stages, then showed his strength by winning the first individual time trial on September 11. The plot line was crystallizing: Hamilton would win this race, his first-ever grand tour, and complete his redemption. Five days later, however, everything changed.

"Hamilton Positive for Blood Doping," the headlines read. It emerged that Hamilton had tested positive not once, but twice: both at the Athens Olympics and at the Tour of Spain.

Much of the cycling world spasmed in disbelief. Hamilton? They could believe almost anyone would dope, but Hamilton? He didn't help matters with his initial press conference, where his denials sounded more careful than categorical. ("I've been accused of taking blood from another person," he said. "Anybody who knows me, knows that's completely impossible.") At one point Hamilton speculated that the positive might have been caused by a surgical procedure, an idea that he did not mention again.

Had Hamilton gone to the dark side? Or, perhaps more disturbing, had he been there all along? (The notorious Cecchini!) Things were not helped a few weeks later, when Hamilton's teammate, the faithful Santiago Perez, became the second-ever cyclist to flunk the new blood-doping test. Or when *L'Equipe* reported on September 23 that Phonak had received two letters from the UCI, warning that blood tests at the Tour de Romandie in May and at the Dauphiné Libéré in June returned "strange fluctuations" in Hamilton's blood values.

Many of Hamilton's fans stuck by their man. Sponsors honored their contracts; Chris Davenport, a fellow Crazykid, set up BelieveTyler.org, a Web site designed to promote Hamilton's innocence and help out with his legal costs. Hamilton was received warmly in October, when he attended the industry's Interbike convention in Las Vegas. Armstrong issued a vaguely supportive statement—he was surprised as anyone, he said. He hoped it wasn't true.*

Bobby Julich, the American rider who won the bronze in Athens, said Hamilton's positives "go against everything I've ever known from the guy. But the rest of us at the Olympics passed the test. Why didn't he? I'm sick of people who cheat, sick of cleaning up their mess and trying to explain it. There is heavy evidence against him. With that much evidence, I don't know how he's going to get out of it."

The answer to Julich's question hinged on the test and the procedures. The blood-doping test was new, and had been administered according to World Anti-Doping Agency (WADA) protocol: two samples were taken, designated A and B. In order for a positive test to be declared, both the A and B sample had to produce identical results.

As it turned out, the Olympics test didn't measure up to this standard. Athens lab technicians had frozen Hamilton's B sample, ruining the cells, so the B test was inconclusive and Hamilton was allowed to keep his gold medal. Exactly why the B sample was frozen—well, that was more complicated. An independent observer's report later showed that Hamilton's A sample was initially ruled negative (clean) but suspicious, and only later reviewed again and reclassified positive. In addition, the report found the test procedure to be fraught with problems: a string of mislabelings, relabelings, and lack of expertise that was, depending on whom you believed, either evidence of incompetence or proof that somebody, somewhere, had decided to go after Hamilton.

---

*Despite the mutual assertions of friendship between Hamilton and Armstrong, I never sensed so much as a scintilla of warmth when they talked about each other. This could be because they were tired of talking about each other, or perhaps because they are indifferent to each other, and are roped into this so-called friendship through proximity and mutual survival.

Of course, we'd never know if it was true, particularly in a sport as complex as cycling, and doubly so with personalities as complex as Armstrong's and Hamilton's. When the Tour was over, Sheryl Crow took the initiative of organizing a party, inviting the Hamiltons and a few others to the café across the street for some cake. Everybody got along, they said, as nice as pie.

Hamilton's A and B samples drawn at the Tour of Spain, however, both tested positive, leaving Hamilton one option: to challenge the accuracy of the test and its protocols. While the Phonak team was forced to release Hamilton to keep in the UCI's good graces, the company spent $800,000 assembling a panel to research the accuracy of the test.

So the story lurched to sports' newest arena: an arbitration tribunal. This particular test was based on the fact that human blood can be distinguished beyond the usual blood types of A, B, and O, according to a highly characteristic pattern of proteins, or antigens, bound to the surface of red blood cells. The test, called flow cytology, involved marking the blood cells with a fluorescent dye, then measuring the reflection signatures from fifty to sixty thousand cells as they pass through a detection tube under ultraviolet light. In a normal individual, every blood cell creates an identical reflection signature. In someone who has received blood from another source, however, those reflection patterns vary. (Transfused blood is detectable for 90 to 120 days, the life span of a red blood cell.)

Dr. Michael Ashenden, the Australian physiologist who helped develop the test for WADA, said that the test was foolproof, able to detect as little as a teaspoonful of foreign blood in a human body. It had been used for years in hospitals to detect fetal/maternal hemorrhage and to test suitability for organ transplants. "If they get it wrong, it's a life or death situation," Ashenden said. "They don't get it wrong. The test works."

The Hamiltons sold their Marblehead house and spent the winter in Colorado, helping to prepare his defense. He hired Howard Jacobs, a California-based attorney who specialized in defending athletes against doping charges, and who had defended American sprinter Tim Montgomery in the BALCO case. The IMAX producers postponed the planned spring release of *Brain Power* for one year, to allow them time to reshoot. The film would no longer be about Tyler, they said; instead, it would feature "several cyclists."

Hamilton kept training, his friends said, riding like a man possessed, climbing mountains on a fixed-gear bike. Haven compared the legal work to doing a complex crossword puzzle. Hamilton spoke quietly as always, but he used a new language of vengeance.

"I'm a nice person and I try to forgive people, but not this time, not with this. I've lost a lot of trust in people because they have backed off from me when I needed them the most. When my name is cleared, I'm going to remember those people. They'd better not come crawling back to me when this is all over."

Hamilton's hearing with the United States Anti-Doping Agency was opened in late February in Denver. Over four days, in front of a three-person arbitration panel (one appointed by Hamilton, one by USADA, and one agreed upon by the other two members), testimony was heard. Hamilton testified for two hours; his team attacked the test on all available grounds, including raising the possibility that his positive result may have been caused by a "vanishing twin," who shared the womb when Hamilton was a fetus. In the following weeks, the panel delayed the release of their decision several times. The delays lent hope to Hamilton supporters, who saw them as proof that the panel was less than united over the validity of the test. Hamilton, aside from infrequent updates on his Web site, remained completely, frustratingly silent.

On April 18, the panel announced their decision: By a 2–1 vote, Hamilton was determined guilty and given the maximum penalty, a two-year ban that would prevent him from racing until April 17, 2007, when he will be thirty-six. "It caught me completely by surprise," Hamilton said of the decision. "Not for a second did I think it was going to turn out that way. I'm innocent." He said he would appeal.

On October 1, an Italian court convicted Michele Ferrari of unlawful distribution of medicines and sporting fraud. He received a prison sentence of eleven months and twenty-one days, which was suspended, and his medical license was revoked for one year.

"I was disappointed to learn of the Italian court's judgment," Armstrong said in a press release officially severing his ties with the doctor. "Dr. Ferrari has been a longtime friend and trusted adviser to me

and the [Postal] team, during which time he never suggested, pre-
scribed, or provided me with any performance-enhancing drugs."

"An historical sentence," read the front page of *La Gazetta dello
Sport*. "October 1 is a date which should remain etched in block letters in the annals of the war on doping."

"Of course I didn't expect this sentence," Ferrari said, "because I
am convinced of my innocence in this whole affair."

Filippo Simeoni said, "On a human level, I'm sorry that Dr. Ferrari has been convicted, but this sentence shows that my testimony
was reliable and that justice exists."

Over the next few months, Armstrong's suits against Walsh,
Ballester, O'Reilly, *L'Express*, the *Sunday Times*, and Martiniere
would inch slowly through the courts. Armstrong's suit against SCA,
the insurance company that had refused to pay the $5 million
bonus, would go through its initial arbitration hearings. By mid-
winter, Armstrong would have ten lawyers in three countries in his
employ, a figure that increased by one when Armstrong became
involved in a legal battle with Mike Anderson, his now-ex mechanic
and assistant.

Armstrong's explanation, told through Stapleton, was that Anderson was fired after he and Armstrong stopped getting along. Stapleton
described Anderson as disgruntled and upset at what he apparently
considered a violation of his contract. According to Stapleton, Anderson, through his lawyers, sought payment of $500,000, along with a
signed jersey, and Armstrong's promise to appear at a bike shop
Anderson might open in the future. Anderson's alleged contract consisted of a 2002 e-mail from Armstrong—an e-mail that, according to
Stapleton, spoke in loose terms about a bike shop, terms that hardly
qualified as a legally binding agreement. In Stapleton's telling, Anderson was the latest incarnation of the classic celebrity hazard: the vindictive, gold-digging ex-assistant.

Anderson told a different story. In his counterclaim and subsequent briefs filed in Travis County District Court, he said he had
enjoyed a good working relationship with Armstrong from the time of
his employment, performing a wide variety of duties in Austin and

Girona. He said that he and Armstrong spoke several times about a bike shop, for which Armstrong would help provide seed money.

In early February 2004, however, Anderson said that everything changed. In his statements, he said he was cleaning the bathroom in Armstrong's Girona apartment when he found a white box bearing a label "like any other prescription drug" but that did not have a doctor's prescription attached. The box, he said, bore a trademark name for Androgen, a banned steroid.

Anderson said he replaced the box in the medicine cabinet. When Armstrong arrived, Anderson said he didn't confront his boss, fearing he would be fired.

"I had a job to do, that's why I kept my mouth shut," Anderson told the Associated Press. "I tried for a very long time to give him the benefit of the doubt. I waited for months to even tell my wife."

According to Anderson, Armstrong began questioning Anderson's honesty the following day, asking for grocery receipts. From there, Anderson says, the relationship slowly disintegrated.

"It is probable that Armstrong knew or suspected Anderson had made the discovery," Anderson's counterclaim reads. "The next morning . . . Armstrong was immediately distant and irritable toward Anderson and his family, which surprised both Anderson and Allison. . . . Since that morning, Anderson and Armstrong's relationship has never been the same."

Anderson also alleged that, in October 2004 in Austin, he and Armstrong discussed the case of Johan Museeuw, the Belgian great who'd recently been banned for doping. According to Anderson's counterclaim, "Armstrong looked directly into the eyes of Anderson and told him, 'Everyone does it.' Armstrong reacted coldly when Anderson did not give him a supportive response."

When Anderson was fired in November 2004, he was asked to sign a confidentiality agreement that would make him liable for $1 million should he violate its terms. Anderson refused to sign. After some heated phone calls with Armstrong, Anderson called a lawyer. The lawyer, Hal Gillespie, contacted Stapleton. The two had a discussion, after which Gillespie sent an offer, which he viewed as confidential, a starting point for negotiating a private settlement. ("Our goal," Gillespie's letter read, "is to NOT file suit.")

Stapleton responded by filing suit against Anderson to contest the validity of his alleged e-mail contract. When asked why Lance Armstrong would file suit against his $36,000-a-year mechanic, Stapleton said, "We were forced to do this because we were threatened with a half-million-dollar lawsuit."

I e-mailed Anderson over the winter, asking if there was anything more he wished to add to the information in the counterclaim.

"As much as I would love to let loose the torrent within, I have to withhold," he wrote. "Acting on anger never serves one well. But damn, that guy is an SOB."

As 2005 rolled around, the rhythms of the season—some old, some new—began to reassert themselves.

Jan Ullrich spent Christmas training in South Africa, leaving his family behind in Germany. It seemed his partner, Gaby, and daughter had caught nasty colds, and a newly vigilant Ullrich didn't want to catch anything. But in February, Ullrich had to miss several weeks of training due to sickness. He announced that he would skip several early-season races, to avoid over-stressing himself. "It is nothing," he said. "There's a lot of time before the Tour."

Floyd Landis trained with his new Phonak team, for which he, in Hamilton's absence, had become the de facto leader. He spoke of the openness of his team, of enjoying a feeling of independence and teamwork. He also went back to Farmersville for the first time in a few years. "It's good to go home," he said. "It's a weird place, for sure. But it's good."

Iban Mayo spent the offseason in Durango. He would train differently this year, he said. He would not ride the Dauphiné; he would go slower and try to build up his form. He had learned his lesson, he said. Next time he would not be so bold.

An early ruling by the British judge struck down one of the *Sunday Times'* key lines of defense in Armstrong's libel suit against the paper, not permitting the *Times* to introduce evidence about cycling's doping culture. Armstrong and Stapleton were elated. Walsh was undeterred, looking forward to the November 2005 court date and holding out hope that *L.A. Confidentiel* would find an English-language publisher. "More damning material is going to come out in the trial, regardless of who wins," he said. "Every day, there's more."

Armstrong spent most of the off-season in Austin. He visited the Letterman and Oprah shows, he launched his satellite-radio show, he held training camps with his team in California, he visited wind tunnels, and he talked of breaking the record for most distance covered in an hour. He was drug-tested four times. His life with Sheryl Crow was equally busy: he presented an award at the Grammys, attended the Oscars, and was honored at a Los Angeles cancer fundraiser. He put his Girona place on the market for $2.5 million; spending more time in the States, he didn't really need a place in Europe, he said. For a few months, Armstrong left open the question of riding for a seventh Tour, until announcing in February that yes, he would be at the start line in Fromentine on July 2.

The morning of the March 6 prologue of the Paris-Nice stage race dawned cold and wintry. The Eiffel Tower gleamed in the distance, but today the riders were headed away from it, to the south and the season's true beginnings. Armstrong showed up, looking mellow and perhaps a touch heavy. He told everyone how he wasn't in shape yet, how he was still jet-lagged from his journey two days previous. This race was strictly for training, he said.

"What is your goal?" someone asked.

A slow smile crossed Armstrong's face.

"To not finish last," he said.

NOTES ON THE SPORT

THE SEASON

Like boxing or horse-racing—or the Catholic Church, for that matter—the professional cycling calendar is organized around a random-seeming sequence of big and small events, all of which are sanctioned by the sport's iron-fisted Vatican, the Lausanne, Switzerland–based **Union Cycliste Internationale (UCI).** Those races can be divided into three categories, each of which exists as its own specialty.

1. **One-day races,** the most storied of which are called classics. Included here are April's famed one-day races, century-old contests held in northern France, Belgium, and Holland, which feature cobblestones, freezing rain, and hundreds of thousands of bellowing, beer-fueled, *frite*-gobbling fans. Foremost among these are the **Tour of Flanders, Flèche Wallonne, Paris-Roubaix, and Liege-Bastogne-Liege.** One-day races are all-or-nothing affairs on the border of macho and masochistic, and thus the domain of "hard men": big, strong, stoic riders capable of spending six hours going full out, then winning with one unmatchable acceleration.

2. **Short stage-races.** Each racing day of a multi-day race is called a stage, and the theatrical analogy works. Each day brings a new show with two heroes: a daily **stage winner,** and an **overall**

leader—the rider with the lowest cumulative time. Overall standings are tracked in the **General Classification,** or **GC.** Short stage-races, which typically last one week, can be thought of as miniature Tour de Frances, placing a premium on strategy, day-to-day recovery, and often on climbing ability. Foremost among these are **Paris-Nice** in March, **Catalan Week** (also in March), the **Tour of Germany,** the **Tour of Switzerland,** and the **Dauphiné Libéré.**

3. **Grand Tours:** three-week stage races, of which there are three: the **Giro d'Italia** (held in May), the **Vuelta a España** (September), and the holiest of holies, the **Tour de France** (July). These races are everything rolled into one, the energy equivalent of running a marathon every day for three weeks. Grand Tours are so demanding so as to be considered their own distinct sport, in which champions do not win so much as they are slowly revealed. "There are no upsets in the Tour de France," is how five-time winner Eddy Merckx put it. "The toughest man always wins." While past champions have won multiple grand tours in a single season, modern riders choose to concentrate on one; it's simply too difficult to remain in top condition for so long.

THE TEAMS

No Yankees or Red Sox here; the model is more a low-budget NASCAR: Pro cycling in 2004 featured a cast of thirty or so Division 1 professional teams sponsored by companies that sell vitamins, flooring, coffee makers, hearing aids, mattresses, bread, and other products that appeal to cycling's mostly older, blue-collar male fan base. It costs about $5–12 million to sponsor a team; each employs about twenty to thirty riders and nearly as many support staff. Teams are sorted along national lines: **Phonak** is Swiss; **Euskaltel-Euskadi** is Basque, **T-Mobile** is German, **CSC** is Danish, and, of course, **U.S. Postal**—which recently became **Discovery Channel**—is American. Minimum rider salary in 2004 was $30,000; top riders made $1–2 million, while most good ones average in the low six figures.

The 2005 season will bring a sea change to pro cycling's structure, with the advent of the **ProTour.** The ProTour is the UCI's attempt to stabilize their sport and concentrate its quality by limiting the number of teams to eighteen. This change requires each ProTour team to enter every one of the twenty-seven designated ProTour events, a commitment that requires bigger rosters and more money. Smaller teams will fend for themselves, racing at smaller regional events and competing for wild-card spots at ProTour events.

Teams are led into battle by a *directeur sportif* (coach), usually a former rider who picks lineup and determines strategy. The director follows the race in the team car, calling orders to the team via earbud radios. Riders are cared for by a support staff of *soigneurs,* who do massage, fill water bottles, and take care of the logistics of hotels, meals, maps, and endless household details (who's got the hotel keys? who's riding in which car?) that make pro racing strongly resemble a giant family camping trip. Because of this, good *soigneurs* have a motherly sensitivity to fundamental needs, always asking if you might want the crusts cut off your sandwich, or if you want a hot cup of tea with lemon for that cough.

Teams are divided into **leaders*** and *domestiques*. The leader is the rider designated to have the best chance of winning the race, that is, accumulating the lowest overall elapsed time. *Domestiques*

---

*In most sports, leaders are easy to spot. But in cycling, which is all about enduring pain, a lot of the toughest riders (with some notable exceptions, including Armstrong) don't seem particularly tough at first glance. They seem quiet, helpful, and, compared to American athletes, as nice as altar boys. This is because they exist in a world beyond normal conventions of toughness. In their world, the truly tough man is not the man who acts tough; it's the one who is so deeply tough that he seems almost bashful or, in an extreme case, sleepy. This latter persona was perfected by none other than another five-time Tour winner, Belgian cyclist Eddy Merckx, the greatest all-around cyclist in history. The photos show it again and again—a small group of men riding over rain-greased cobbles or up a godforsaken Alp, each face a desperate mask of pain, and there's Merckx at the front, mouth closed, eyes half-lidded, the face of a drowsy man reading a particularly uninteresting book. The sleepy/nice personalities can make for some confusion. On meeting these skinny, reserved, well-dressed young men, many women (particularly Americans) walk away perplexed, mistakenly convinced that a high percentage of pro cyclists must be gay. Which, in a way, is perfect.

("servants" in French) are the support riders. They haul water, shelter the leader from the wind, give up their bikes if his breaks, and, in general, sacrifice their overall standing for their leader. For their efforts, they receive bonuses and prize money (the entirety of the Tour's $400,000 first-prize award is traditionally passed on to the leader's *domestiques*). Sometimes *domestiques* can suddenly transform themselves into leaders, as when Jan Ullrich won the 1997 Tour. But it doesn't happen often.

By whim and tradition, different races require teams to start different numbers of riders. It varies from five per team in some races to a maximum of nine in the Tour de France. There is thus a constant selection process within each team to see whom the director will select for each race. Once the race starts, however, no substitutions are allowed.

TYPES OF TOUR DE FRANCE STAGES

Stages come in two flavors: **time trials** and **road stages.** In bike racing, as in all things European, everything is measured in kilometers, each of which is roughly half a mile (0.62 miles per kilometer, if you're keeping track).

Time trials, for which racers use specially designed aerodynamic bikes, come in three varieties:

Individual time trial—the rider alone for a long ride (usually fifteen to fifty kilometers). Competitors start in reverse order of overall standings. **Drafting,** riding in another racer's slipstream, is strictly prohibited.

Team time trial—the team riding as a unit; all of those who finish together are given the same finishing time—which means the leader is only as fast as his team.

Prologue—a short individual time trial (usually less than ten kilometers) that serves to kick off a stage race.

In a road stage, all the riders start as a group, or **peloton** (platoon). In time trials, riders compete against the clock.

RACE TACTICS

Time trial tactics are simple: go fast. Riders who produce the most power with the least aerodynamic resistance win.

Road tactics, on the other hand, are a chess game that stems from a single truth: it's easier to ride just behind someone than in front. A lot easier. At twenty-five miles per hour on the flats, the trailing rider uses **30 percent less power** than the leader. To ride at the front is the equivalent of attaching a sizable parachute to your bike; the faster you go, the more air it catches. The peloton is **always faster** than smaller groups of riders, because they have more power (more legs) pushing relatively less air.

The second truth of bike racing is that somebody always tries to defy the first truth and break away; or **attack.** The heroic impulse, the Greeks would have called it, an impulse that sets up the two questions that lie at the heart of every race: Who is going to get away? And who is going to spend the energy required to catch them?

On the Tour's flat stages, the answer to the first question is often Joe Nobody—a rider who's not thought to be a threat in the overall. Contenders rarely attack on the flats—it's too easy for another contender to tag along and follow them, or **wheelsuck.** (Strong headwinds or sidewinds sometimes create an exception to this rule.)

Steep hills and mountains, however, are prime places for contender attacks. The steeper it is, the more efficiently an attacker can gain distance (and the less the air-resistance advantage of the chasing pack). Climbing ability is measured by **power-to-weight ratio,** in watts per kilogram: basically, how much power each gram of your body can produce. Among two climbers of equal power, the lighter one has a large advantage. Being skinny is not a body type; it's a tactical necessity.

Who's going to chase the breakaway? Usually the team with the most to lose. In the Tour de France, it's often the team with the yellow jersey, which wants to preserve its status. In other races, it's often the team with good sprinters who won't get a chance to show their stuff unless the breakaway is reeled in. On flat stages, the peloton often comes together, and the stage is won by a **sprint specialist,** a powerful rider who is often **"led out"** by teammates who form a line in front of him, launching the sprinter from their slipstream with a few hundred meters left.

How fast can the chasing peloton **close the gap on the breakaway?** On flat stages, the rule of thumb is that the chasing peloton can gain **ten seconds per kilometer.** Thus breakaways are often a temporary balance of opposing wants: the photogenic glory desired by the escapee (*fuggitivi,* in Italian) and the stability desired by the peloton (who know that if they keep the gap within bounds, they're probably going to catch up). Attacks in the mountains, however, are frequently unanswerable; and are where Tours are won and lost.

HOW TO WIN THE TOUR DE FRANCE

At the end of each Tour de France stage, the rider with the best overall (GC) time is awarded the *maillot jaune,* the **yellow jersey.** Other races have different colors for the leader's jersey: **pink** for the Giro d'Italia, **golden** for the Vuelta a España. In grand tours, the contenders mark each other on flat stages, not permitting each other in breakaways. Thus, the ways to make time on rivals generally fall into three categories:

1. **Climb faster.** Gaps in climbing stages can be big: one- or two-minute chunks.
2. **Time-trial faster.** During his run of Tour victories, Armstrong has usually thumped most of his rivals in this discipline. Five-time Tour winner Miguel Induráin rarely won a climbing stage, but he crushed everyone in the time trials.
3. **Win a few time bonuses.** The winner of a Tour stage gets twenty seconds bonus; second gets twelve seconds, third gets eight. There are also bonuses for intermediate sprints (pulse-quickening, pre-designated spots along the course where race organizers reward the first riders through), but they're smaller.

OTHER TOUR DE FRANCE PRIZES

It's easy to get the impression that there's only one winner in the Tour; in fact there are dozens. (If there weren't, three weeks would get pretty dull.)

King of the Mountains (K-O-M). Each climb is categorized as follows:

- **Category 4.** Usually less than two miles long, and not so steep
- **Category 3.** Slightly steeper, up to three miles long
- **Category 2.** Three to six miles long, more than 4 percent grade
- **Category 1.** Very tough: between six and twelve miles long, more than 5 percent grade
- **Hors-catégorie.** Even longer and even steeper, sometimes at the end of a stage

The first few riders to reach the summit of each categorized climb are awarded points; the harder the climb, the more points. At the end of each day, the rider with the most climbing points is awarded the *maillot de pois,* the **polka-dot jersey.** Winning K-O-M has turned into a specialty; Frenchman Richard Virenque has won seven.

Best Sprinter. The winner of finishing and intermediate sprints is awarded points on a similarly graded scale. The points are totaled daily, and the leader awarded the *maillot vert,* the **green jersey.**

Best Young Rider. Tour riders tend to mature later; the **white jersey,** the *maillot blanc,* is traditionally awarded to the best GC-classified rider who is twenty-five or younger.

Most Combative Rider. A Tour jury awards this daily to the rider who shows the most competitive spirit; i.e., attacks the most. It's designated by a red race number on the rider's jersey.

Winning a stage. To win a stage of the Tour can be the biggest event of a season, a career, and frequently a lifetime. Also a chance to spend quality time with the **podium girls,** the models hired by race sponsors to award the bouquets, trophies, and victory kisses.

CHEATING

Cycling, like the human mind, is partly reptilian. While the sport's early days were a festival of overt cheating (Maurice Garin, who won the first Tour in 1903, was disqualified the following year, having been caught employing the simple but spectacularly effective method of taking the train), most modern cheating happens inside the body.

Performance-enhancing drugs fall into a few categories: there are **stimulants, steroids, human-growth hormone,** and **erythropoeitin, (EPO).** Of these, EPO seems to be the most prevalent; it stimulates the bone marrow to produce more oxygen-carrying red blood cells, which results in an increased endurance.

In 1997, to control rampant EPO abuse, the UCI introduced the **50-percent hematocrit limit.** Hematocrit is the percentage of total blood plasma taken up by oxygen-carrying red blood cells; a percentage that varies in the general population from 42 to 48 percent. The 50-percent rule (any rider whose hematocrit exceeds 50 percent is prohibited from racing) has been criticized for being little more than an incentive to cheat, but as of this writing, the UCI has yet to come up with a better solution. (The UCI started testing directly for EPO in 2001, but the substance is only detectable for a few days after its use.)

Blood doping is an old-time method that has recently returned to vogue. Used legally (if very quietly) by American cyclists in the 1984 Olympics, blood doping involves banking red blood cells (either the athlete's or someone's of identical blood type), then infusing them just before an event to boost oxygen-carrying capacity, and thus endurance. Just before the 2004 Tour, the UCI introduced a new test for detecting **homologous transfusions** (from another source). There is no test for detecting **autologous transfusions,** in which the athlete banks and then transfuses his or her own blood.

FOOD AND LOVE

Riders eat and drink the equivalent of three Thanksgiving dinners a day during the Tour: during races they use **feed zones**—specified areas, usually on the flats, where *soigneurs* hand off their *musettes*, cloth bags filled with food and drink. It's considered unsportsmanlike to attack near a feed zone.

When it comes to bathroom breaks, similar rules apply. Riders stop as a group to pee, or sometimes will let fly while on the bike. To keep things seemly, photographers discreetly refrain from capturing such moments.

Love, of course, is similarly regulated. Wives and girlfriends are traditionally barred from hotel rooms and team dinner tables during races; a rule that is violated at risk, unless your name happens to be Lance Armstrong or Sheryl Crow. Last year, a Spanish rider was fired from his team for sneaking a woman into his room during a race. Likewise, Tour de France podium girls are officially forbidden to fraternize with the riders, a rule that has been broken with happier results. During the 2003 Tour, Postal rider George Hincapie met podium girl Melanie Simonneau. In November of 2004, their daughter, Julia Paris Hincapie, was born.

ACKNOWLEDGMENTS

Writing this book involved relocating our family to Spain from Alaska, a feat that would have been impossible if not for *muy grande* amounts of help on both sides of the world. In Girona, we'd like to thank Casilda Cruz Poyatos, Francisco Moreno Troyano, Xavi Moreno Cruz, and Alba Puig Comerbal at the Apartaments Historic, Oscar Sanchez at Medina Bicycles, and Judit Guix Gascons at Viaugusta Café. In Alaska, the ever-resourceful Gary Thomas helped keep the home front under control—or as close to it as we ever get—as did the Beach, Bursch, Kizzia, Schneider, and Stuart families. We'd especially like to thank Cristina Ortega Perez, the Newson-Smith Gomez de Bonilla, Dyce, and King families for sharing cava and friendship.

Professional cycling is often referred to as a closed, secretive world—an impression that quickly evaporates if you're in the company of able guides like Frankie Andreu, Luuc Eisenga, Bryan Nygaard, Louise Donald, Dave Bolch, Freddy Viane, Bob Roll, Dirk Spiers, and Stefano Ferrari. Thanks particularly to Jonathan Vaughters for indulging a thousand questions with patience and interest—and for finding some good wine in the process.

Many journalists helped along the way, not least for their excellent reporting that I sometimes relied upon for quotations. Thanks to Andrew Hood, Edward Pickering, Bonnie DeSimone, Bob Ford, Sebastian Moll, Neal Rogers, Bill Westbrook, Jaime Nichols, Martin

Hardie, Sam Abt, Rupert Guinness, Beth Seliga, Richard Pestes, Tim Maloney, John Henderson, Juliet Macur, Evan Smith, Joe Lindsay, Andreas Burkert, Bernd Volland, Markus Goting, Stephen Farrand, Christi Valentine-Anderson, Brion O'Connor, and Eric Hagerman. Thanks to Hal Espen, Mary Turner, Elizabeth Hightower, and Larry Burke at *Outside* magazine for their ever-stalwart support and ideas. Thanks especially to the indefatigable Bruce Hildenbrand, who kept his finger on various pulses (including mine) and lent his eagle eye to the manuscript.

Stephen Cheung, Joe Friel, Alejandro Lucia, Conrad Earnest, Andrew Coggan, and John Cobb were patient teachers when it came to decoding the sometimes tangly science behind the sport. A special thanks—and at least one steak dinner—to the supremely able Scott Daubert at Trek.

For help with logistics and travel, I'm indebted to a far-flung crew, including Susan Chung, Margot Marsh, Brett Potash, Mathieu Desplats, Ray and Lisa Kennedy, Megan and Mollie MacEachern, Alain Bruyneel, Tom MacAdam, Ralph Spielman, Scott Coady, and Belgium's own Stefaan Wybo, who may be the only person to ever pilot a rental car with fake press credentials alongside the peloton during the Paris-Roubaix race.

Cycling is a difficult sport to watch in person; it helps to have an audio/visual maestro like Philip Taylor in your corner, as well as the gracious and helpful people at Outdoor Life Network, especially Leslie LaLuna and the unflappable John Carter. Thanks also to Ken Dice at the Discovery Channel for the champagne in Paris.

A talented team of readers helped hone early drafts of the manuscript, including my amazingly intuitive brother, Maurice Coyle, the ever-wise Laura Hohnhold, and the superlative Mike Paterniti. And to Todd Balf, whose understanding of the book and its subject matter may have exceeded my own, I can only offer a tip of the chapeau, and the solemn vow to score at least one Tony Graffanino sighting next spring.

I'd like to thank our families—Maurice and Agnes Coyle, and Fred and Beeb Fisher, for their love, support, and nearly always welcome editing advice. Thanks also to Jon Coyle, Rob Fisher, and Tom Humphrey for their smart counsel and readings.

Thanks to my agent, David Black, a world-class *directeur sportif* if ever there was one, and to his outstanding squad, including Joy Tutela, Jason Sacher, Gary Morris, and Lauren Escobar. Thanks also to Miles Doyle, Emily McDonald, Nick Trautwein, and David Hirshey at HarperCollins, who took on many tasks, including making sure I got to all the right places with all the right credentials. And a big *gracias* to Clare Hertel for her whiz-bang advice.

Without my editor, Mark Bryant, this book would not exist. Thanks for your faith, your friendship, and your matchless ability to steer at high velocity.

Finally, thanks to my remarkable wife, Jen, who makes everything go. It's been a wonderful tour, and we're just getting rolling.

THE ROAD TO PARIS

4 **April 23** Georgia, USA

One day after Armstrong wins two stages of the Tour of Georgia, the U.S. Postal Service announces they are ending their support of Armstrong's cycling team. A search for a new sponsor ensues.

Atlantic Ocean

Stage 8

Stage

June 11 Southwestern France

At an undisclosed location, *L.A. Confidentiel: Les Secrets de Lance Armstrong* is printed in French. The 385-page book alleges that Armstrong may have been systematically using performance-enhancing drugs.

6

July 16 Stage 12, La Mongie

Lightning Strike: In a thunderstorm, the Tour reaches the Pyrenees. Several contenders crack, but not Armstrong. The following day, he begins an unprecedented run of four consecutive mountain victories.

Stage 1

9

February 21 Algarve, Portugal

2 Armstrong race-tests top-secret $250,000 time-trial bike, code-named Narrowbike, estimated to gain Armstrong more than 1 second per mile.

3 **March 10** Tenerife, the Canary Islands

Top-secret Narrowbike is unexpectedly abandoned after a one-hour test supervised by Armstrong's trainer, Dr. Michele Ferrari. "This bike, it is a bullshit bike," Ferrari decrees.